IMAGES
of America

LENOIR CITY

I0792664

ON THE COVER: This photograph was one of a handful rescued from a fire at the General Lenoir Hotel in Lenoir City on March 6, 1999. Although the identity of the men in the photograph is a mystery at this time, the automotive repair shop in which they stood was probably located on Broadway Street, Lenoir City's main street. (Lenoir City Museum.)

IMAGES
of America

LENOIR CITY

Kate Clabough with a foreword by
Joe Spence, Loudon County Historian

ARCADIA
PUBLISHING

ISBN 978-0-7385-6641-2

Published by Arcadia Publishing
Charleston, South Carolina

Printed in the United States of America

Library of Congress Control Number: 2009928933

For all general information contact Arcadia Publishing at:
Telephone 843-853-2070
Fax 843-853-0044
E-mail sales@arcadiapublishing.com
For customer service and orders:
Toll-Free 1-888-313-2665

Visit us on the Internet at www.arcadiapublishing.com

This book is dedicated to my darling husband, David; my three wonderful children, Beth, Ian, and Kacy; and my parents, Richard and Beverly Klamm, all of whom have loved, supported, and inspired me through a myriad of projects over the years.

Contents

ACKNOWLEDGMENTS

I would like to express my deepest appreciation to Loudon County historian Joe Spence. Without his expert help and guidance, this project would have never come to fruition. His efforts in preserving the area's history should be applauded by all. And thanks to the Lenoir City Museum for access to these wonderful photographs that tell the history of the city so beautifully. Unless otherwise noted, all images are courtesy of the museum.

Special thanks to my editor at Arcadia Publishing, Maggie Bullwinkel, for working with me on a second book. I would also like to thank my husband, David, for his untiring help no matter how many times I asked for it.

FOREWORD

The town of Lenoir City was incorporated in 1907, but the Lenoir family came to the area in 1810. Maj. William Ballard Lenoir and his wife, Elizabeth Avery, settled on 5,000 acres of land granted by North Carolina to his father, Gen. William Lenoir, for his services in the Revolutionary War.

By 1820, a farm was cleared and the Lenoirs built a large brick house, still standing in downtown Lenoir City. The Lenoir plantation grew into a prosperous and well-managed estate. The farm projects were extensive; cattle and hogs were raised in large numbers, and the Lenoir hams were famous throughout the South. The first industry was a mill to make cotton yarns and batting. Completed prior to 1837, the business was profitable and uninterrupted for 50 years, except during the Civil War. When the East Tennessee, Virginia, and Georgia Railway was completed through Lenoir's Station in 1854, trade increased.

When William Ballard Lenoir died in 1852, his four sons—William, Israel Pickens, Benjamin Ballard, and Waightsill Avery—formed William Lenoir and Brothers, which controlled around 2,700 acres of the estate. The remainder of the land was given to their sisters. Acquiring more land, the Lenoir brothers built a large flour and gristmill, sawmill, and planing mill.

The Lenoir estate was devastated during the Civil War. Although there were no major battles in the immediate vicinity, many soldiers traveled through the area on a direct route from Knoxville to Chattanooga and onto Atlanta and the Deep South. The Confederate general James Longstreet and the Union general Ambrose Burnside lead their armies through the Lenoir area prior to the battle of Knoxville on November 29, 1863. The Union forces seized over $70,000 of supplies from the Lenoir family. According to Dr. J. G. M. Ramsey, "The enemy . . . took whatever of supplies they chose to of all kinds. They exhausted the smokehouse and cellar of all the necessities of life, cut down the forests as they pleased, and erected in their fertile fields villas of cabins for their soldiers."

Despite their losses, the Lenoir family resumed their businesses. A large depot and store was completed, and a new burr and roller flour mill was built to replace the one burned in 1860. When Israel Pickens Lenoir died, the Lenoir Manufacturing Company was chartered as a stock company in 1877. It eventually became the property of five individuals, until it was sold to the Lenoir City Company in 1890, with an initial holding of 2,743 acres. Owned by prominent businessmen from Knoxville and New York City, and one from Lima, Ohio, this company surveyed the land, divided it into lots and streets, and hoped to develop a planned community. When their plans failed, Lenoir City was incorporated by an act of the state legislature in 1907.

With the coming of the Tennessee Valley Authority (TVA) and the construction of Fort Loudon Dam in the 1940s, the town continued to prosper. However, Lenoir City's unprecedented growth began following the construction of Tellico Dam in the late 1970s with the development of Tellico Village. With the recent construction of a new hospital on Highway 321 near I-75, a virtual explosion of both business and residential development occurred, which continues unabated today.

—Joe Spence
Loudon County Historian

INTRODUCTION

Like so many other towns in East Tennessee, Lenoir City can trace its roots back to the Revolutionary War, as it was common practice at the time for soldiers to be paid for service with a land grant in the Southwest Territory. Gen. William Lenoir received such a grant, but it was his son Maj. William Ballard Lenoir who actually settled the land. The town itself did not get its start until 1890, when the Lenoir City Company was formed.

Although there are plenty of records, documents, and old photographs chronicling the early years, they were scattered around until a Lenoir City High School American studies class started collecting them under the guidance of teachers Joe Spence, Nancy Majors Braun, Phyllis Wilburn, and Sandra Towns. As the American history and American literature classes began studying local history using state and community resources, the students and teachers created a heritage room at the high school to display their collection.

Upon the retirement of Joe Spence in 1996, former student and current mayor Matt Brookshire contacted local attorney Harvey Sproul to secure three rooms above the Sproul and Hinton law offices in which to move the historical collection and create a small museum. Coincidentally, the law offices happened to be housed in a building that served as Lenoir City's first city hall.

The museum stayed in those rooms for about three years until it outgrew its surroundings. In 1999, an agreement was made with the city for the museum to be moved to its current home in the Lenoir City Company building on Depot Street, which is yet another appropriate space for a museum chronicling the town's history.

The museum, which is staffed by volunteers, gives visitors a chance to experience Lenoir City's past with displays showcasing the people, businesses, events, and buildings that give this town its unique face. The photographs in this book all came from the museum's archives. Although there are certainly plenty more photographs and documents that reside in other places or are yet to be found, those represented here in these pages give readers, at the very least, a small glimpse into Lenoir City's lengthy past.

The book is divided into 10 chapters, but many of the photographs could easily represent more than one category. They are sprinkled throughout the book in a somewhat organized fashion. Most of the chapters are in rough chronological order. Others may have photographs taken at approximately the same time that serve as illustrations for a single story. Still other chapters may be a little more hit and miss, as a pattern was not always obvious. Whatever the format, this book is a possibly incomplete but wholly heartfelt historical gift from this humble author to you. And although I am far from an expert on Lenoir City, it has been both an honor and a privilege to be given the opportunity to work on this worthwhile project.

—Kate Clabough
Author

Lenoir City, like many or even most small towns throughout the southeast, has seen its share of change. Much of that change has happened just within the last 50 years or so with the arrival of such institutions as the Tennessee Valley Authority and the national interstate system. This rapid change is all the more reason why it is so important for communities such as ours to preserve and promote their history. This book, with its many wonderful old pictures, does just that. It helps us to remember who we once were and helps us to better understand who we are today.

—Matt Brookshire
Lenoir City Mayor

One

The Early Years

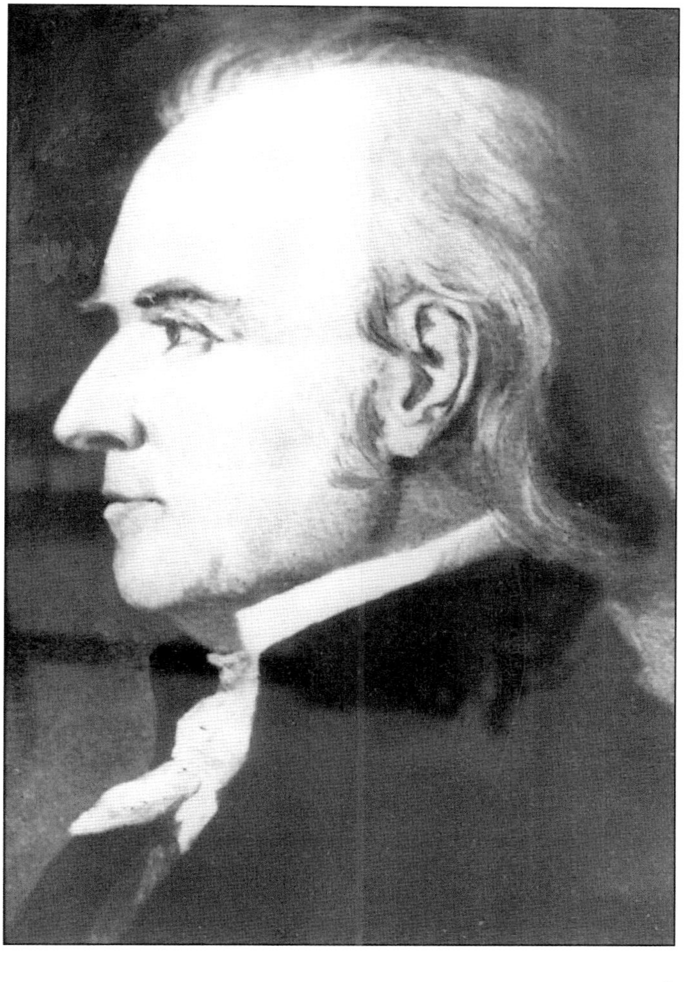

Gen. William Lenoir was born in Brunswick County, Virginia, on May 8, 1751, to Thomas and Mourning Lenoir. The Lenoirs moved to Tarboro, North Carolina, where the aptly named Mourning was widowed with 10 children. General Lenoir married Ann Ballard in 1771. He fought under Col. Benjamin Cleveland in the battle of King's Mountain during the Revolutionary War and received the property that would later become Lenoir City for his service.

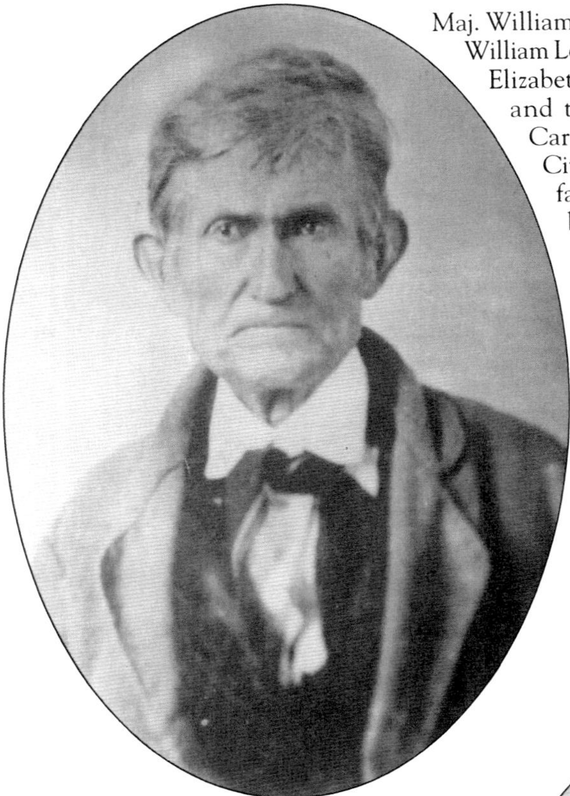

Maj. William Ballard Lenoir was the oldest son of Gen. William Lenoir and Ann (Ballard) Lenoir. He married Elizabeth Avery in 1802. Major Lenoir, Elizabeth, and their four children moved from North Carolina to the Lenoir property (later Lenoir City) deeded to him by his father. The Lenoir family prospered in the woods of Tennessee, building a fine brick home and clearing land for a prosperous farming estate.

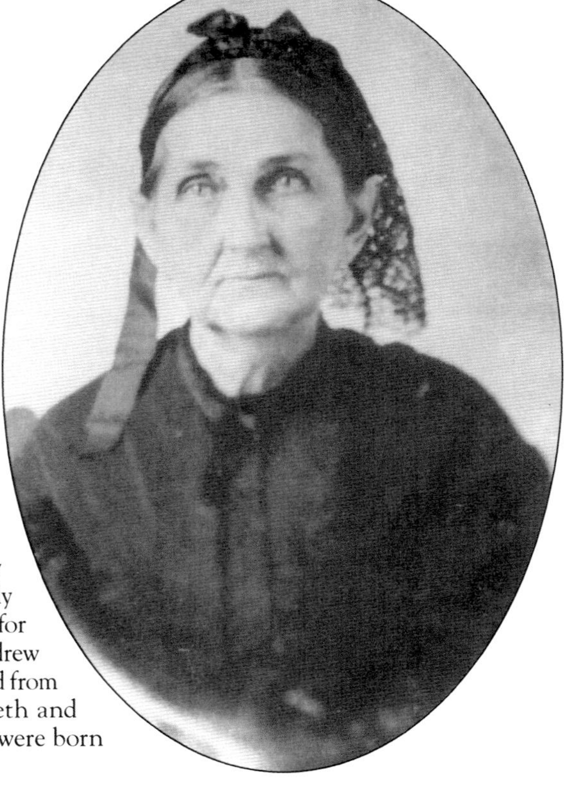

Elizabeth Avery, wife of Maj. William Ballard Lenoir, was the daughter of Waightsill Avery and Leah Probart Francks. Avery was an early American lawyer and soldier. He is noted for fighting a duel with future U.S. president Andrew Jackson in 1788. The Avery family descended from the Plantagenet Kings of England. Elizabeth and Major Lenoir had 12 children, 8 of whom were born on the Lenoir estate in Tennessee.

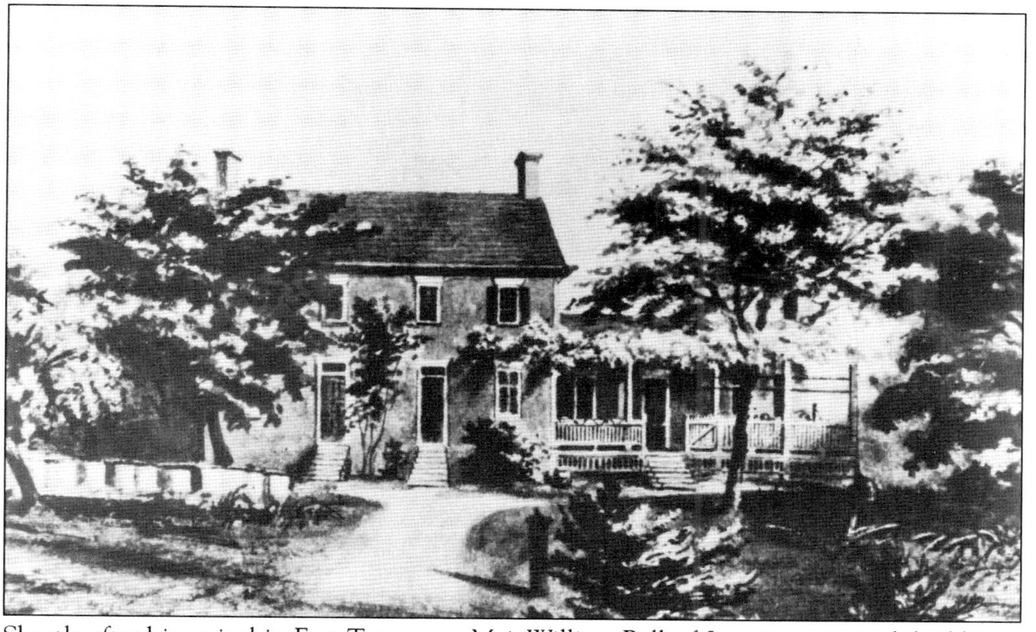

Shortly after his arrival in East Tennessee, Maj. William Ballard Lenoir set to work building a fine brick home to accommodate his growing family. Included in the home was a large "preacher's room" built to the side of the house. It was outfitted with two beds to host itinerant or circuit-riding preachers that traveled around the area.

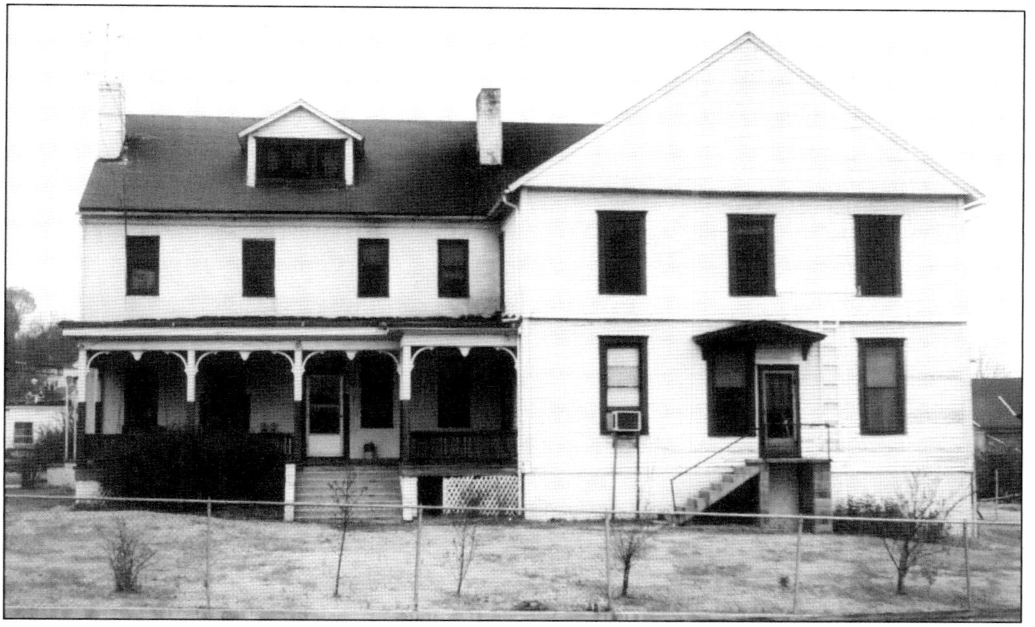

The Lenoirs continued to make improvements to the family home, and many additions were made over the years. The building, which still stands on Depot Street, became the Lenoir Inn, and travelers were always a welcome sight. In the attic of the older part of the home, Roman numerals are visible on the beams; they were used as a numbering system to help workmen fit the hand-hewn roof beams together properly.

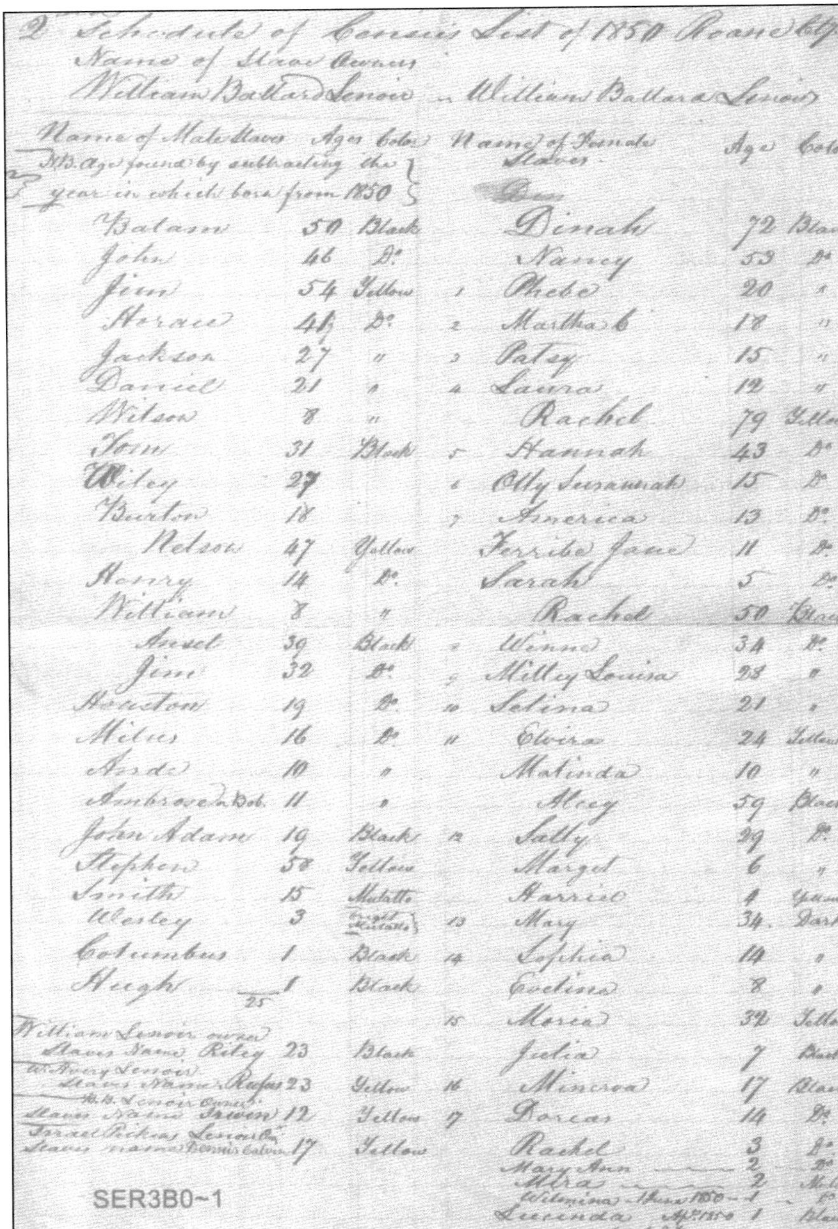

2 Schedule of Census List of 1850 Roane Cty
Name of Slave Owners
William Ballard Lenoir — William Ballard Lenoir

N.B. Age found by subtracting the year in which born from 1850

Name of Male Slaves	Ages	Color		Name of Female Slaves	Age	Color
Balam	50	Black		Dinah	72	Black
John	46	Do		Nancy	53	Do
Jim	54	Yellow	1	Phebe	20	"
Horace	41	Do	2	Martha C	18	"
Jackson	27	"	3	Patsy	15	"
Daniel	21	"	4	Laura	12	"
Wilson	8	"		Rachel	79	Yellow
Tom	31	Black	5	Hannah	43	Do
Wiley	27		6	Olly Savannah	15	Do
Burton	18		7	America	13	Do
Nelson	47	Yellow		Ferribe Jane	11	Do
Henry	14	Do		Sarah	5	Do
William	8	"		Rachel	50	Black
Ansel	39	Black	8	Winnie	34	Do
Jim	32	Do	9	Milley Louisa	23	"
Houston	19	Do	10	Selina	21	"
Miles	16	Do	11	Elvira	24	Yellow
Andre	10	"		Malinda	10	"
Ambrose in Dob.	11	"		Alcey	59	Black
John Adam	19	Black	12	Sally	29	Do
Stephen	58	Yellow		Margret	6	"
Smith	15	Mulatto		Harriet	4	Yellow
Wesley	3	bright Mulatto	13	Mary	34	Dark
Columbus	1	Black	14	Sophia	14	"
Hugh	1	Black		Eveline	8	"
25			15	Maria	32	Yellow
William Lenoir owned Slaves Name Riley	23	Black		Julia	7	Black
W. Avery Lenoir Slaves Name Rufus	23	Yellow	16	Minerva	17	Black
B.B. Lenoir Owner Slaves Name Irwin	12	Yellow	17	Dorcas	14	Do
Israel Pickens Lenoir Owner Slaves name Dennis Calvin	17	Yellow		Rachel	3	Do
				Mary Ann	2	Do
				Mira	2	Mulatto
				Wilimina Since 1850	1	Do
				Lucinda Apr 1850	1	Black
				total 34		

SER3B0~1

According to the 1850 census, the Lenoir family owned a large number of slaves. The list of male slaves included the following: Balam, John, Mim, Horace, Jackson, Daniel, Wilson, Tom, Wiley, Burton, Nelson, Henry, William, Ansel, Jim, Houston, Miles, Andre, Ambrose, John Adam, Stephen, Smith, Wesley, Columbus, Hugh, Riley, Rufus, Irwin, and Dennis. Female slaves were as follows: Dinah, Nancy, Phebe, Martha, Patsy, Laura, Rachel, Hannah, Olly Savannah, America, Ferribe Jane, Sarah, Rachel, Winnie, Milley Louisa, Salina, Elvira, Malinda, Alcey, Sally, Margret, Harriet, Mary, Sophia, Eveline, Maria, Julia, Minerva, Dorcas, Rachel, Mary Ann, Mira, Wilimina, and Lucinda. They ranged in age from 4 to 72. The census listed approximate age in addition to a description of skin color such as black, yellow, mulatto, and dark.

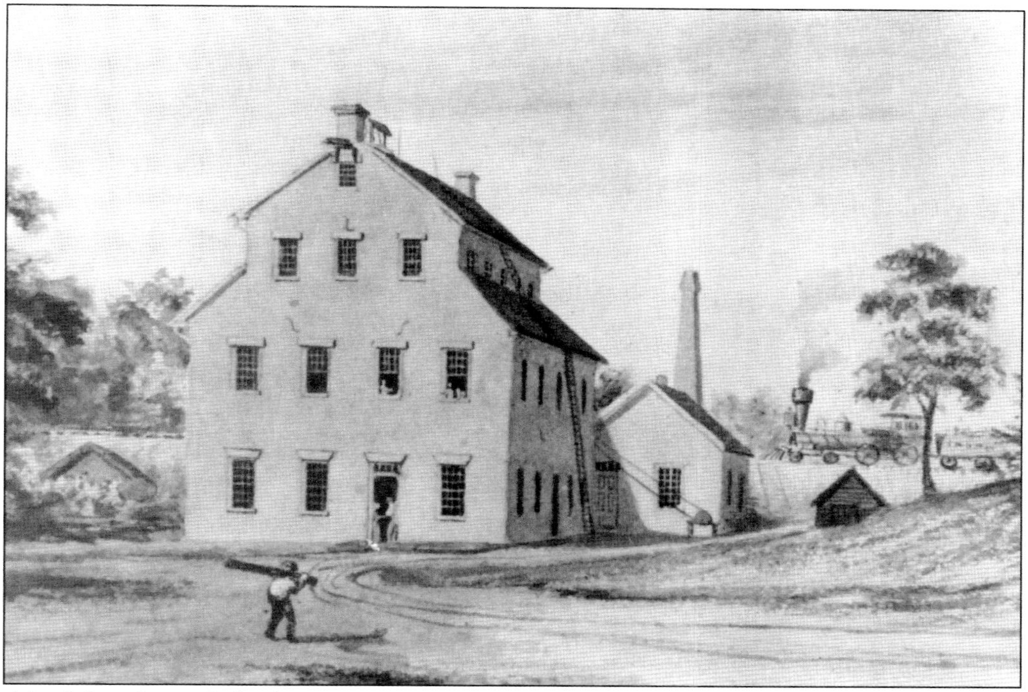

After Major Lenoir's death in 1852, his four sons—Dr. Benjamin Ballard, Waightsill Avery, Israel Pickens, and William Lenoir—continued to prosper. The hard-working and enterprising family harnessed water power from Town Creek, which flowed through their property to run various industries, including this cotton mill where cotton yarn and batting was produced. The mill building was to be restored until a fire destroyed it in 1991.

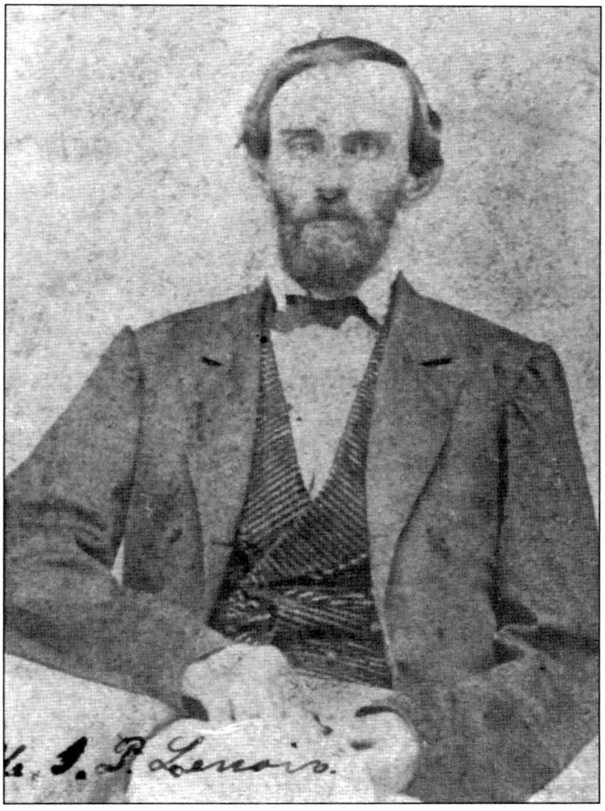

During his famed march through East Tennessee, Gen. Ambrose Burnside was so impressed with the abundance of provisions, productive soil, superb climate, and picturesque scenery at Lenoir's Station, he offered to buy it from the Lenoir family. Isreal Pickens Lenoir, son of Maj. William Ballard Lenoir and Elizabeth (Avery) Lenoir, told him, "General, it would take considerable boot to get us to swap it for the state of Rhode Island."

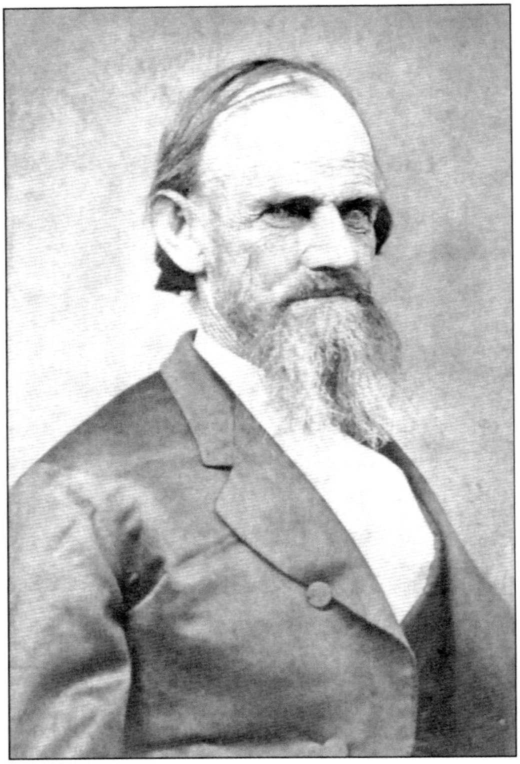

Dr. Benjamin Ballard Lenoir was born on March 5, 1821, in Lenoir's Station to Maj. William Ballard Lenoir and Elizabeth (Avery) Lenoir. On November 27, 1855, he married Henrietta Rutledge Ramsey. As if dealing with the realities of the Civil War was not enough, Dr. and Mrs. Lenoir suffered the tragedy of losing two young sons, Jimmie and Charlie, in October 1863 while the doctor was away in Knoxville serving with the Confederate forces.

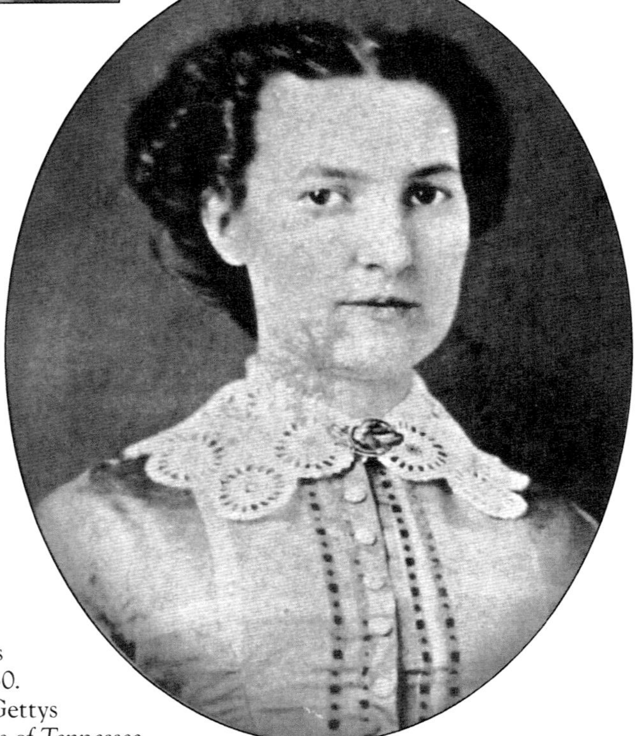

Henrietta Rutledge Ramsey Lenoir prevented the theft of money by Union forces from Lenoir's Station (later Lenoir City) by removing it from the safe at the family's business. She hid the money under some yarn in a basket. She then took it home and buried it under a bush in the front yard. Henrietta died before the war's end on May 25, 1864, at the age of 30. She was the daughter of Dr. James Gettys McGready Ramsey, author of *Annals of Tennessee*.

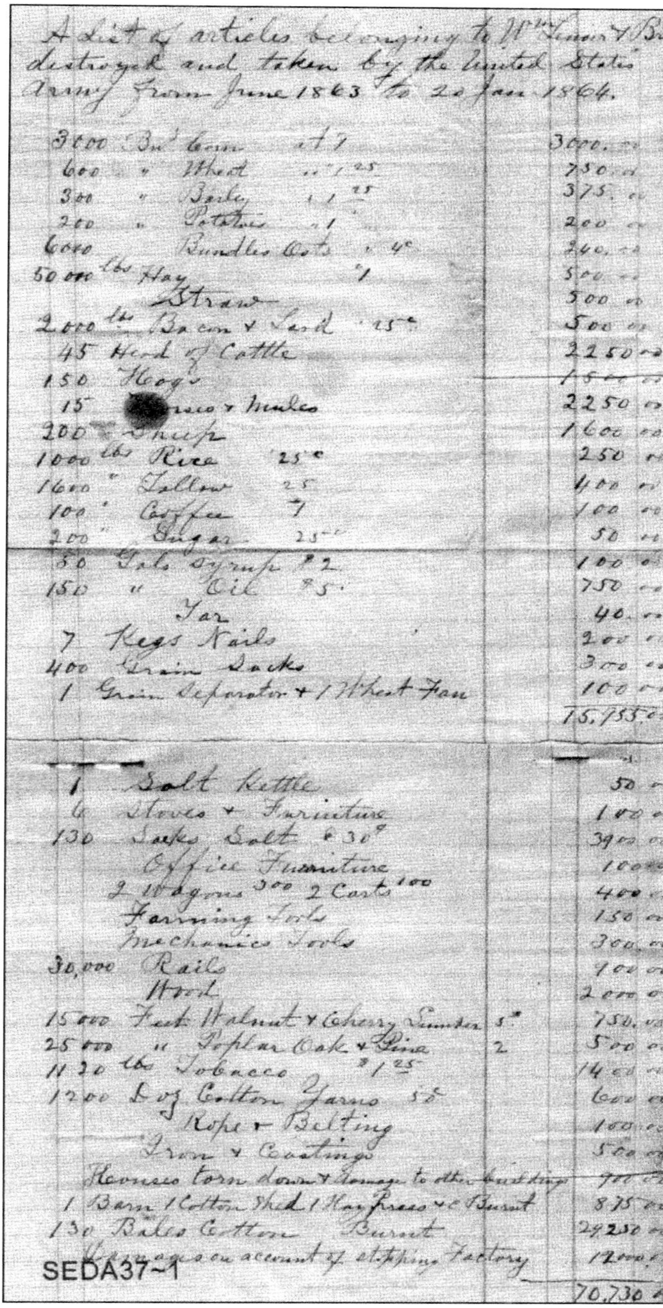

A List of articles belonging to Wm Lenoir & Bro destroyed and taken by the United States Army From June 1863 to 20 Jan 1864.

3000 Bu Corn at 1	3000.00
600 " Wheat " 1.25	750.00
300 " Barley " 1.25	375.00
200 " Potatoes " 1	200.00
6000 Bundles Oats " 4c	240.00
50 000 lbs Hay 1	500.00
Straw	500.00
2000 lbs Bacon & Lard 25c	500.00
45 Head of Cattle	2250.00
150 Hogs	1500.00
15 [illegible] & Mules	2250.00
200 Sheep	1600.00
1000 lbs Rice 25c	250.00
1600 " Tallow 25	400.00
100 " Coffee 1	100.00
200 " Sugar 25c	50.00
50 Gals Syrup $2	100.00
150 " Oil $5	750.00
Tar	40.00
7 Kegs Nails	200.00
400 Grain Sacks	300.00
1 Grain Separator & 1 Wheat Fan	100.00
	15,155.00
1 Salt Kettle	50.00
6 Stoves & Furniture	100.00
130 Sacks Salt $30	3900.00
Office Furniture	100.00
2 Wagons 300 2 Carts 100	400.00
Farming Tools	150.00
Mechanics Tools	300.00
30,000 Rails	900.00
Wood	2000.00
15 000 Feet Walnut & Cherry Lumber 5c	750.00
25 000 " Poplar Oak & Pine 2	500.00
1120 lbs Tobacco $1.25	1400.00
1200 Doz Cotton Yarns 50c	600.00
Rope & Belting	100.00
Iron & Castings	500.00
Houses torn down & damage to other buildings	900.00
1 Barn 1 Cotton Shed 1 Hay Press &c Burnt	875.00
130 Bales Cotton Burnt	29250.00
Damages on account of stopping Factory	12000.00
	70,730.00

SEDA37-1

Like many families in the South during the Civil War, the Lenoirs suffered great financial loss. The family submitted a list of belongings, such as nails, syrup, wheat, furniture, and rope, which were destroyed or taken by Union troops, along with a request for reimbursement in the amount of $70,730. The War Department wrote, "In reply to your letter of February 25, 1880, I am directed by the Quartermaster General to inform you that the case of the Lenoir Bros. of Loudon County, Tennessee was closed by Treasury Settlement No. 497 of March 28, 1878 for $991.87, which closes the case so far as this office is concerned."

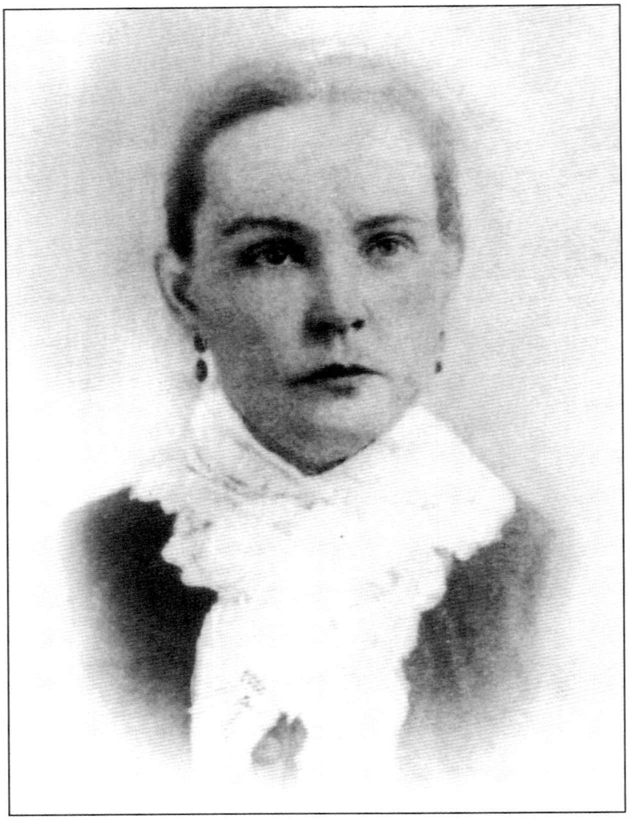

Eliza Hume Lenoir, daughter of Waightsill Avery Lenoir and Isabella (Hume) Lenoir, married Dr. George Madre Burdett on June 17, 1873. George enlisted in Company D, 15th Georgia, in 1861. He served four years as a surgeon with the Confederacy. George and Eliza, granddaughter of Maj. William Ballard Lenoir, had at least nine children, including a set of triplets (Lora, Lois, and Laurence) who died in infancy.

The Lenoirs and other families who lived in the area around Lenoir's Station suffered great loss during the Civil War. Many of the buildings were burned or otherwise destroyed, fields and storehouses emptied, and merchandise and foodstuffs confiscated. As soon as they were able, the Lenoirs set to work rebuilding what was lost, including the depot, which also contained a warehouse and general store.

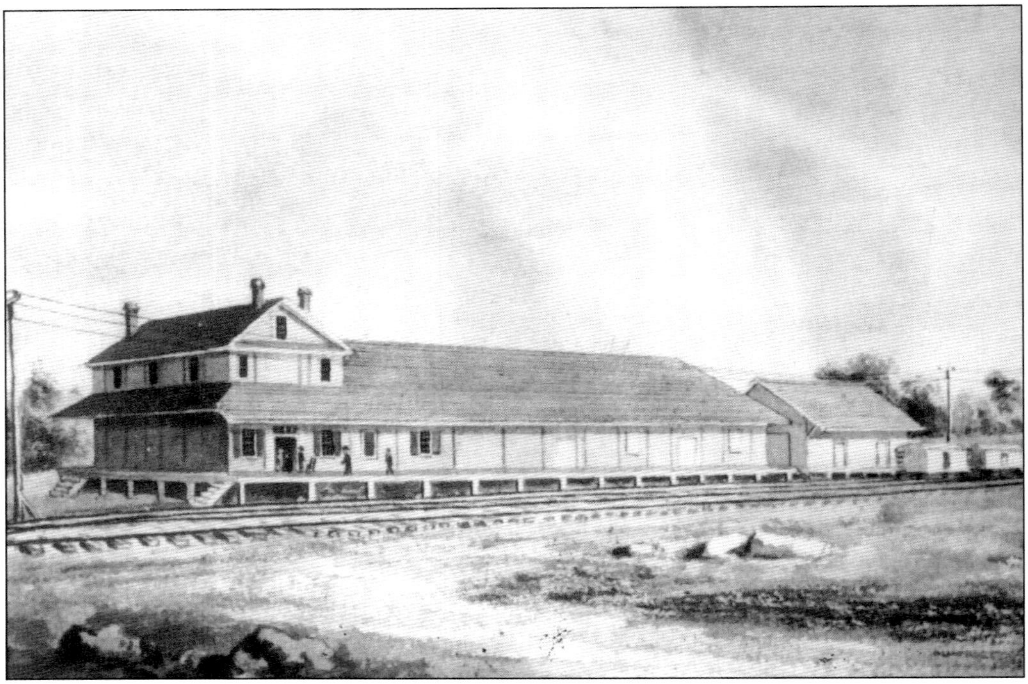

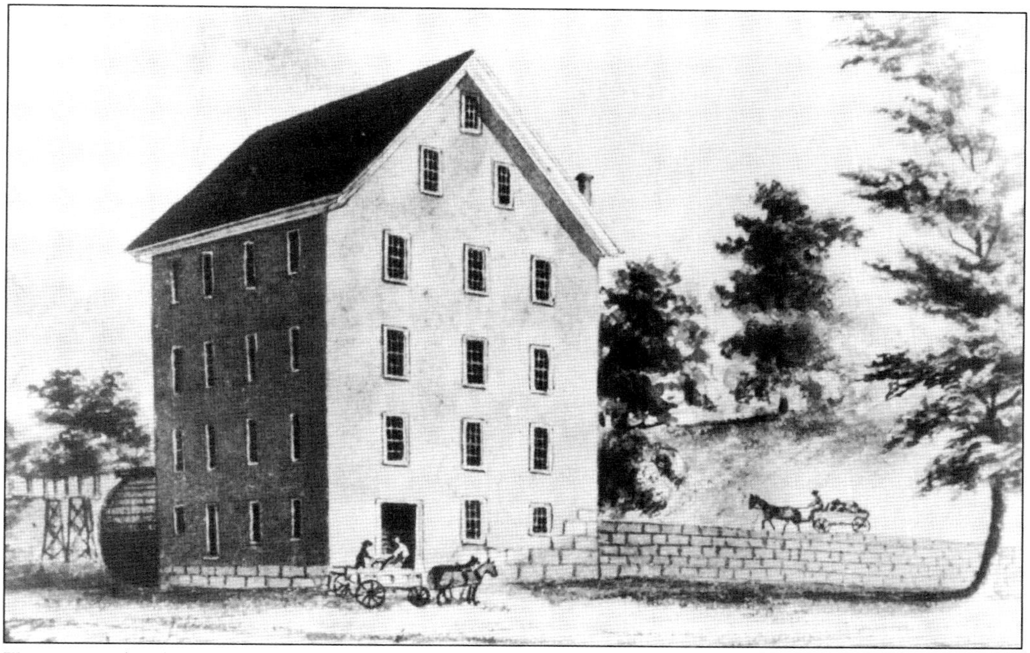

Town Creek offered an unending source of power to run area mills and other local industries. This flour mill was built by the Lenoir family in the 1870s and provided not only flour, but work for families in the area. It is believed to be the first burr and roller flour mill in the area. The building, which stood near McGhee Boulevard, burned in 1915.

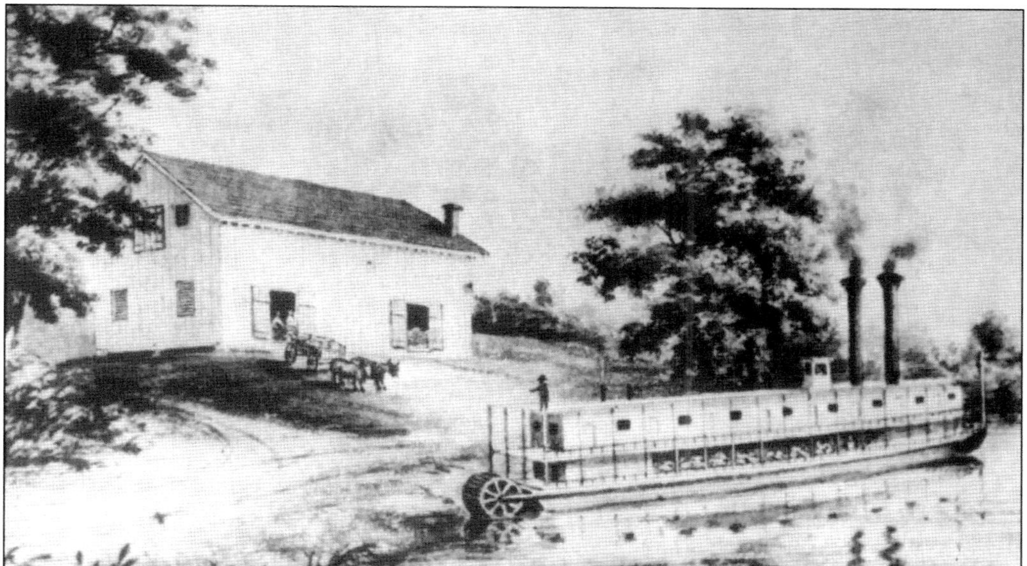

The Lenoir Cotton Mill Warehouse, located at the junction of Bussell Ferry Road and Lee Drive, was built around 1830. The warehouse was used as storage for raw cotton for the Lenoir Cotton Mill. In 2004, Family Pride Corporation restored the building, and it was placed in the National Register of Historic Places. Remnants of the original structure, which is now a private residence, are still visible on the main floor.

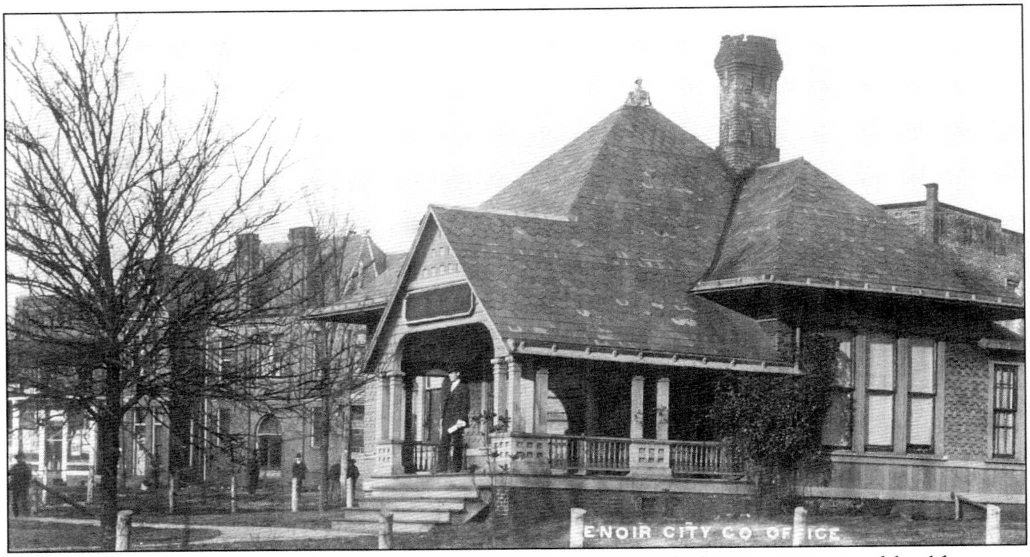

In 1890, the Lenoir brothers sold the entire Lenoir estate, including property and buildings, to a syndicate of New York and Knoxville businessmen who created the Lenoir City Company. Company officials had plans of creating an industrial town utilizing industries started by the Lenoirs. The company had its office in this building at 110 Depot Street, which now hosts the Lenoir City Museum.

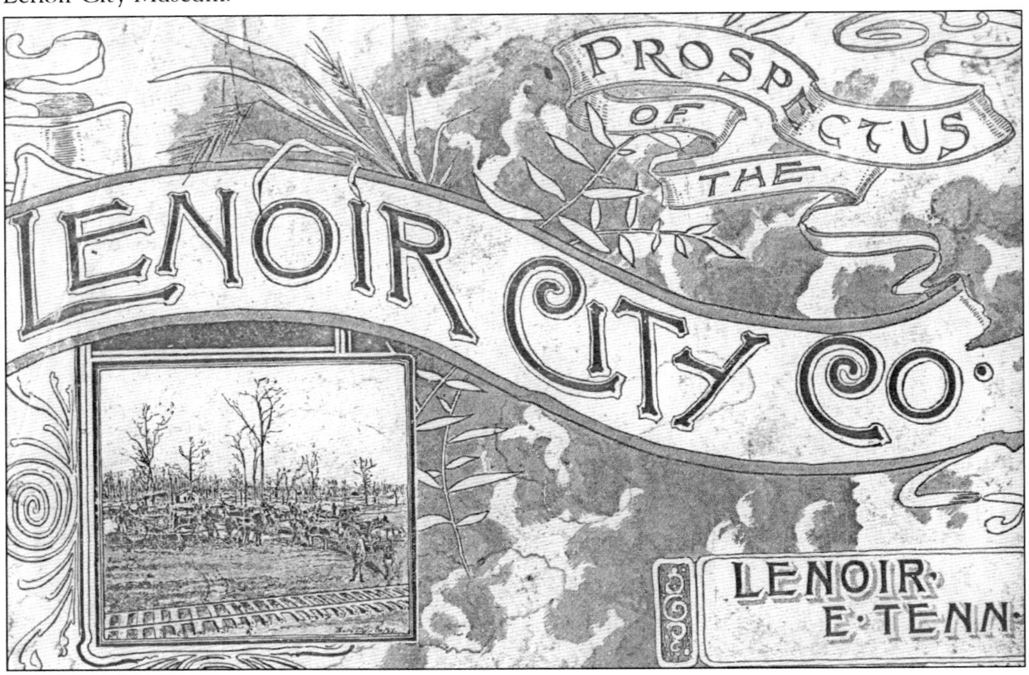

To entice investors, the Lenoir City Company published a prospectus. The booklet emphasized the area's virtues, describing the landscape as a "charmingly picturesque environment, embracing rare scenery by river and shore, of wooded hills and fertile plains, of majestic rivers and distant mountains." The prospectus also promised schools and churches open to the public and the prohibition of the sale of alcohol within city limits.

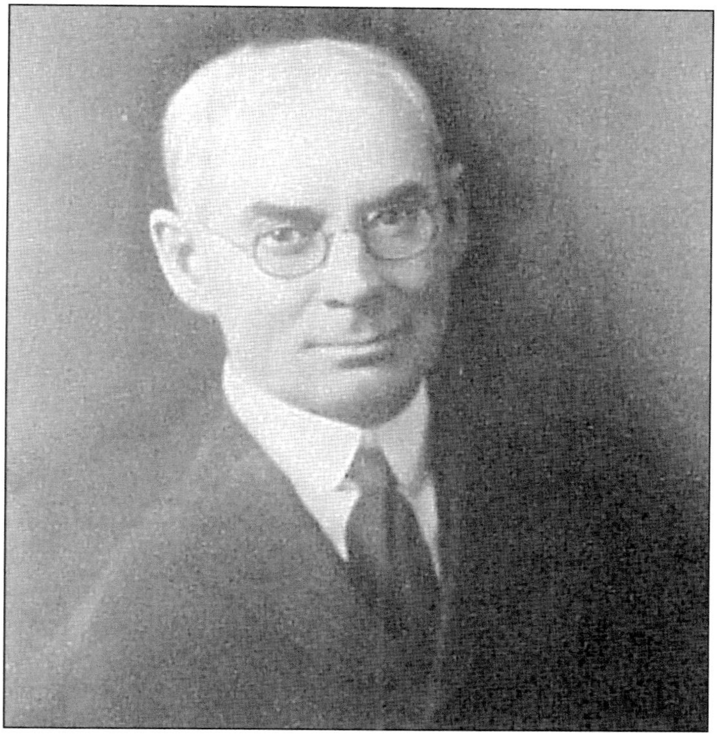

Frank Austin Weiss was born in Warren, Ohio, in 1871. He journeyed south, where he found a job with the railroad. He eventually made his way to Lenoir City and worked at the Bass Foundry. As his fortunes increased, he founded the Holston Manufacturing Company. When Lenoir City incorporated in 1907, he was elected as the town's first mayor; he served four terms in that office.

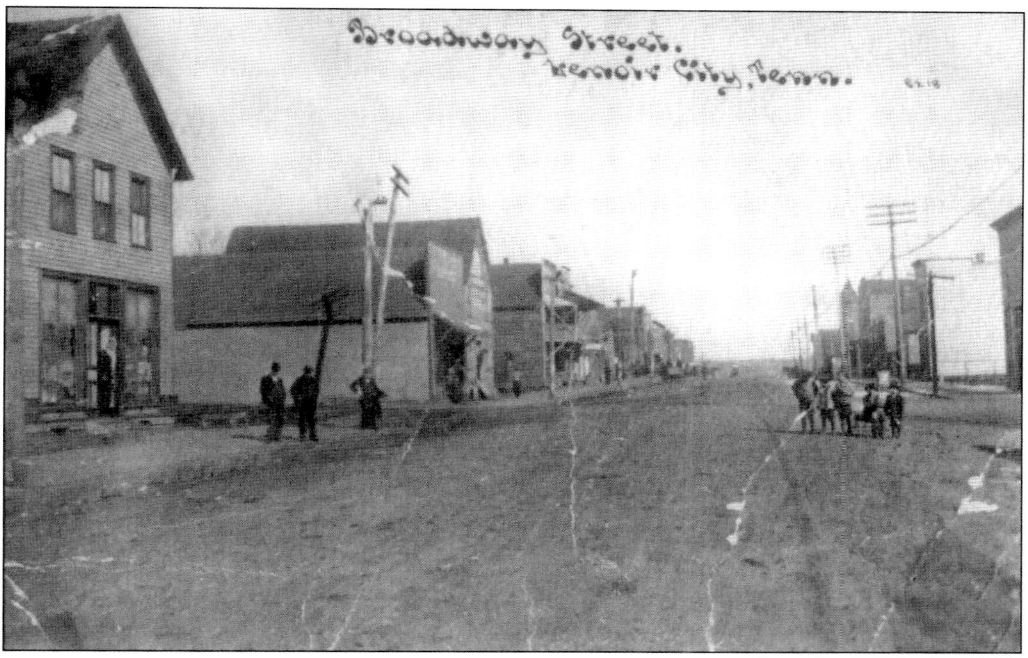

This photograph was taken at the corner of B and Broadway Streets facing east. According to John D. Eldridge, founder of the *Lenoir City News* in 1904, early Lenoir City was "just a thinly scattered collection of frame buildings on the wooded hillside with mud streets held in place by wooden poles laid endwise. No water system, no sewers, not a foot of hard surface road."

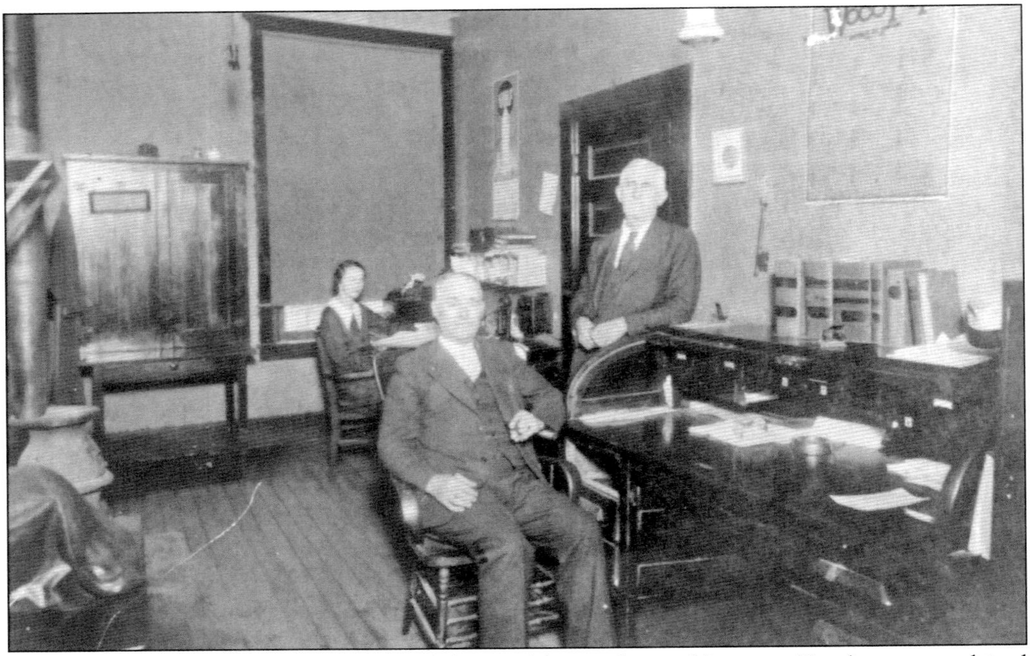

As Lenoir City continued to grow, so did the need for good record keeping. Employees were hired to staff the city hall. Pictured here in the mid-1920s are, from left to right, the following: Artie Markwood, city clerk; Horace Bacon, city treasurer; and Charles Price, city recorder. A Woco Pep Oil Company poster hung over the roll top desk.

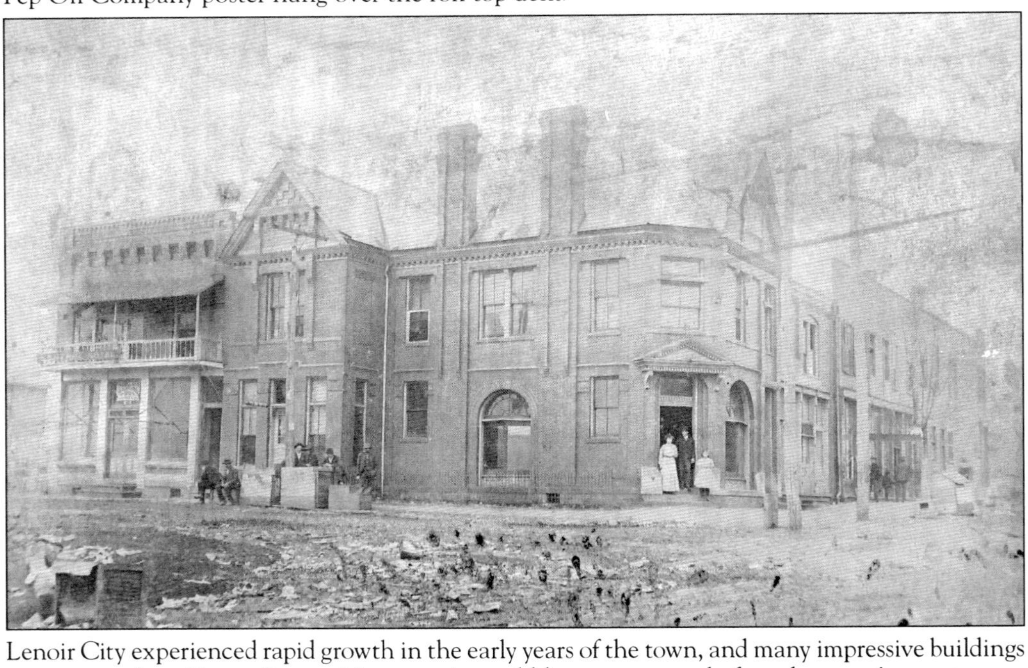

Lenoir City experienced rapid growth in the early years of the town, and many impressive buildings were erected on Depot Street. However, it would be many years before the town's streets were paved. Hardware store owner Roy G. Cardwell Sr. described the main thoroughfare as "either a cloud of dust or a lot of mud holes, depending on the weather."

Two

Car Works and Hosiery Mill

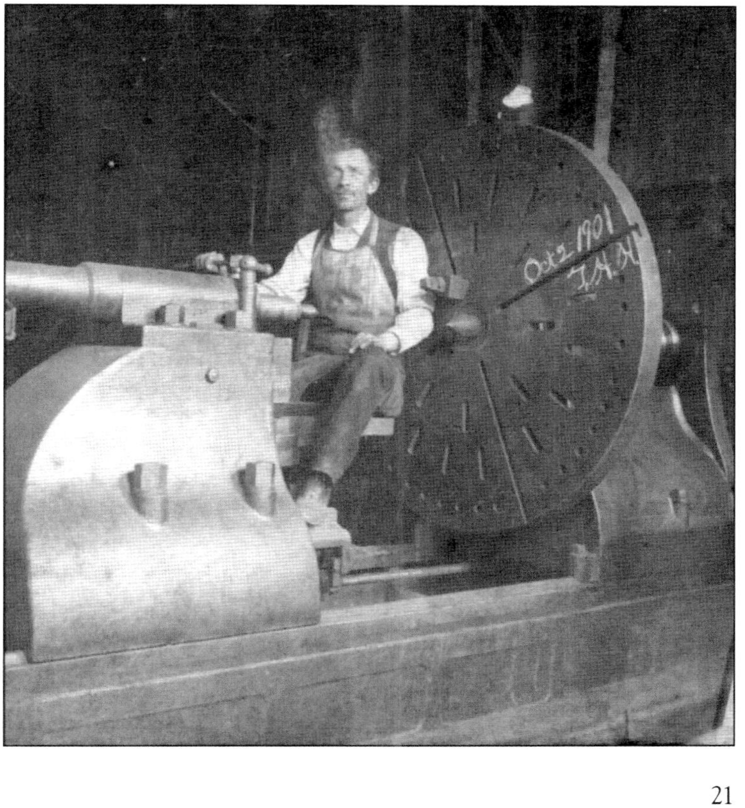

One of Lenoir City's earliest industries was the Bass Foundry, established in 1892 by John Henry Bass of Fort Wayne, Indiana. The foundry made railroad car wheels and gray iron castings. This photograph, taken October 2, 1901, is of J. Wesley Brown, foundry pattern shop superintendent. In 1905, Bass sold his business to the Lenoir Car Works, owned by Southern Railway, which made parts for and built 10 to 12 railroad cars per day.

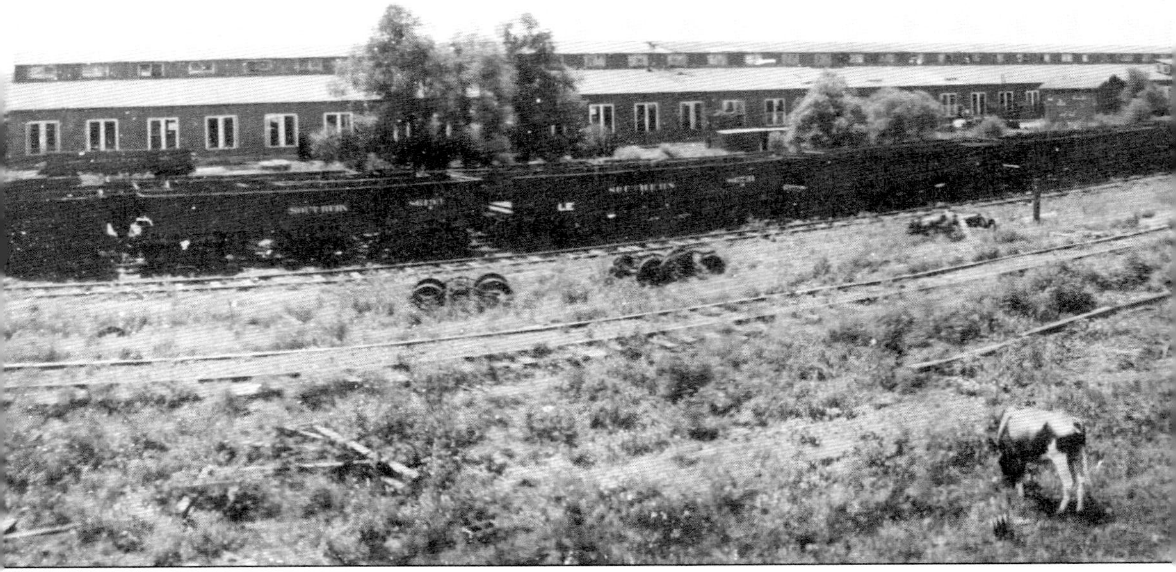

Railroads became an integral part of American history, linking east to west and north to south. They allowed for easy transportation of both people and goods, and as railway lines increased, the demand for railroad cars and parts increased as well. Situated on the East Tennessee, Virginia, and Georgia Railroad and the Tennessee River, Lenoir City offered the perfect location for a railroad-centric industry. The Lenoir Car Works complex occupied 93 acres along the

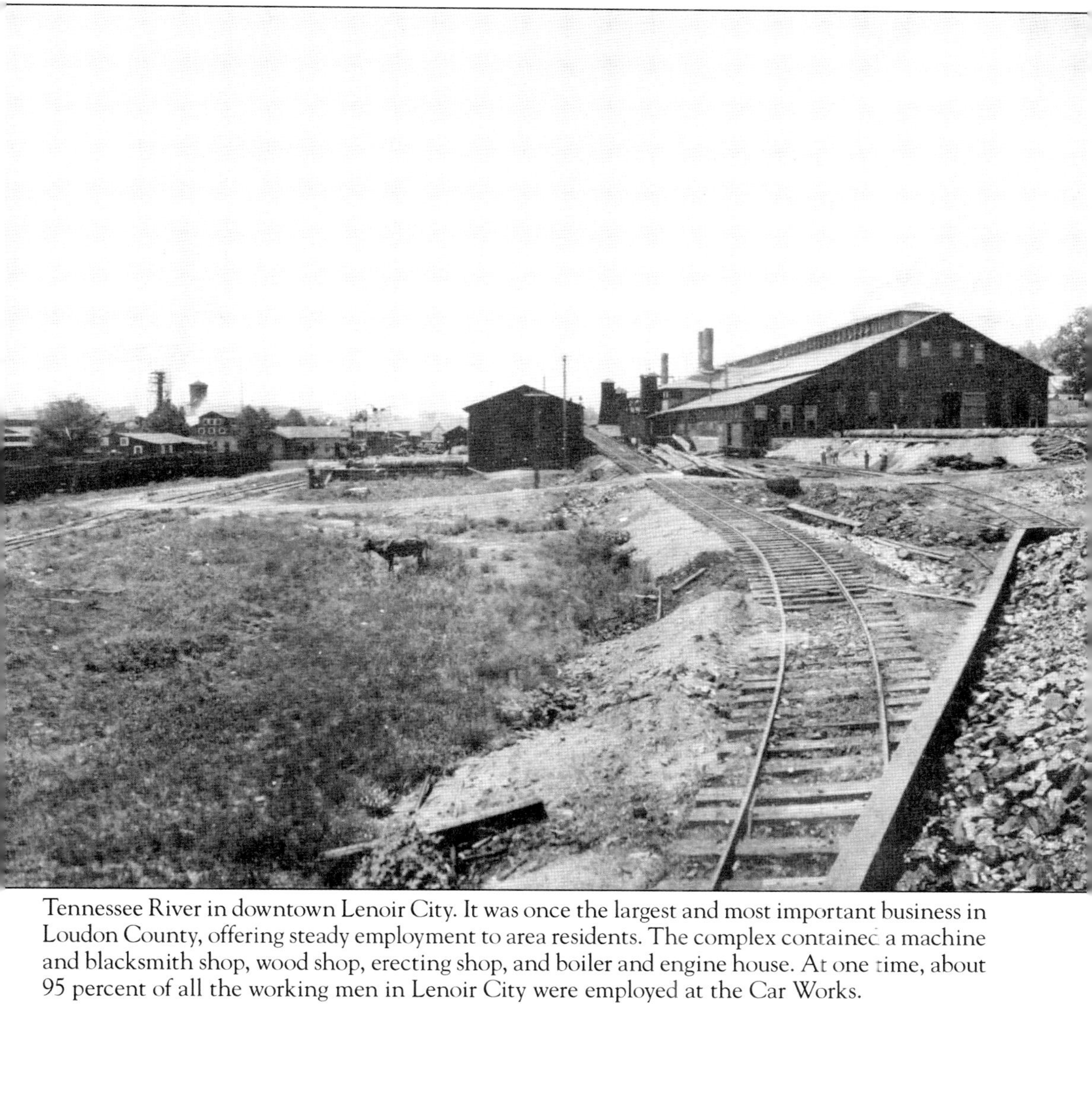

Tennessee River in downtown Lenoir City. It was once the largest and most important business in Loudon County, offering steady employment to area residents. The complex contained a machine and blacksmith shop, wood shop, erecting shop, and boiler and engine house. At one time, about 95 percent of all the working men in Lenoir City were employed at the Car Works.

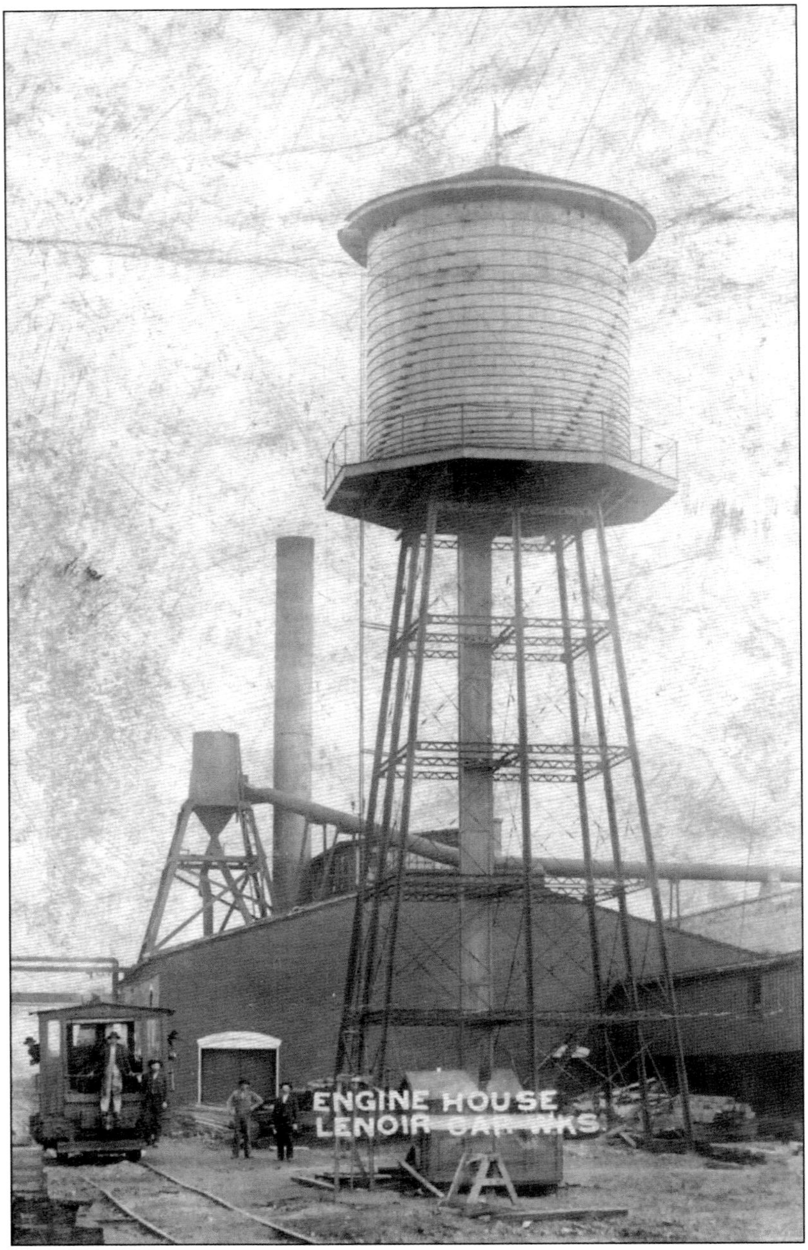

The Lenoir Car Works, a small plant for building and repairing freight cars, was founded in 1904 and purchased by Southern Railway the following year. Soon after, the Bass Foundry became part of the Car Works. By 1907, the Lenoir Car Works covered about 33 acres and employed approximately 500 men. The business continued to grow and expand thanks in part to World War I, when the workforce swelled to between 1,800 and 2,700 employees. Not only did the company build railcars, but the foundry portion also turned out car wheels and other castings in brass, gray iron, and steel. The engine house, with its imposing smokestack, powered the Car Works complex and supplied electricity to parts of Lenoir City. Car making ended at the plant in the 1940s, and the steel foundry ended operations in 1963.

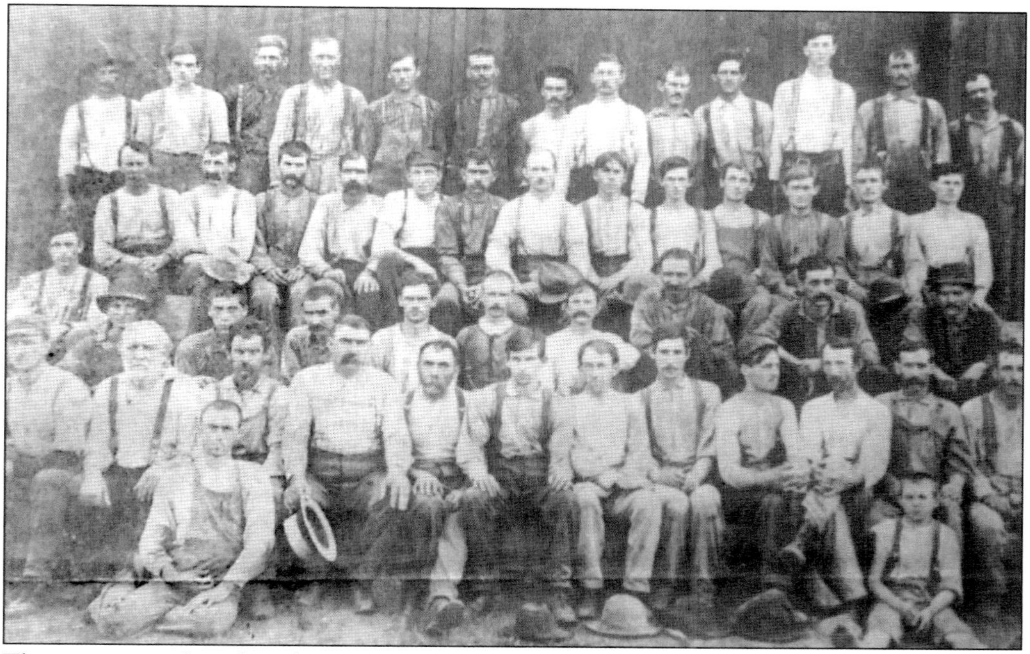

The average number of employees at the Lenoir Car Works, like these unidentified workers, varied between 800 and 900 men, and most area families depended on the plant for economic survival. The only major strike occurred in the early 1920s, which resulted in the death of one striker and the involvement of the Ku Klux Klan. The local Klan sent threatening notes to nonunion "scabs" and burned crosses in their yards.

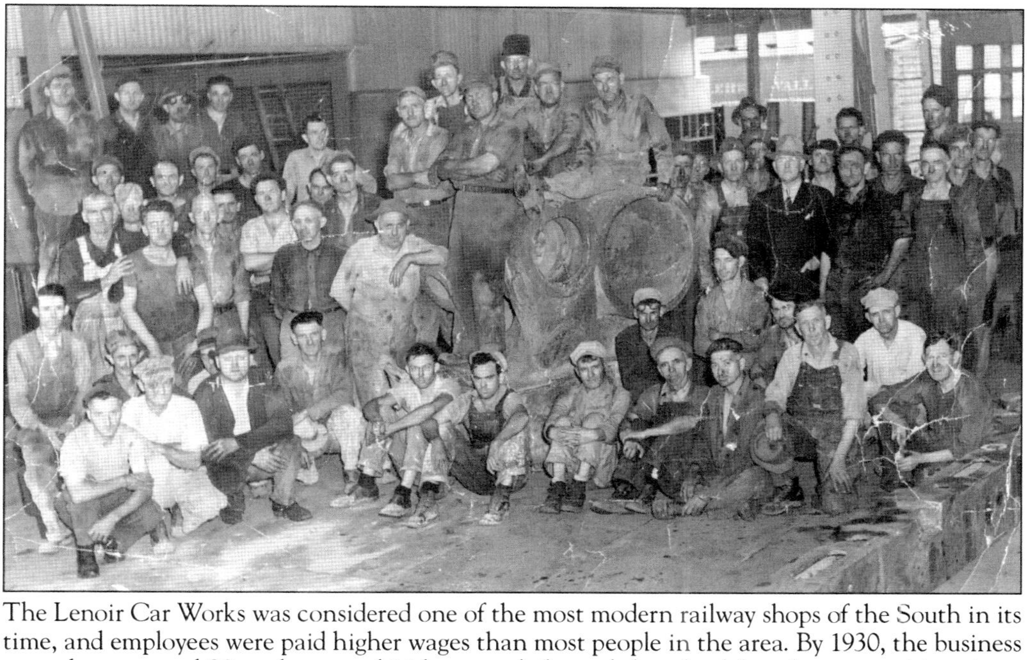

The Lenoir Car Works was considered one of the most modern railway shops of the South in its time, and employees were paid higher wages than most people in the area. By 1930, the business turned out around 20 coal cars and 16 boxcars daily, and the wheel foundry was making about 400 wheels per day. These unidentified workers kept the facilities running at peak capacity.

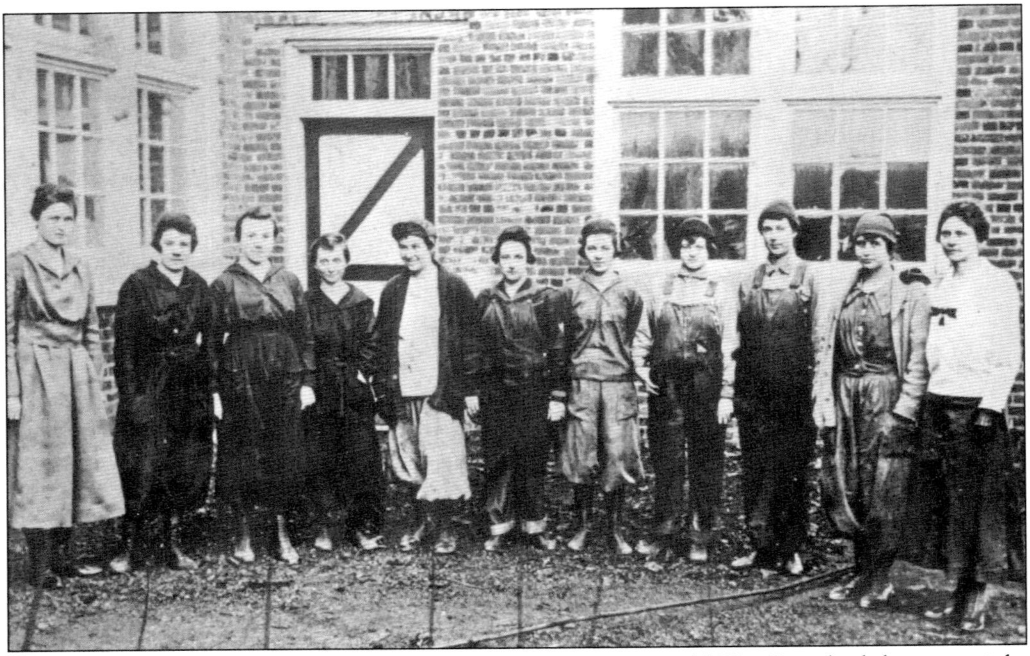

Although women traditionally held the role of homemaker, World War II pushed them into jobs usually filled by men, like those at the Lenoir Car Works. As local fathers, brothers, and sons were drafted, women stepped into jobs in order to support their families while the male breadwinners were away. Several of these unidentified Car Works employees were wearing dresses or skirts, despite the physically demanding nature of the job.

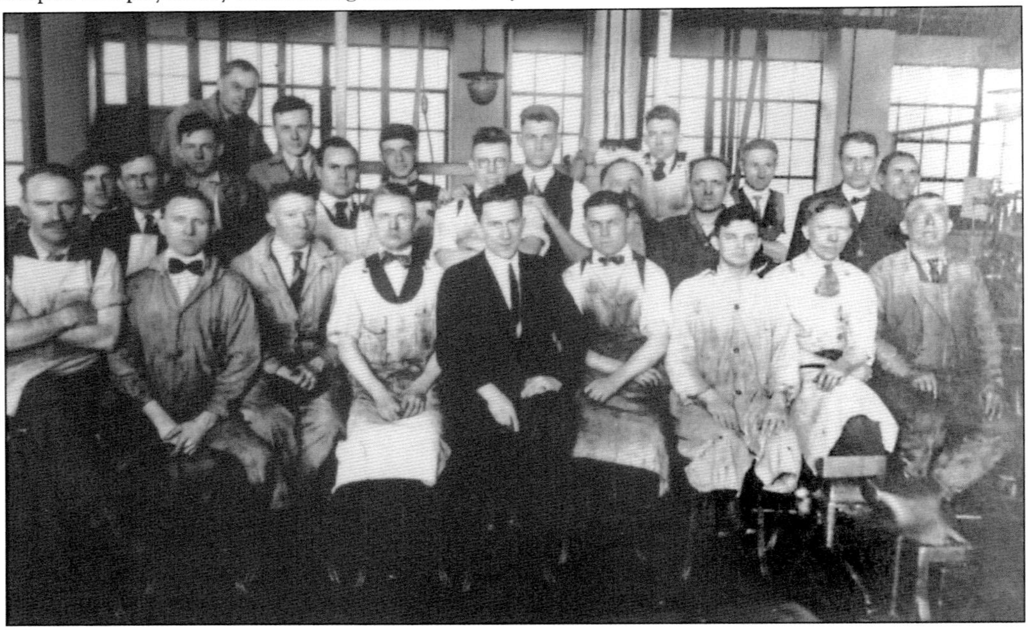

These unidentified Lenoir Car Works pattern department employees sported suits and ties under protective aprons and smocks. It was the job of these men to draft the blueprints for the railroad cars, wheels, and other parts first on paper, then in wood models before finally being cast in metal.

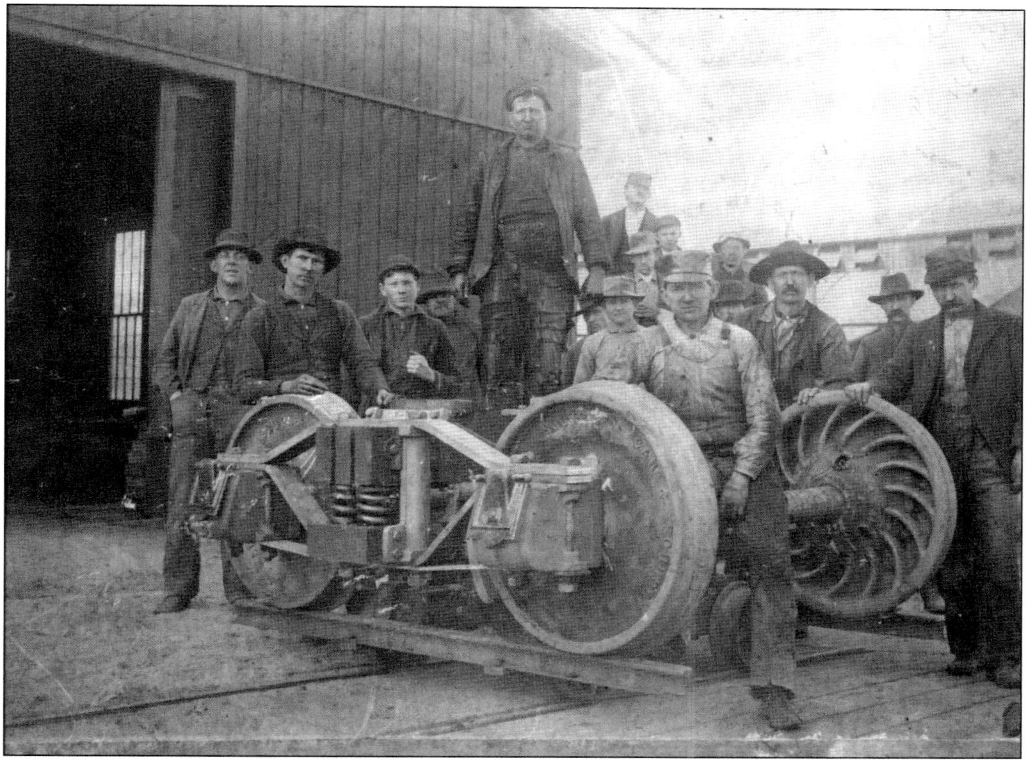

Southern Railway, which was created in 1894 largely from the Richmond and Danville system and the East Tennessee, Virginia, and Georgia Railroad, benefited from the Lenoir Car Works location. Situated on 93 acres of Southern Railway-owned land, the Lenoir Car Works churned out boxcars, coal cars, train wheels, and other railroad items. These unidentified employees made a good living working here.

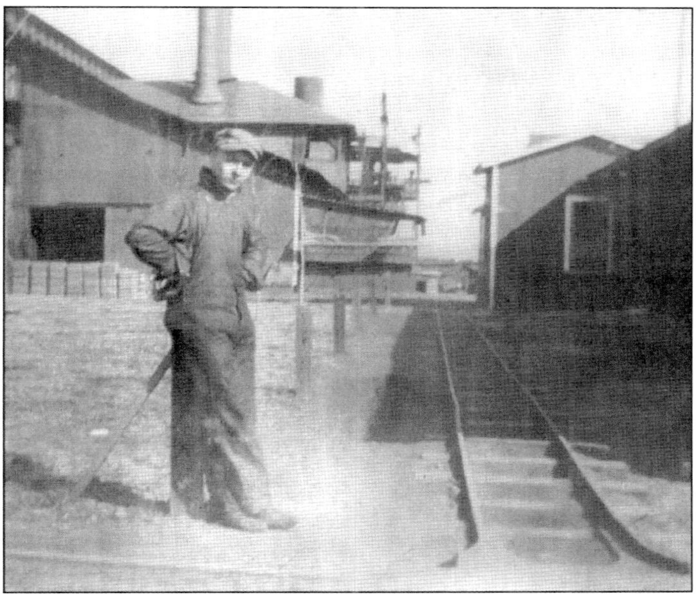

Despite long hours and grueling work, the Lenoir Car Works offered employees, like this unidentified fellow, job security and a healthy paycheck during its peak years. It took a constant stream of quality parts to keep Southern Railway's many trains running smoothly, and the Lenoir Car Works had the manpower and equipment to deliver.

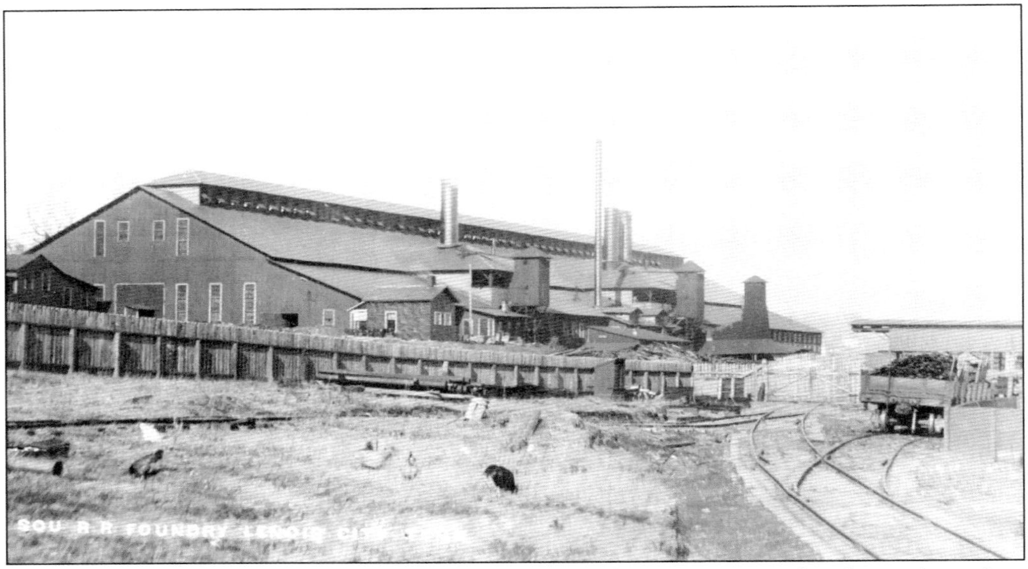

Lenoir City and the Lenoir Car Works began at roughly the same time, and each was dependent upon the other. The town supplied workers for the Car Works, and the Car Works supplied a reliable income for the residents. In the early years, the Car Works turned out 10 to 12 cars daily, more than tripling that number within three decades before it started its decline.

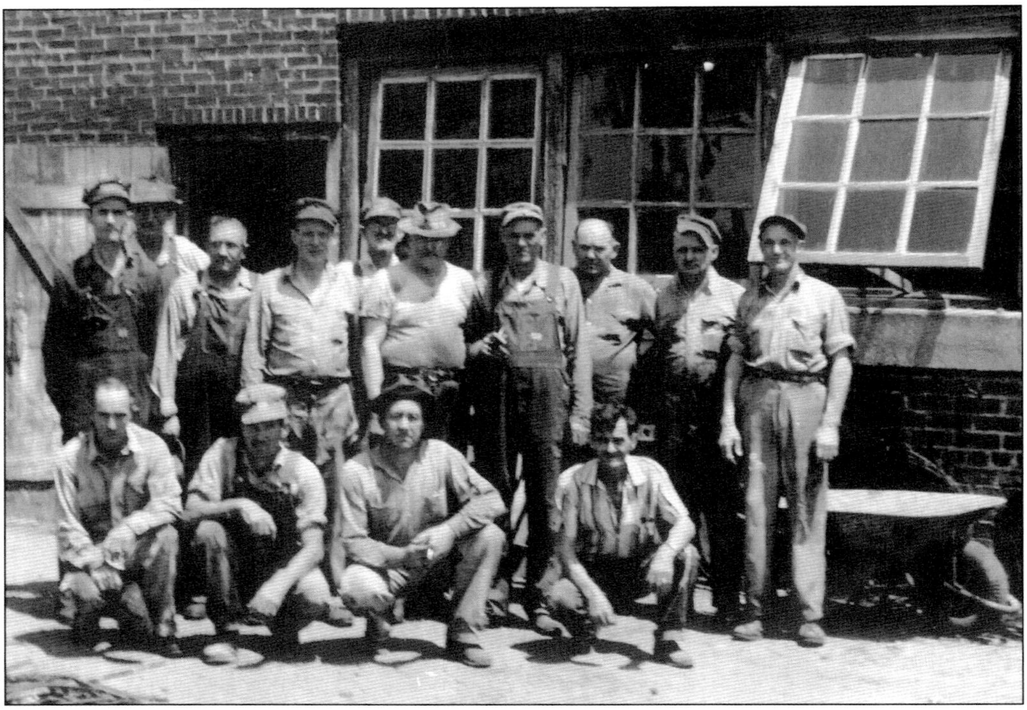

By the 1930s, automobiles, airplanes, and the Great Depression led to a decline in railroad ridership and mileage. The Lenoir Car Works began to feel the effects. It took fewer employees to meet the production demands at the Car Works, and jobs began to dwindle. Those who were lucky enough to still have a job, like these unidentified Car Works employees, stayed on as long as they could.

In addition to the Lenoir Car Works, residents were able to seek employment at area mills including what would eventually become the Charles H. Bacon Company hosiery mill. Charles Harrison Bacon was the son of Nathaniel P. and Martha Bacon, farmers from Loudon, Tennessee. Charles served in World War I and served as a delegate to the Democratic National Convention in 1924. He owned hosiery mills in both Loudon and Lenoir City.

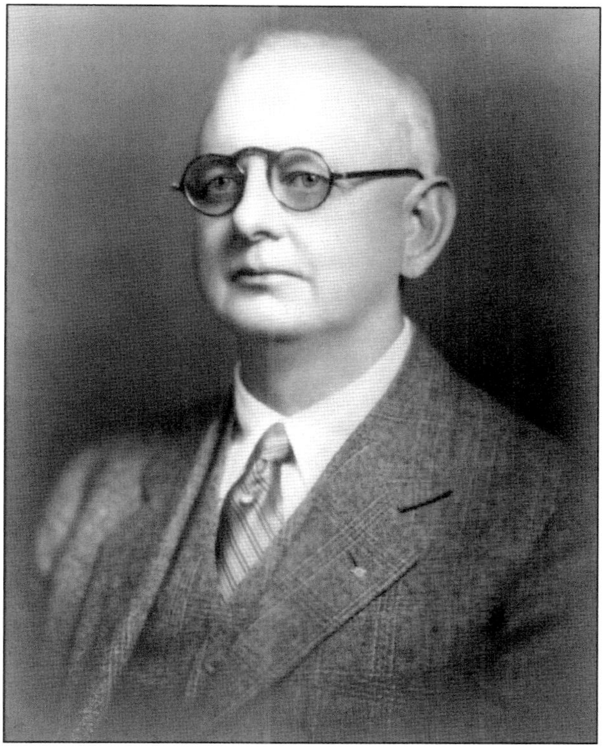

The hosiery mill in Lenoir City got its start in 1897 when Frank A. Weiss, the town's first mayor, decided to go into business for himself. Weiss originally called the business Dixie Mills but later changed it to the Holston Manufacturing Company. There were 600 employees at the hosiery mill in Lenoir City in 1907, and in 1918, Weiss sold the mill to Taubel-Scott.

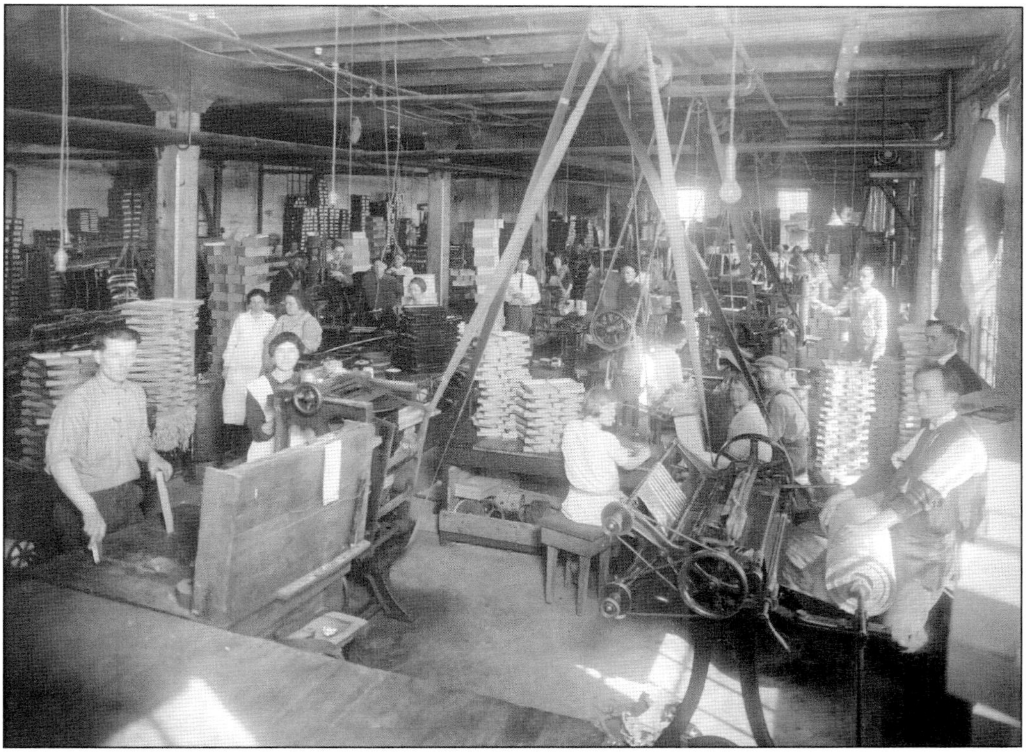

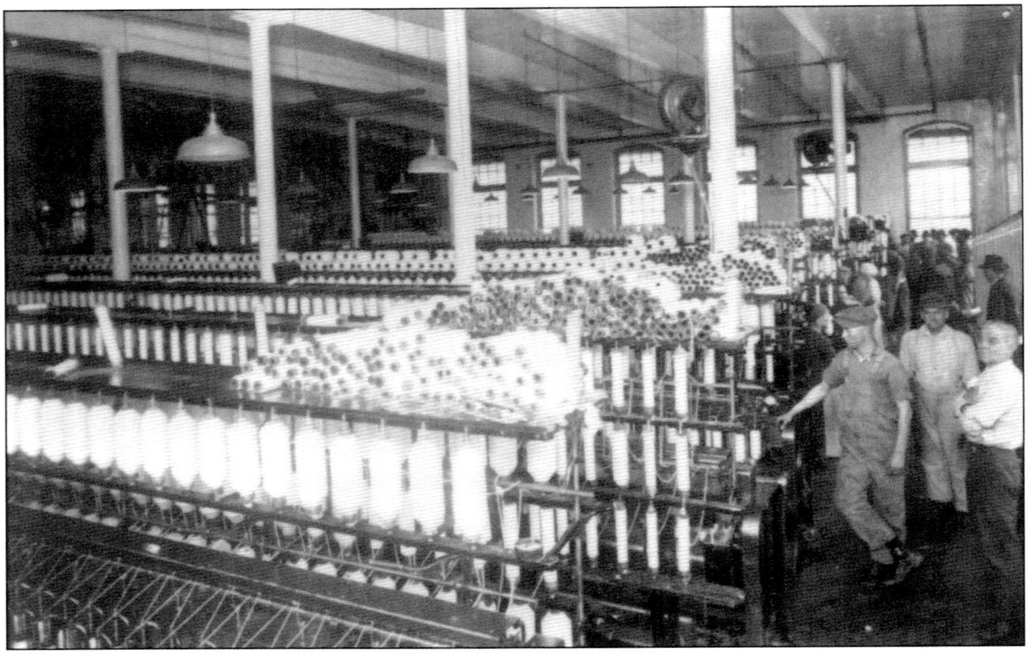

In 1924, the Taubel-Scott hosiery mill merged with the mill in Loudon, and the two businesses incorporated under the name Charles H. Bacon Company. The mill flourished, and new equipment was installed in the early 1930s, making mill jobs less hazardous by replacing floor to ceiling pulley belts with self-contained electric motors. By the 1970s, the two mills employed more than 1,400 people.

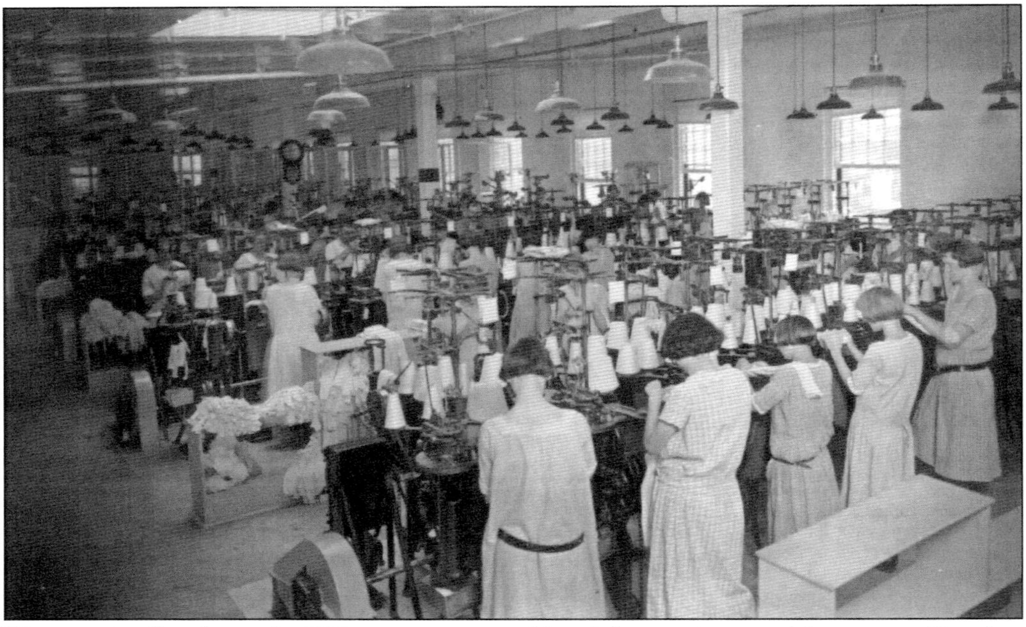

The typical mill worker in the 1920s was an unmarried female living at home with her parents. She often helped to support younger siblings and contribute to the family coffers. With the passing of the 19th amendment in 1920, women were given the right to vote. Many cut their hair in a "shingle bob," like these unidentified women at the Charles H. Bacon hosiery mill, and became more independent.

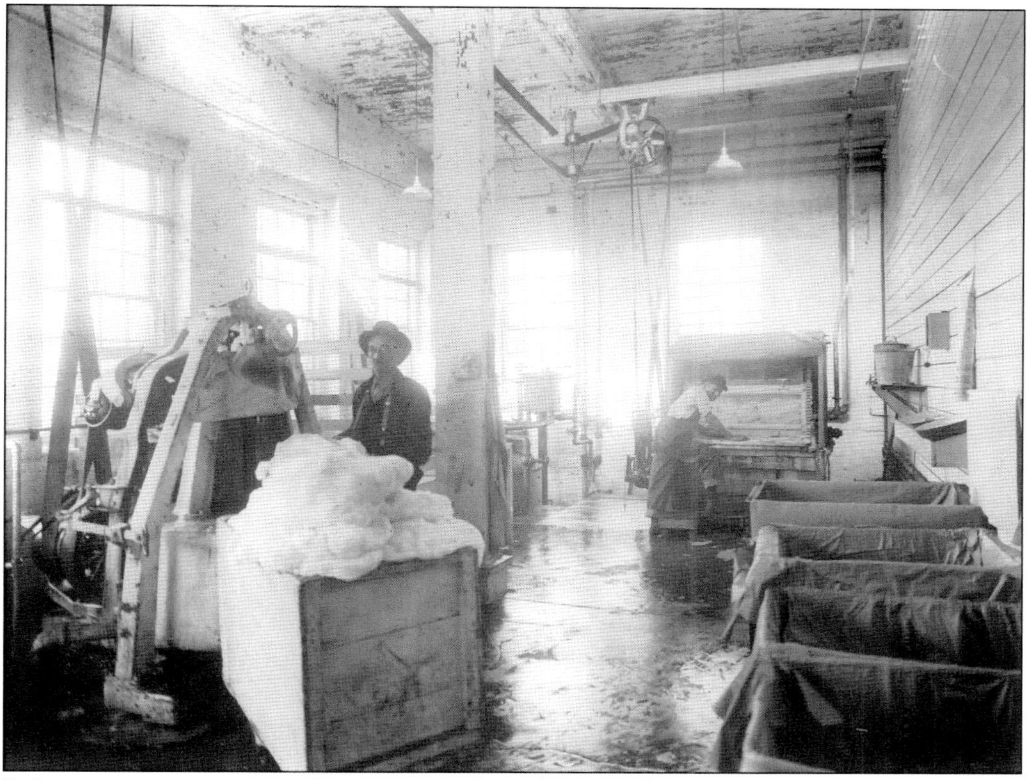

Before it was spun into yarn, the cotton was cleaned or ginned to remove trash. Carding separated the fibers and removed the remaining debris and short fibers, then the yarn was scoured or washed and dried. Scouring was a hot, steamy job, particularly in the summer months when East Tennessee humidity is especially brutal thanks to the myriad waterways in the area.

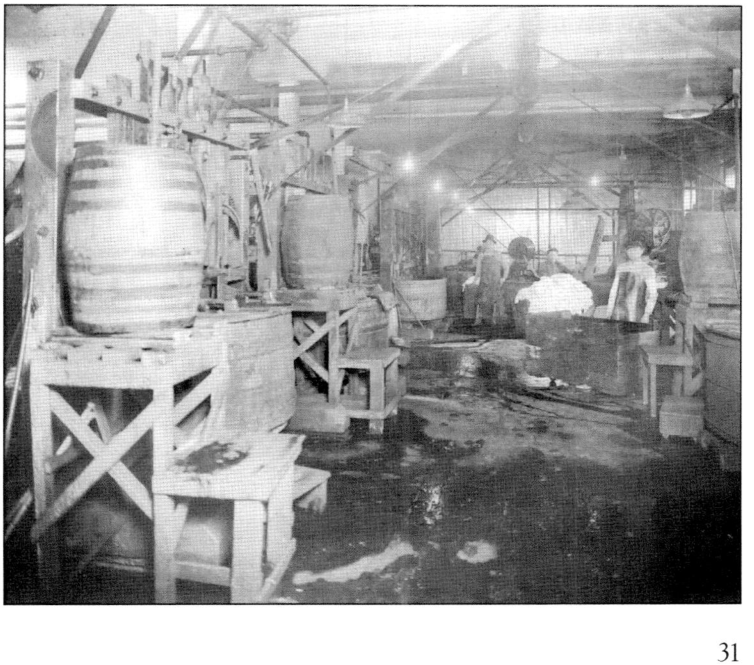

For colored stockings, the yarn could be dyed after washing or scouring, or even after the stocking was sewn. Large white pine barrels were used for this task. Like the washing room, the dying room offered damp conditions and slippery floors. Workers, like these unidentified hosiery mill employees, had to take great care not to fall.

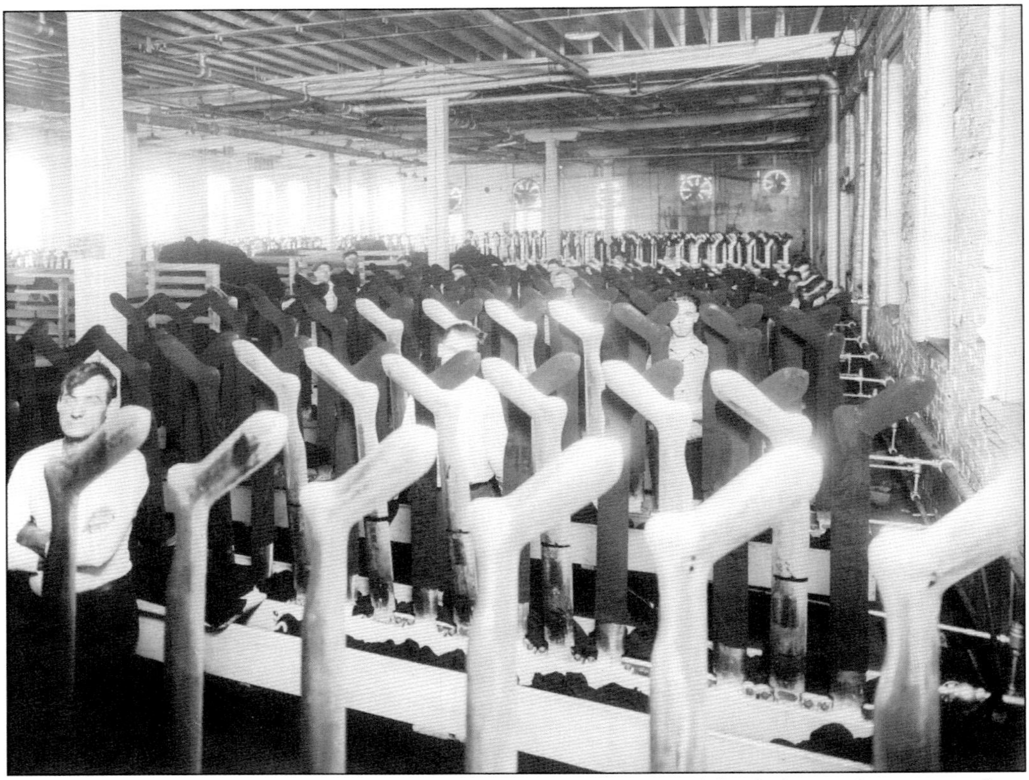

Once the cotton was cleaned, washed, woven, sewn together, and dyed, the stockings were then stretched on steam-heated metallic forms for drying and shaping. These forms may have been purchased from the Paramount Hosiery Form Drying Company, which held a patent on this type of form and offered demonstrations at their offices in New York City, according to an article printed in the *Textile American* in 1917.

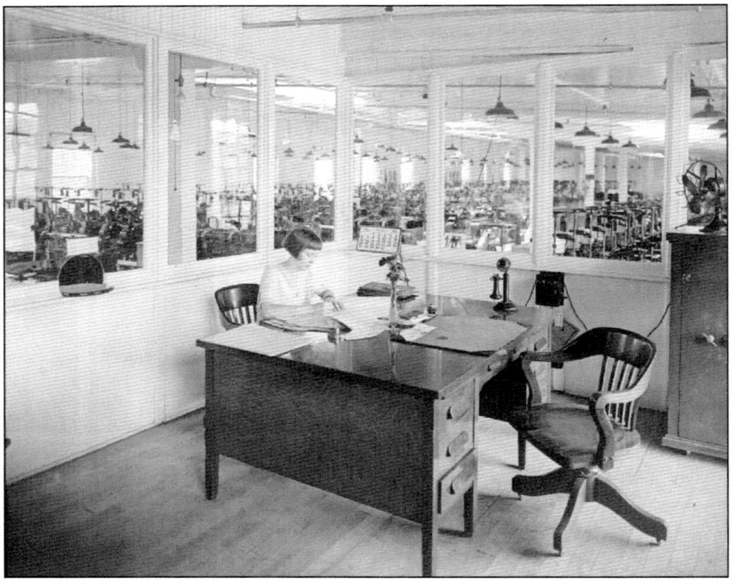

Although the hours were long and the jobs often hazardous, Charles H. Bacon Company hosiery mill offered employees, like this unidentified office worker, a steady income. A calendar in the background of this glassed-in office showed a date of July 1924. Note the electric fan and modern candlestick telephone with wall ringer; a telephone book hung below.

Three

Other Businesses

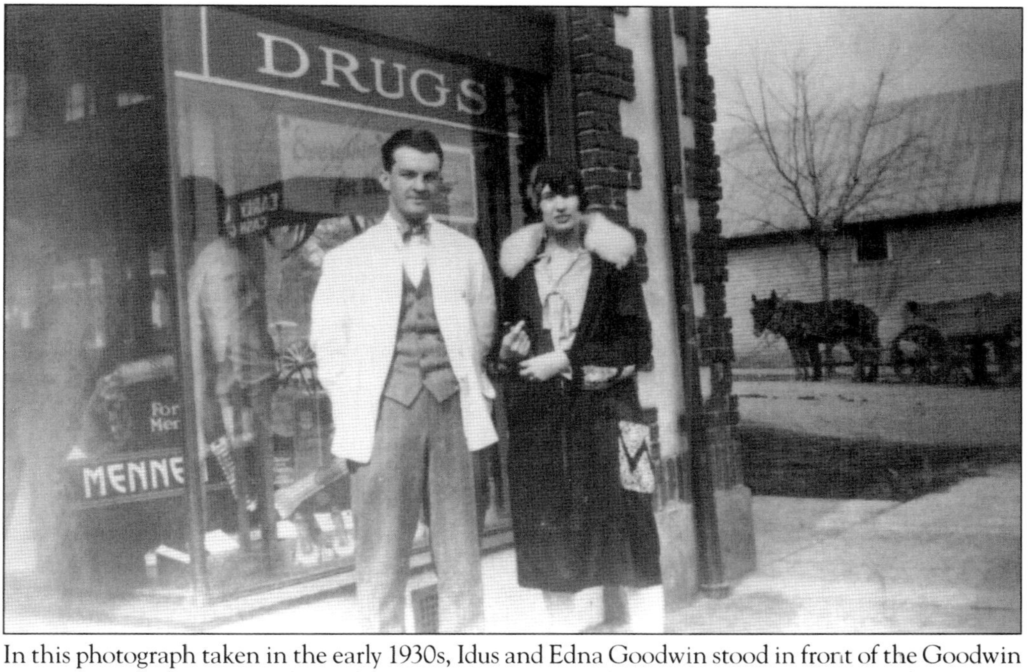

In this photograph taken in the early 1930s, Idus and Edna Goodwin stood in front of the Goodwin Drug Store on the corner of Broadway and B Streets. The business offered patrons a soda fountain and became a local gathering spot. Edna wore a fashionable cloche hat and fur-trimmed coat. In the background was a horse drawn wagon. The Goodwin Drug Company was founded in 1884 by William H. Goodwin.

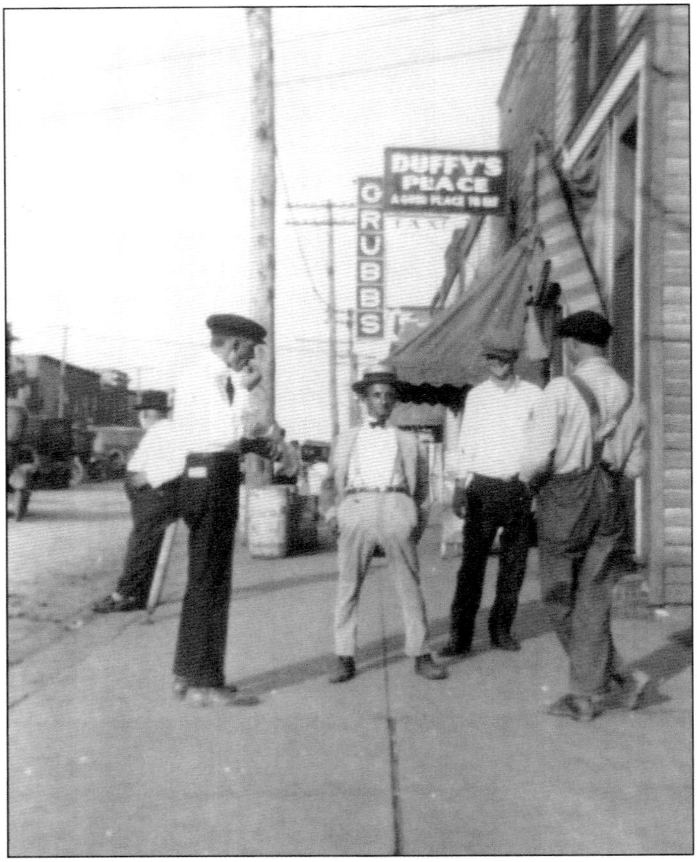

The aptly named Charlie Hatfield (center, wearing a straw hat) and his unidentified companions were loafing around in downtown Lenoir City in this 1920 photograph. Behind them, the signs for Duffy's Place—"A Good Place to Eat"—and Grubbs Variety Store are visible. Hatfield was a textile worker at the hosiery mill.

The staff of the Porter and Campbell Grocery Store looked neat, clean, and ready to serve you in this 1934 photograph. They are, from left to right, Porter Campbell, Roy DeRieux, and James Boyd Porter. In the 1930s, shoppers would have paid about 39¢ per pound for ham, 18¢ for a dozen eggs, and 19¢ for 10 pounds of potatoes.

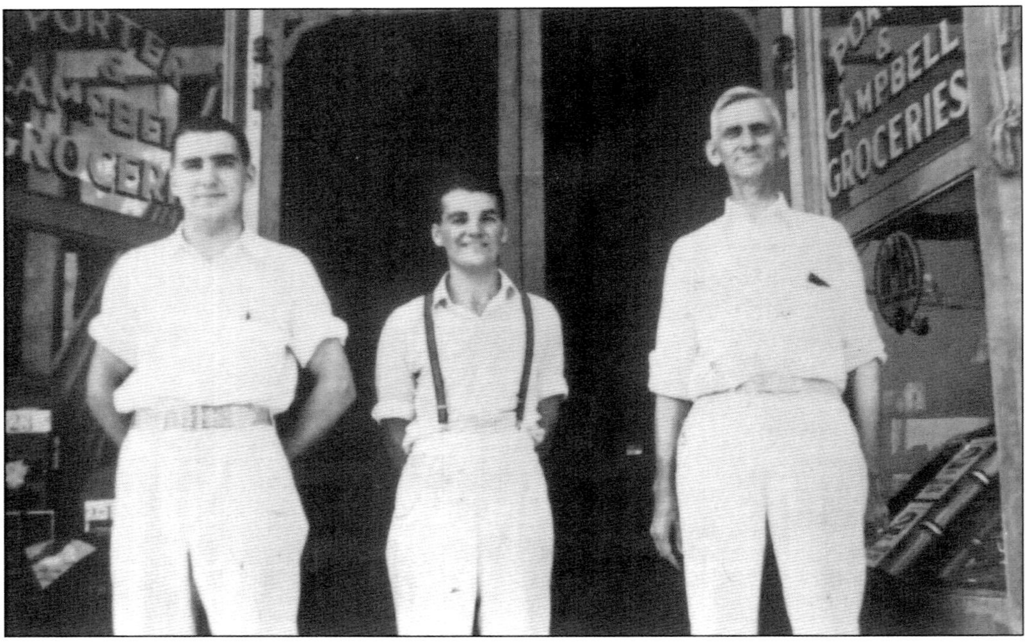

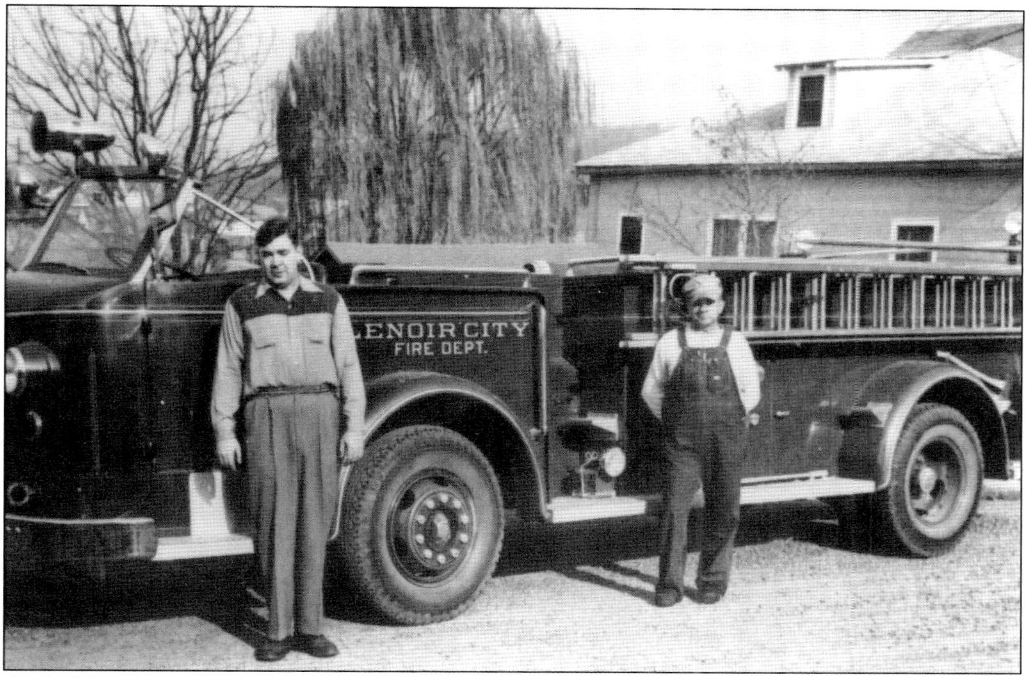

A good fire department was essential in an industrial town like Lenoir City. Here Bill Fritts (right) and Fred "Butter" Nelson stood beside the city fire truck in this 1959 photograph. These men, along with other paid and volunteer firefighters, were ready to put their lives on the line to save the people and buildings in their community.

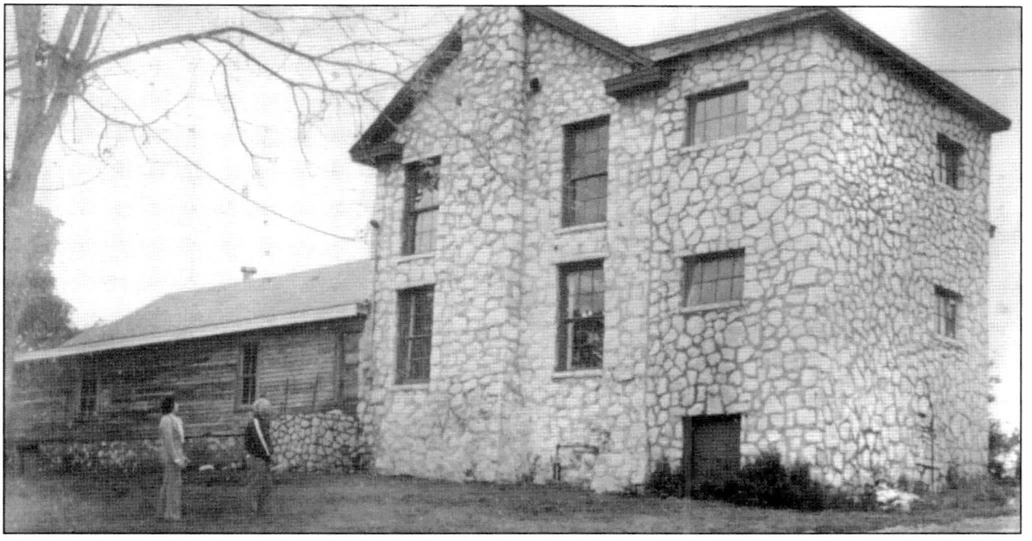

The Armstrong Candy Factory was built around 1929 by Eugene Armstrong Sr. The company sold candy to schools in Tennessee, Georgia, Kentucky, and Alabama for fund-raising events. Salesmen traveled among schools promoting contests with the top selling schools receiving sports equipment. The Lenoir City Museum has metal templates used by the company to print the candy wrappers.

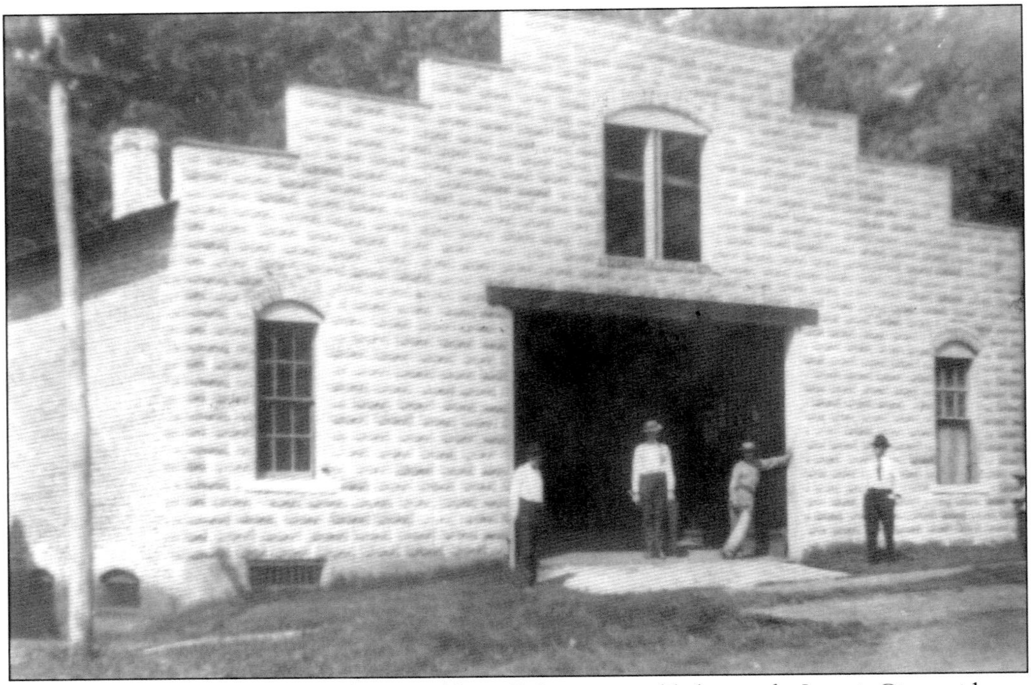

William H. Ghormley built this livery stable on B Street to stable horses for Lenoir City residents. In 1911, a year after this photograph was taken, the building housed Lenoir City's first Ford automobile franchise. The building was later used as a mortuary by Harvey Hawkins. The only people identified in this photograph are Nelson "Nell" Bishop (standing in the center of the doorway) and Clyde Ghormley (on the far right).

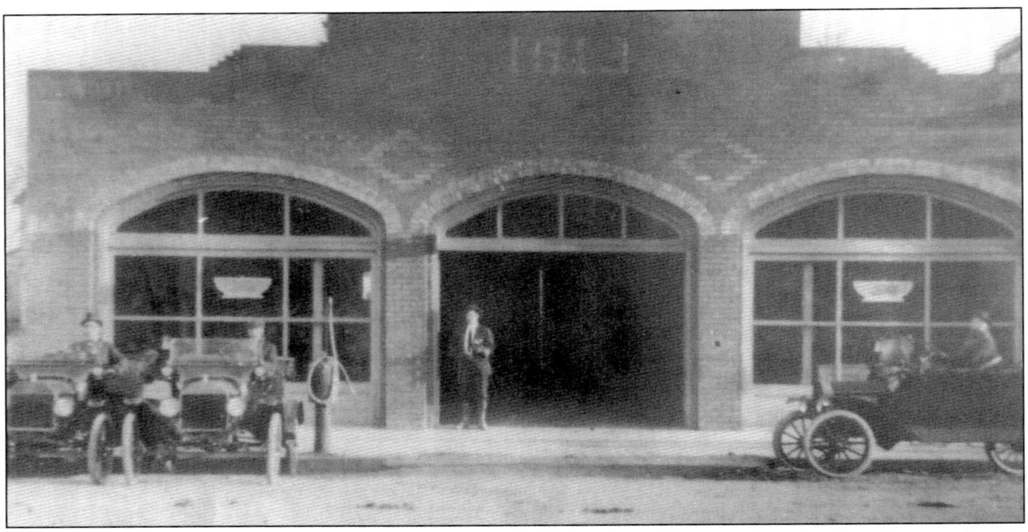

In 1913, William H. Ghormley and Sons built a new 50-foot-by-140-foot facility on the south side of Broadway Street opposite Kingston Street to accommodate their Ford franchise. Progressive businessmen, the Ghormleys were the first dealers for Ford automobiles in Loudon County. Ed Ghormley had the distinction of being the first person to sell a Ford automobile in Loudon County. In addition to selling cars, the business offered a parts department and repair service.

This building, built by William H. Ghormley, originally housed the Ghormley Ford dealership. After the death of Thomas Ghormley in 1951, his widow, Julia, and son David continued to operate the Ford dealership until 1954, when they sold it to Gillus Purdy and R. L. "Cotton" Easter.

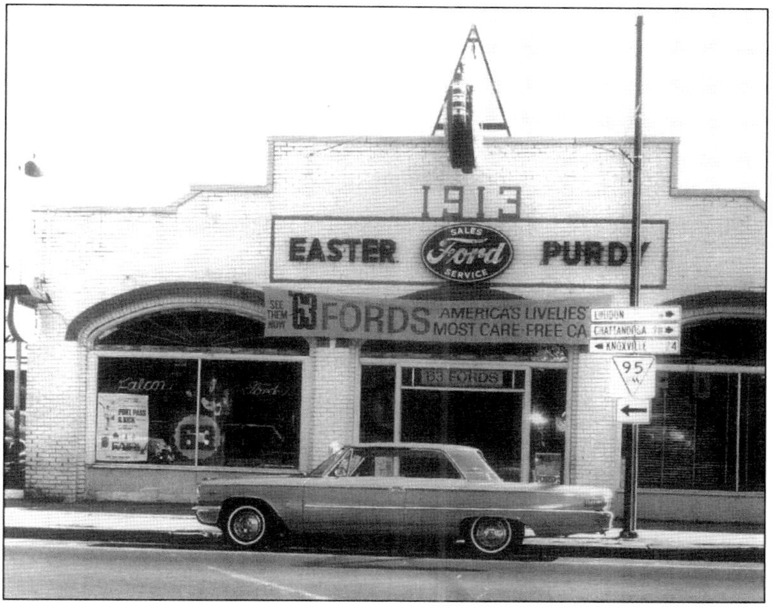

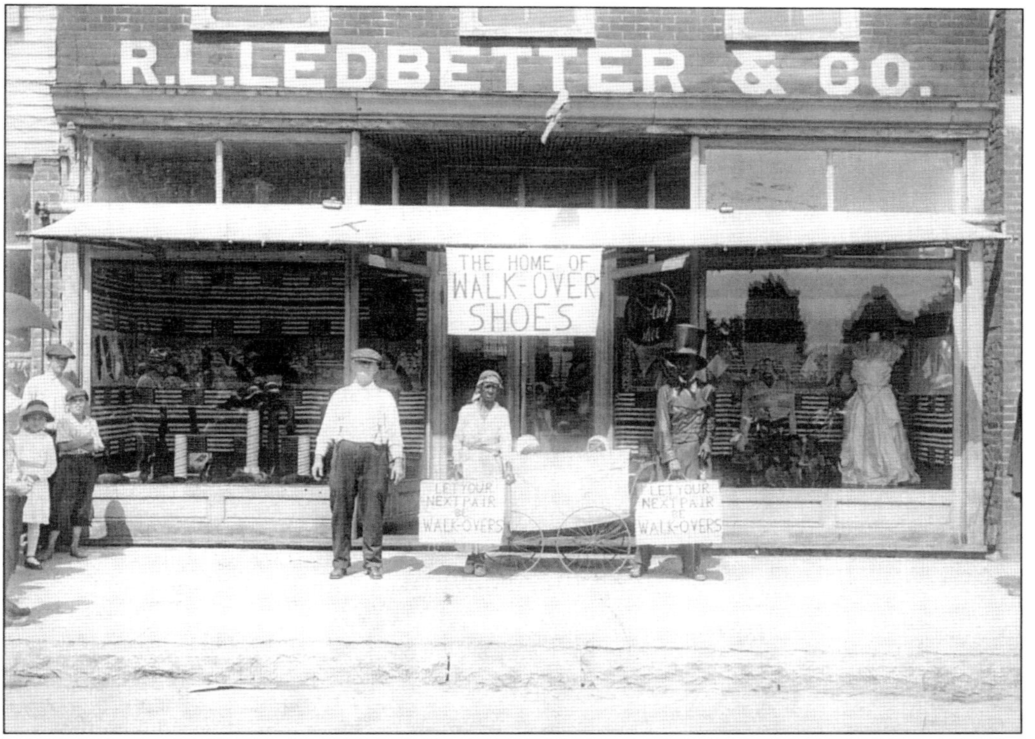

This July 4, 1916, photograph taken in front of the R. L. Ledbetter and Company dry goods store shows a live performance art advertisement for Walk-Over Shoes. Standing in the center are, from left to right, Robert L. Ledbetter (owner), Roy B. Ledbetter (in black face), and unidentified (in top hat). The children in the buggy are George Ledbetter and Florence Mae "Pon" Ledbetter Walker.

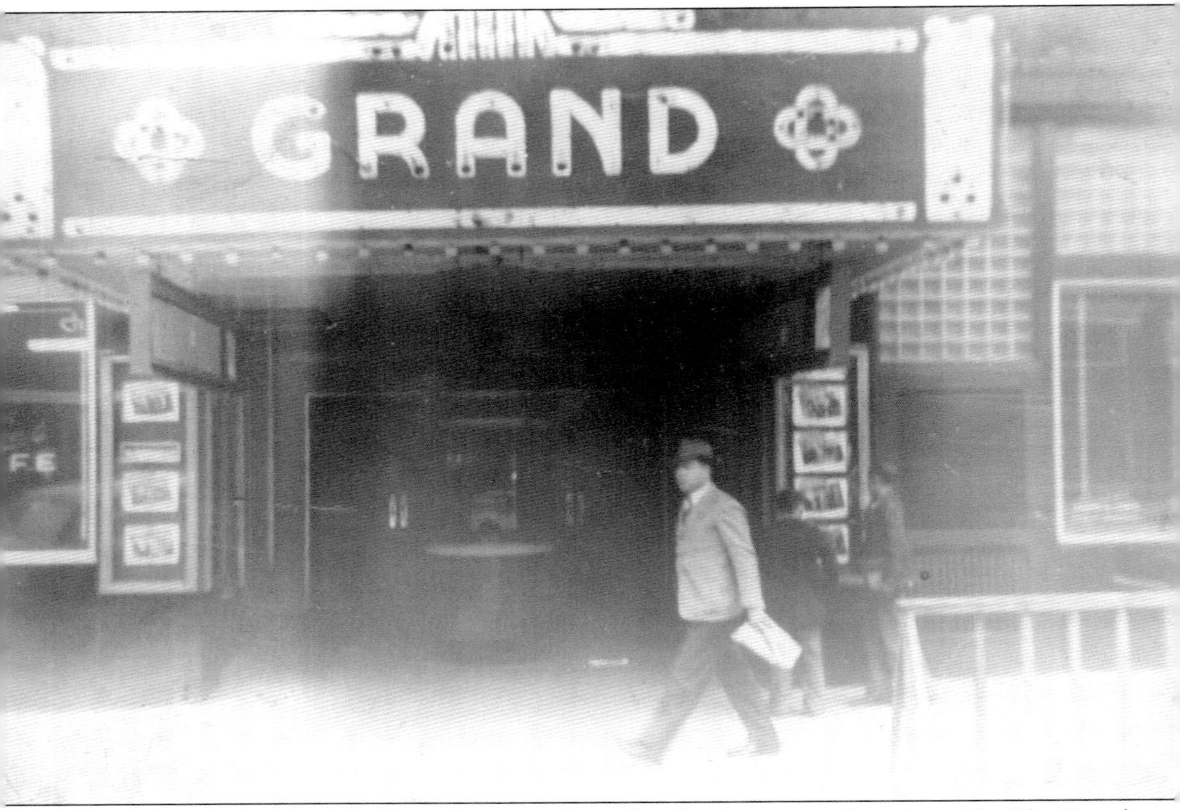

There is nothing grander than taking your best gal to the theater on a Saturday night. The Grand Theater in Lenoir City was operated by Consolidated Amusements in the 1930s and offered films as well as live entertainment. It had a single screen and could seat 715 people. It has since been closed and demolished. The people in the photograph are unidentified.

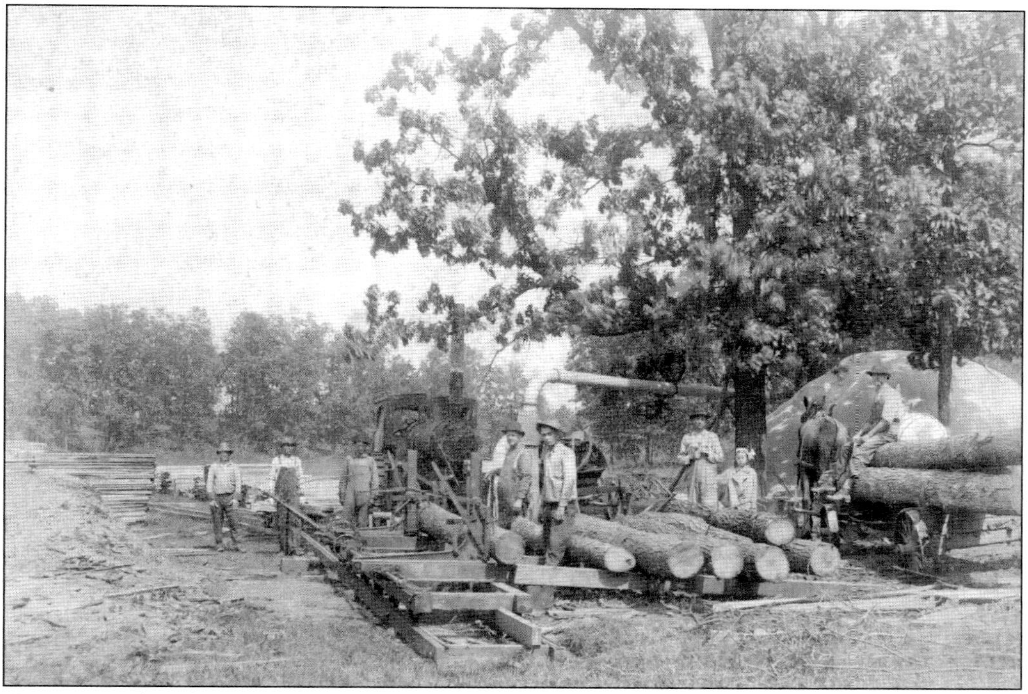

Trees were abundant in East Tennessee when the Lenoir family and early settlers of Loudon County came to the area. Sawmills were an important part of everyday life, providing wood for homes, barns, and businesses. These unidentified sawmill workers are utilizing both mechanical and live horsepower to transport trees that have been recently felled.

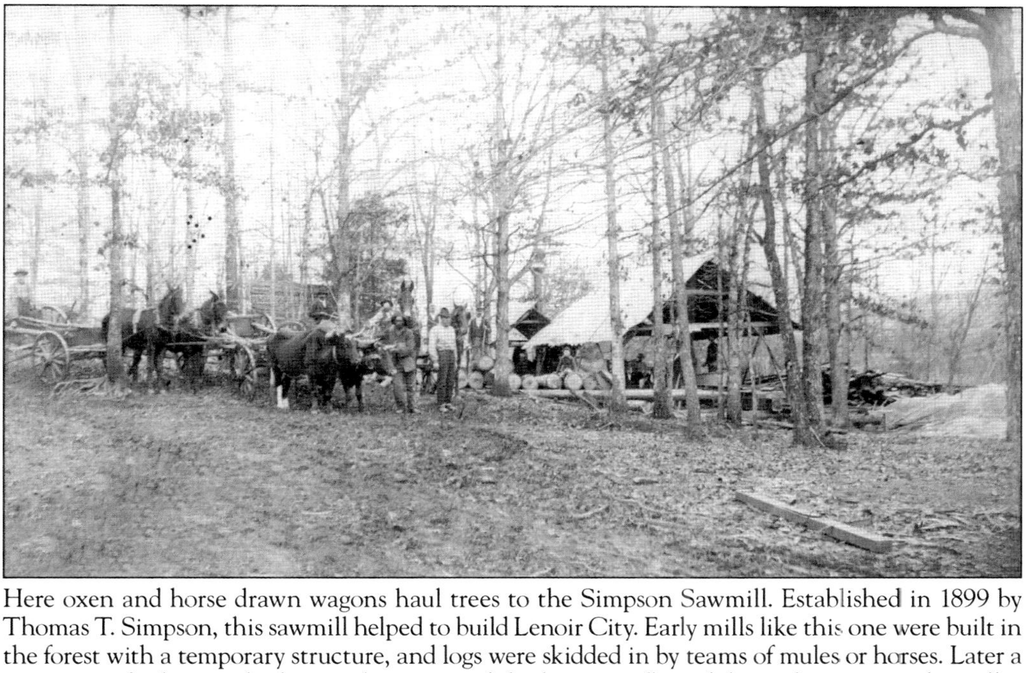

Here oxen and horse drawn wagons haul trees to the Simpson Sawmill. Established in 1899 by Thomas T. Simpson, this sawmill helped to build Lenoir City. Early mills like this one were built in the forest with a temporary structure, and logs were skidded in by teams of mules or horses. Later a permanent facility was built near the river, and the logs were floated down the water to the mill.

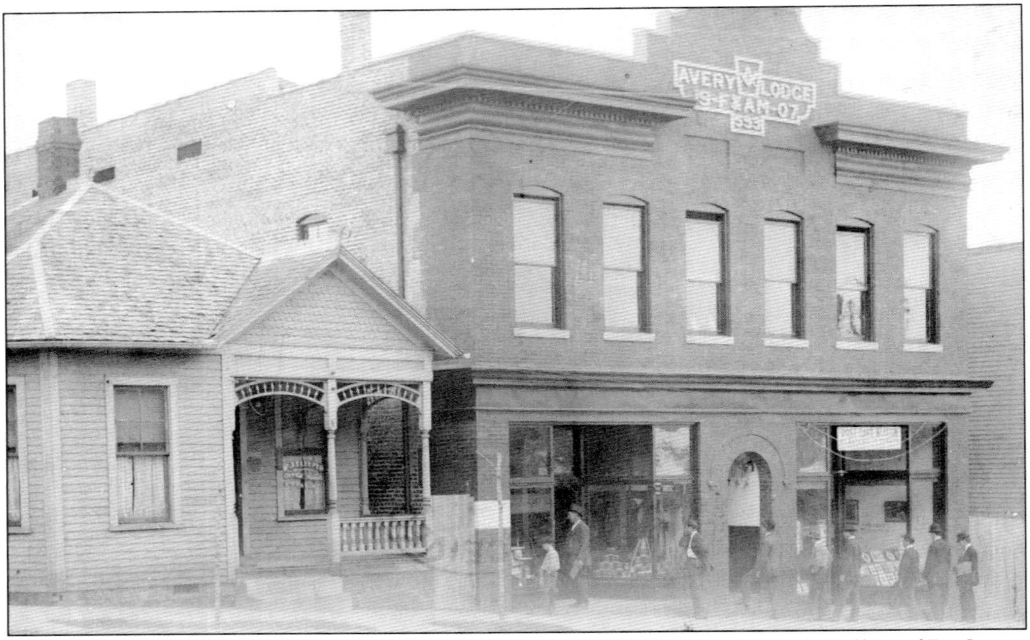

On January 31, 1906, the city council met in the small building on the left, the office of Dr. James Thomas Leeper, to discuss the incorporation of the town. After a year of planning, Lenoir City was incorporated on February 7, 1907, and a town charter was approved detailing city boundaries, duties of city officials, and other such things. The building on the right is the Avery Masonic Lodge.

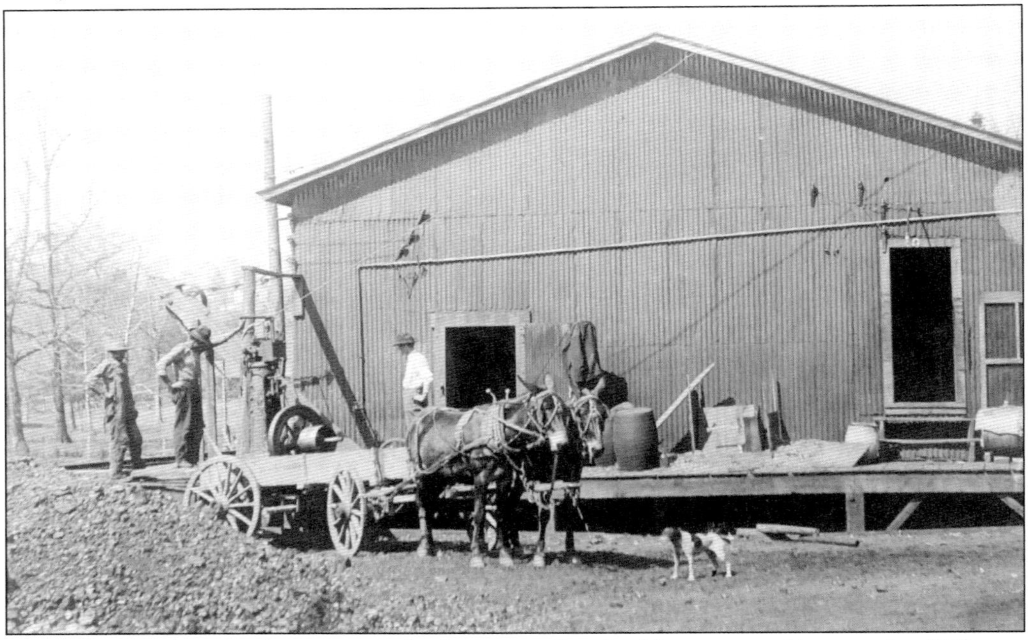

Located across from Rock Springs Park, the Lenoir City Ice Plant pictured here in the 1920s was owned by Henry Foster Sr. The plant produced 300-pound blocks of ice that were delivered to businesses and homes by horse drawn wagons. Before the advent of mechanical refrigeration, people relied on spring houses to keep perishable items cold.

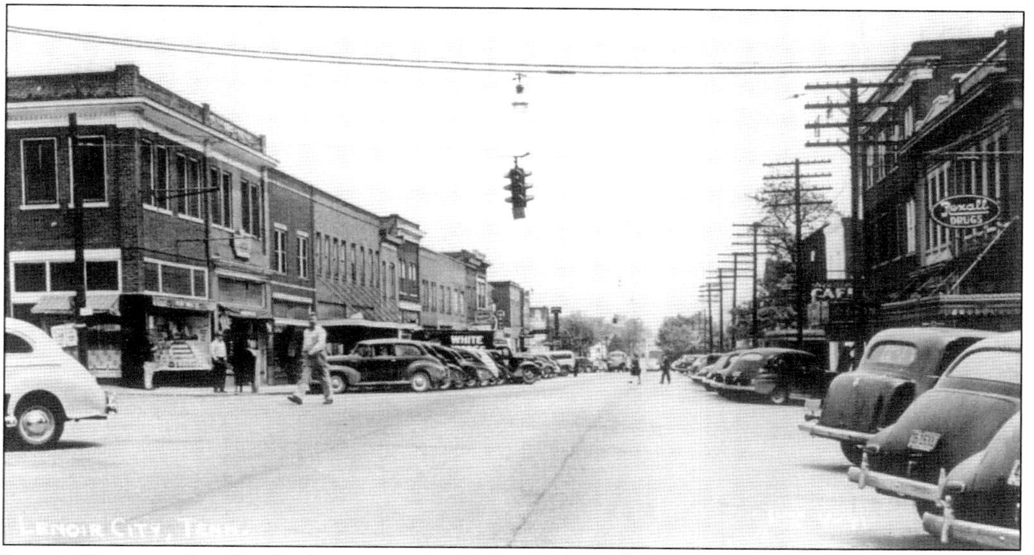

Lenoir City was a bustling little town in the 1940s. On Broadway Street, residents could shop at the White Store, eat at Keener Café, attend a movie at the Grand Theater, or pick up a prescription at the corner drugstore. Traffic lights and streetlights, strung on wires at the intersections, kept both cars and pedestrians in order. At that time, parking was diagonal.

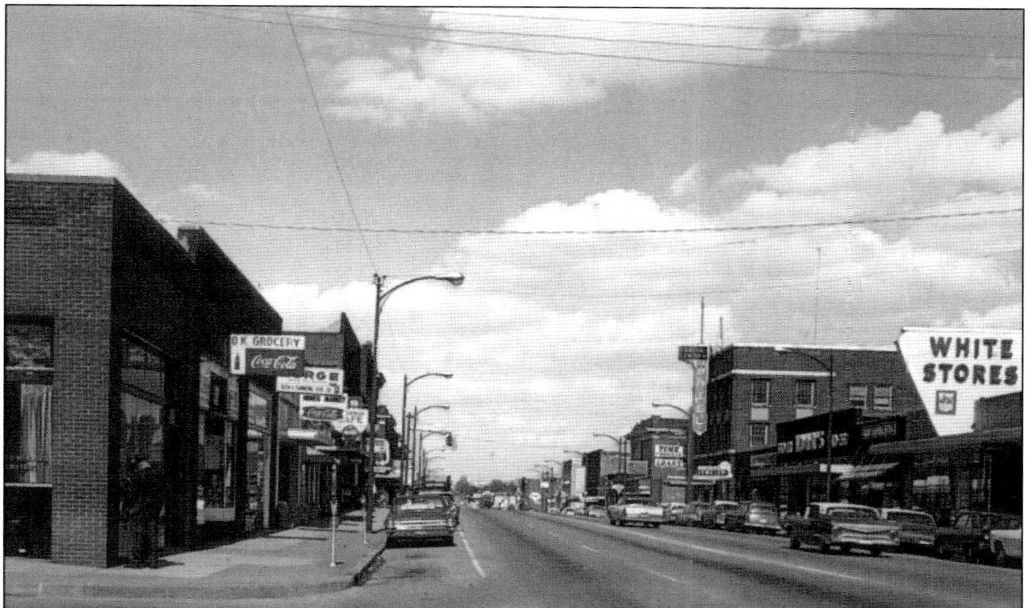

By 1960, parking had been changed to parallel on Broadway Street. Residents could still shop at the White Store or OK Grocery, drink a soda at the café, or check their balance at the First National Bank. Visitors could book a room at the General Lenoir Hotel and then stop by the jewelry store to pick up a gift for their sweetie.

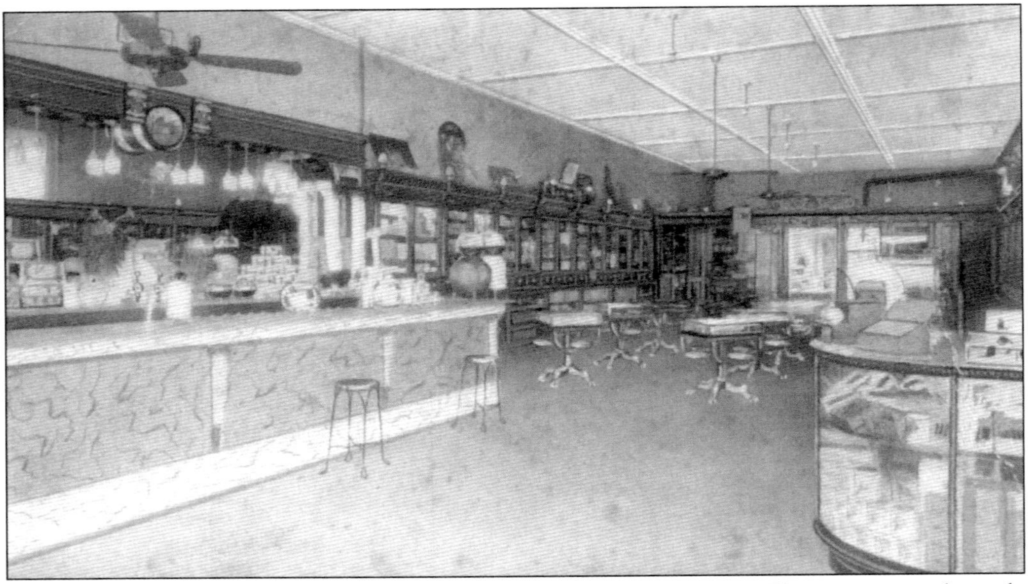

This postcard shows a detailed drawing of the Lenoir Drug Company. The counter at the soda fountain was the perfect place for teenagers to gather after school for a cherry phosphate, chocolate malt, or root beer float. The back of the card reads, "Just to remind you of the place where you use [sic] to get good 'dopes.' " The word dope was slang for soft drink.

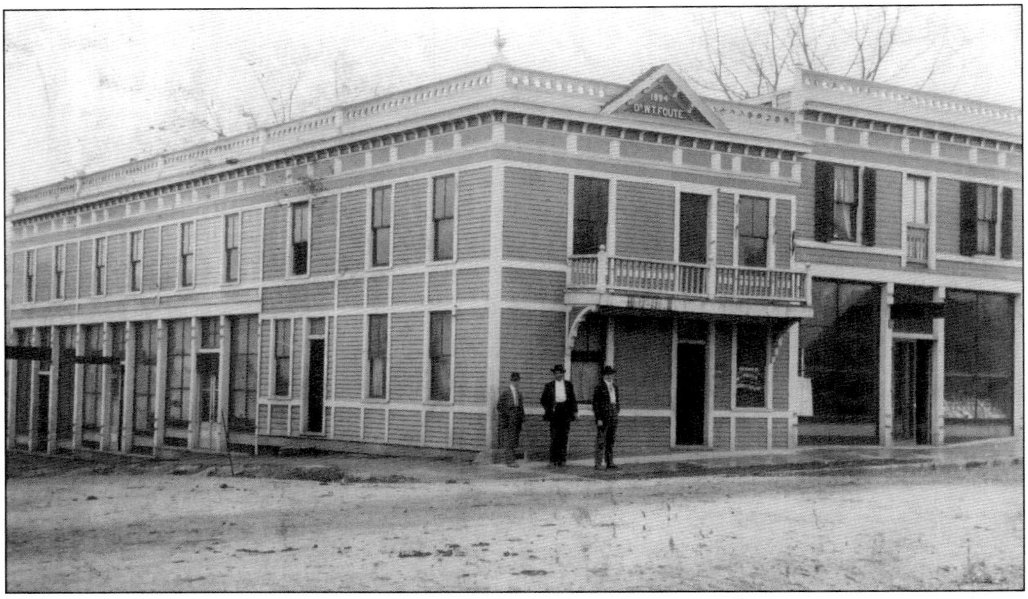

Dr. William Taylor Foute was born in Loudon County. He attended college at Tennessee Wesleyan in Athens, Tennessee, and Southern Medical College in Atlanta. In 1882, he moved to Lenoir's Station and went into partnership with Dr. Benjamin Ballard Lenoir for several years. He and Dr. Ballard parted company on good terms, and Dr. Foute opened his own private office in this building in 1894.

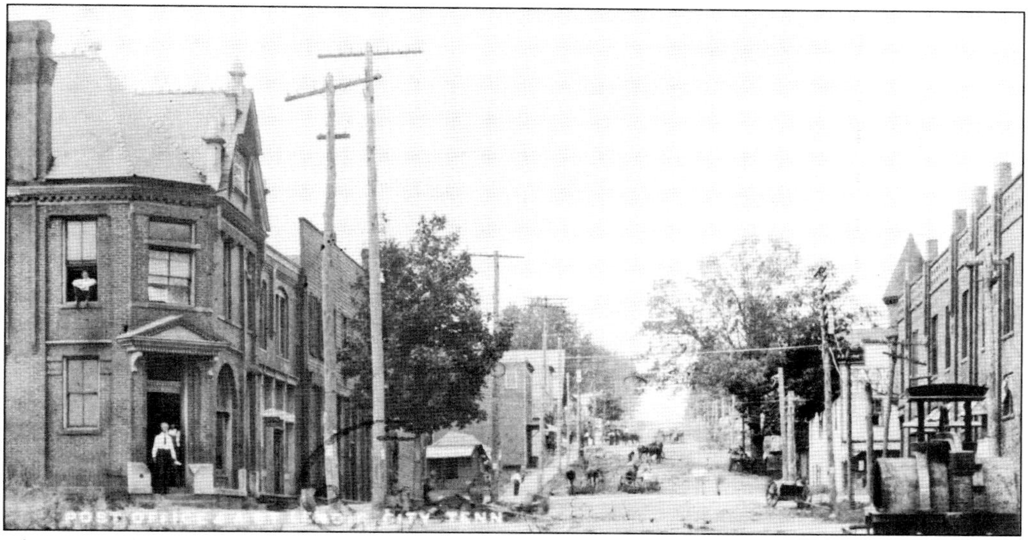

The original Lenoir City post office was an imposing two-story brick building located on Depot Street, where John J. Duff was the first Lenoir City postmaster. In the late 1890s, at the time this building was built, postage cost 2¢ per ounce for domestic letters and a penny per ounce for postcards. On April 16, 1900, the United States Postal Service issued its first books of postage stamps.

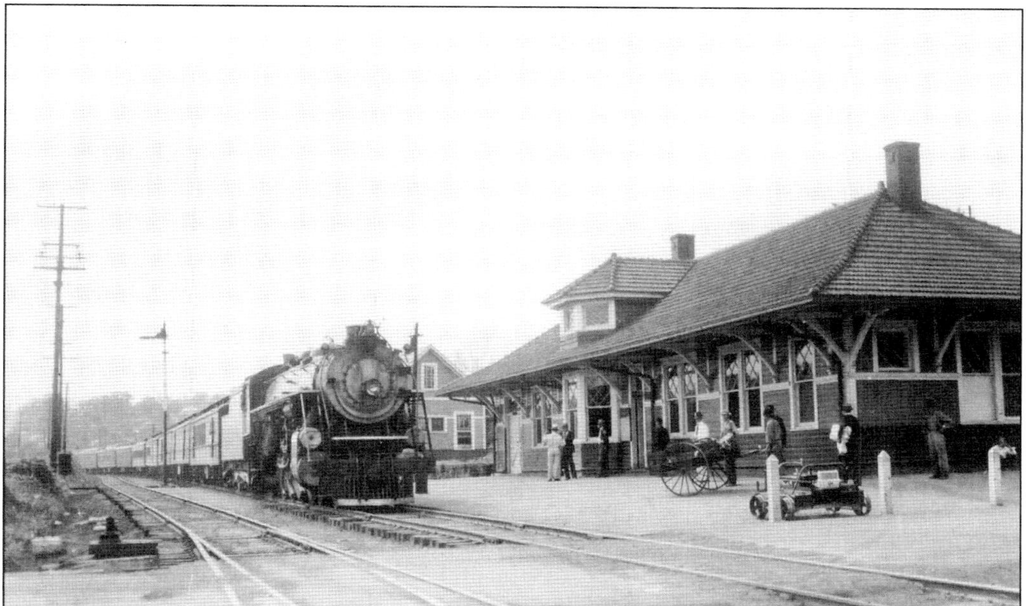

Lenoir City sat directly on the East Tennessee, Georgia, and Virginia Railroad, which was later bought out by Southern Railway. The railroad brought jobs to the city via the Lenoir Car Works, and the depot, with its red tile roof and beveled glass windows, was a vital part of early 20th century life, providing affordable transportation for people and goods.

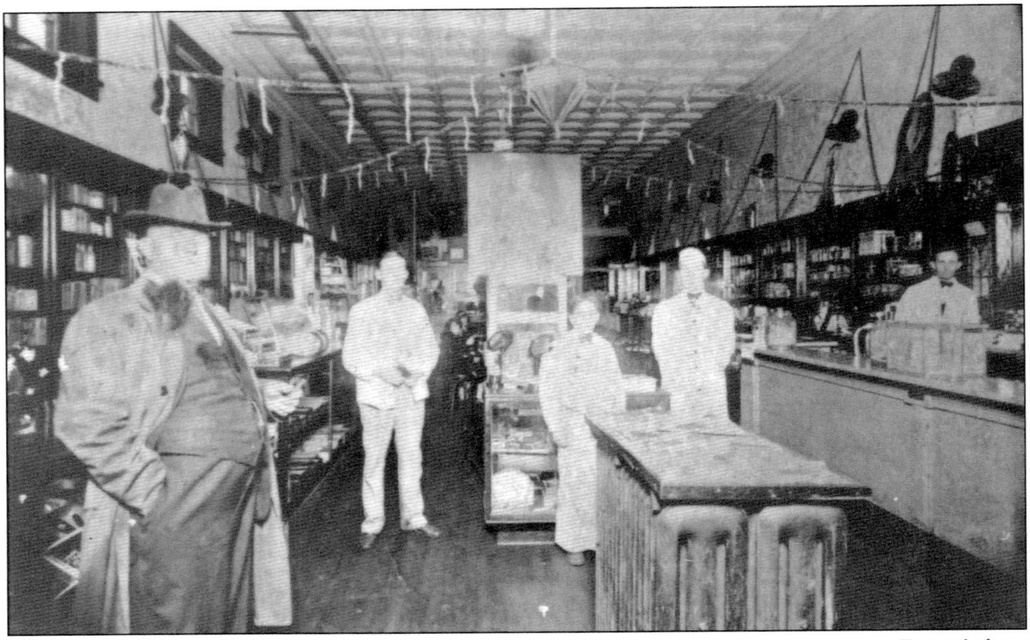

This 1929 photograph was taken inside the Goodwin and Moore Drug Company. From left to right are the following: ? Kittrell, Jim Bailey, Porter Campbell, Millard Glass, and Martin Moore. In addition to medicines, tinctures, salves, and sundries, customers could buy drinks and ice cream from the soda jerk at the store's soda fountain.

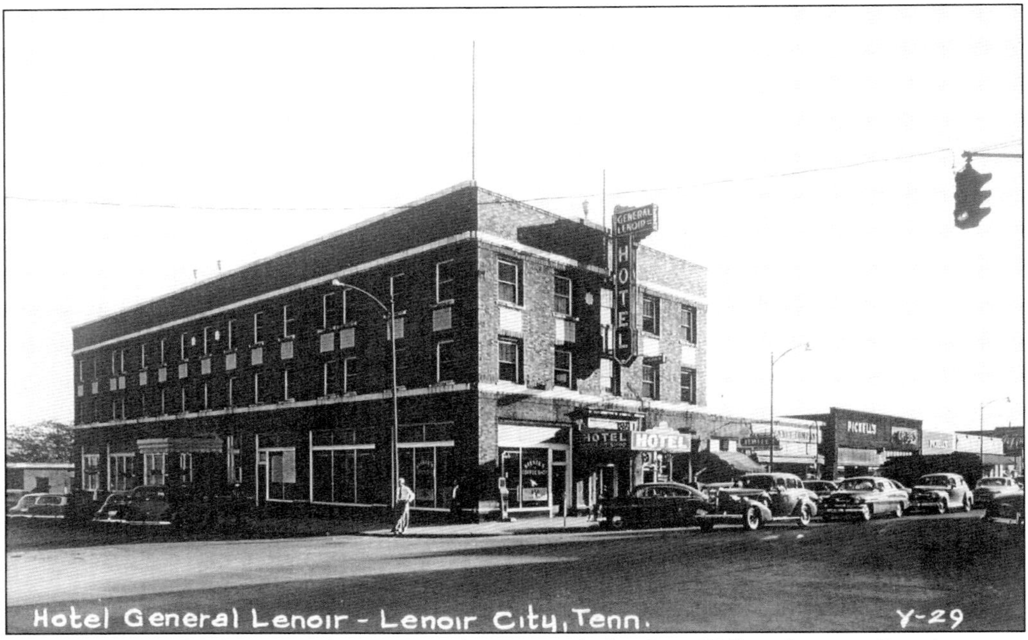

Like the town itself, the General Lenoir Hotel was named after Gen. William Lenoir, a Revolutionary War soldier who fought at the Battle of King's Mountain. Keener's Coffee Shop occupies the left corner of the hotel's first floor. This photograph postcard was taken in the 1940s and shows a view of Broadway Street also known as U.S. Highway 11.

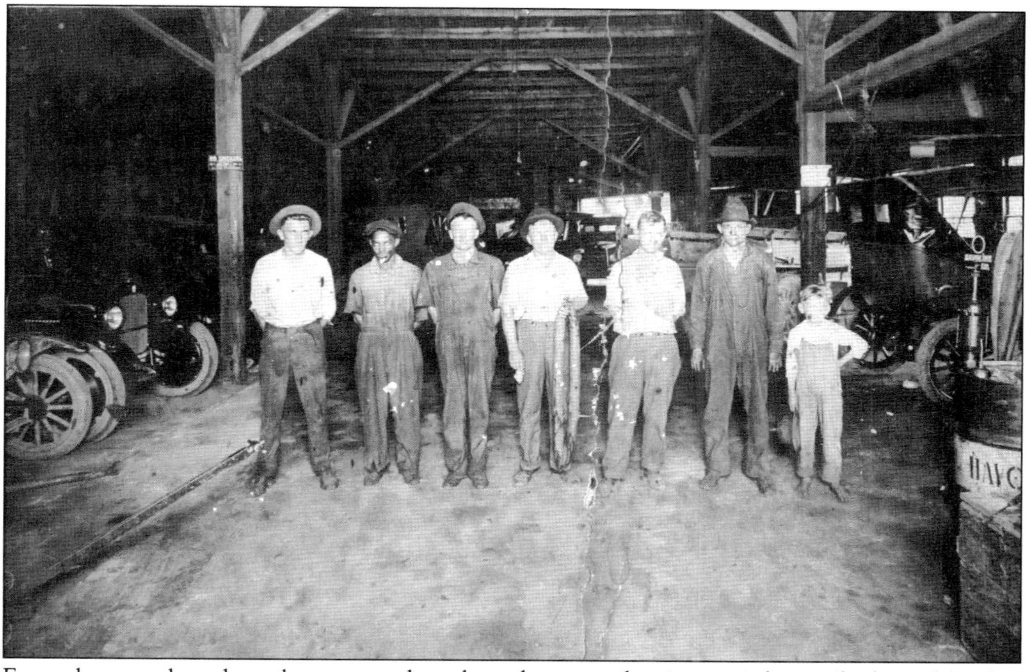

For as long as there have been cars, there have been mechanics to tinker with them, like this unidentified bunch in an early 1920s garage in Lenoir City. The man in the center holds a long thin rubber tire that probably needs a patch, and a Havoline oil barrel sits at the far right.

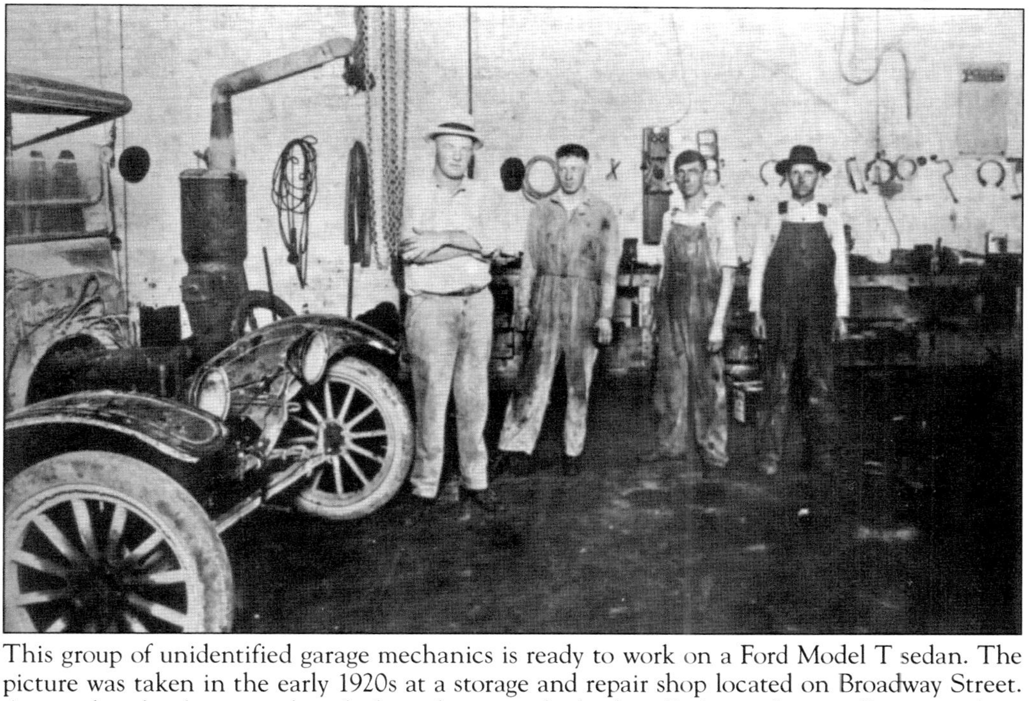

This group of unidentified garage mechanics is ready to work on a Ford Model T sedan. The picture was taken in the early 1920s at a storage and repair shop located on Broadway Street. Assorted tools, chains, and a telephone hang on the back wall. A woodstove offers warmth in the open building on cold winter days.

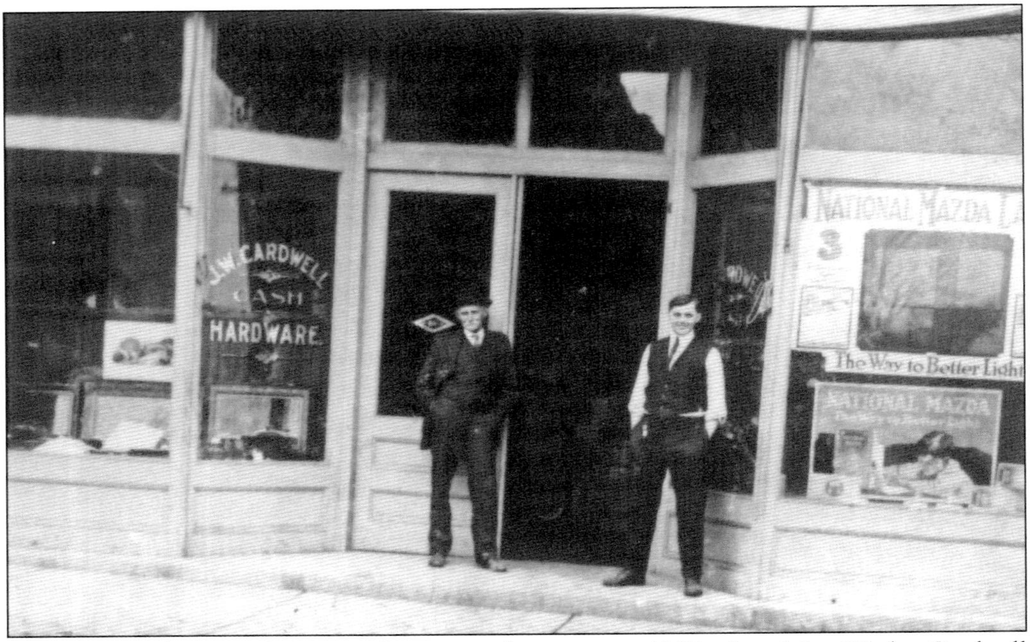

Cardwell Hardware and Grocery Stores got their start in 1907, when John Wesley Cardwell bought goods from a general merchandising firm. In 1908 and 1910, the Cardwells built new brick buildings to house both stores. The family sold the grocery business in 1912 and concentrated their efforts on the hardware store. This photograph shows John Wesley Cardwell (left) and Roy G. Cardwell Sr. in front of their newly built hardware store.

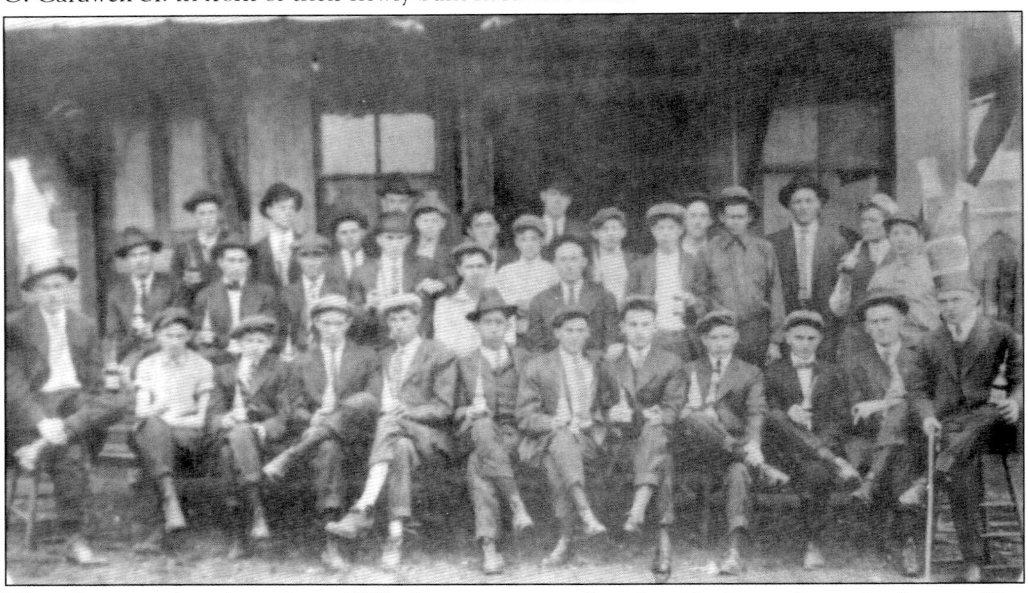

This photograph, taken about 1919, shows a group of unidentified men from the Lenoir City knitting mill holding bottles of Chero-Cola for a promotion hosted by the soft drink manufacturer. Chero-Cola was created in early 1905 by Claud A. Hatcher, a young pharmacist from Columbus, Georgia. In 1924, Hatcher changed the name of the company to Nehi, which eventually became the Royal Crown Cola Company still in business today.

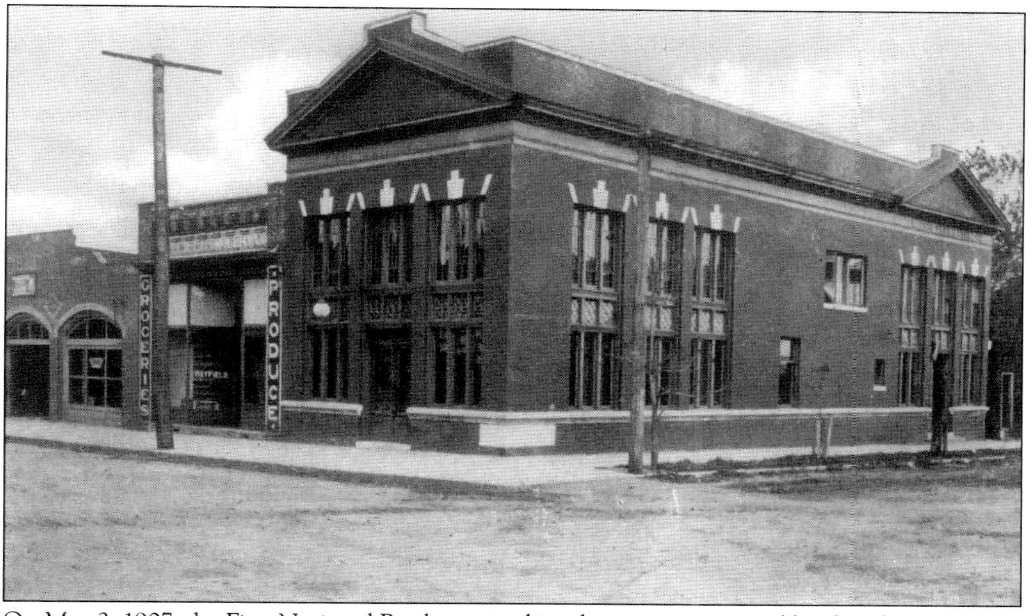

On May 2, 1907, the First National Bank received its charter as a national bank, taking over the assets of the Farmers and Traders Bank that was organized in 1904. Deposits for the opening day totaled $4,542.84, and the total loans made on that date were $595.

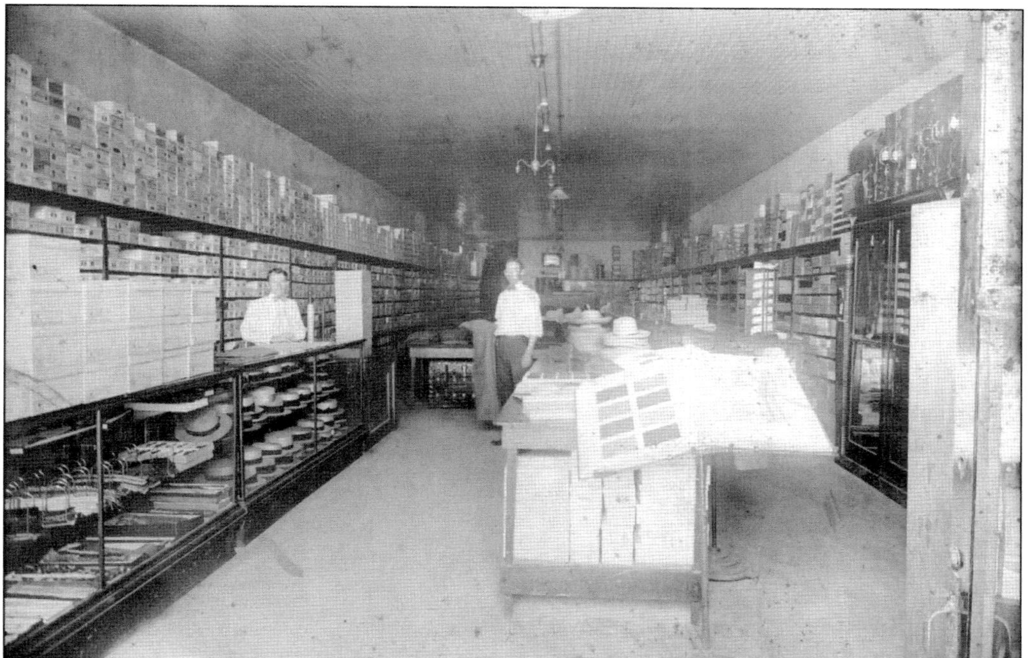

Paul Alexander Bailey (left) and William Walter "Bud" Fisher are ready and waiting for customers at Fisher's Men's Store. In addition to upscale brand names, Fisher's also offered tailored suits. Swatchbooks in front show samples of materials for custom orders. Piles of straw boater hats fill the glass display cases along with boxes of neckties.

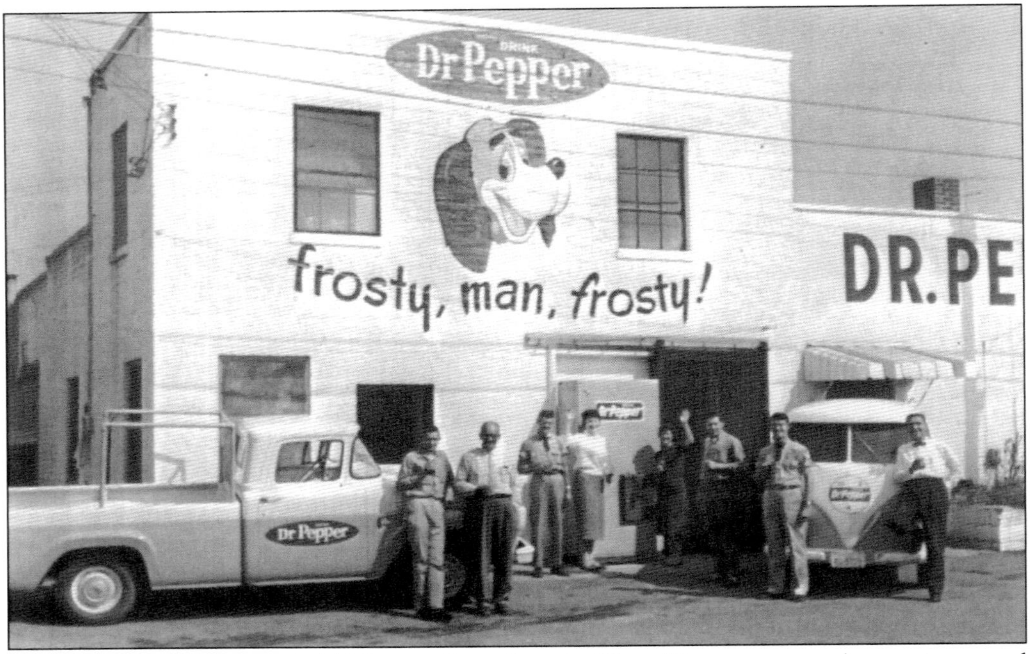

In 1885, at Wade Morrison's Old Corner Drug Store in Waco, Texas, a young pharmacist named Charles Alderton experimented with a variety of formulas for making soft drinks to serve to soda fountain customers. His most requested concoction, known then as the Waco, was soon renamed Dr Pepper by Morrison. The drink became so popular that Morrison hooked up with Robert S. Lazenby, owner of the Circle A Ginger Ale Company. Alderton opted out of the venture, but Morrison and Lazenby pressed on and presented Dr Pepper at the 1904 World's Fair in St. Louis. The drink was a perfect complement to ice cream cones and hamburgers. Dr Pepper enjoyed steady growth in sales and began to spread in popularity across the country. Bottling plants opened nationwide, like the one shown here in Lenoir City.

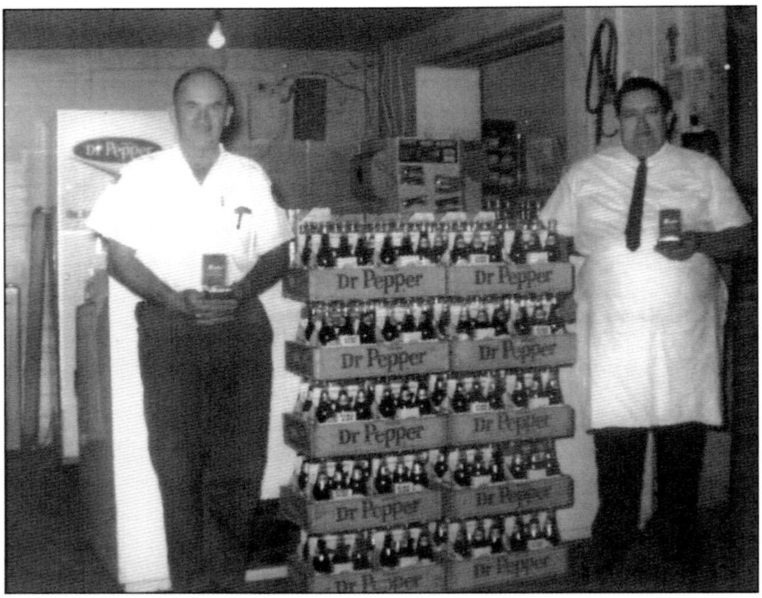

Four

Education

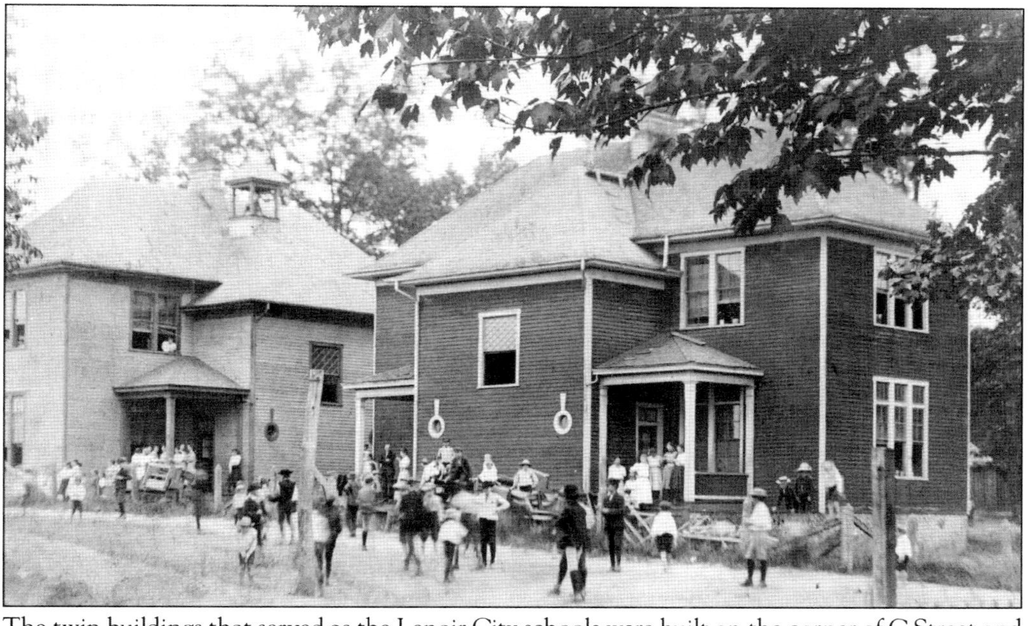

The twin buildings that served as the Lenoir City schools were built on the corner of C Street and Second Avenue between 1902 and 1904. The identical two-story buildings played host to local school children for many years. The structures were replaced by Nichols Elementary School in 1924.

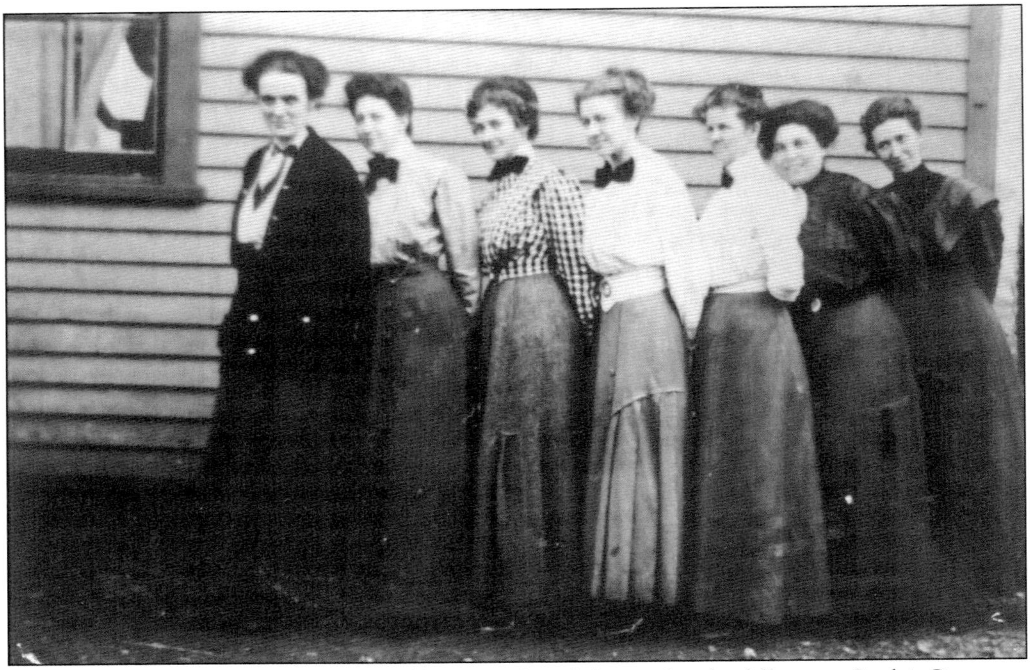

The Lenoir City schoolmarms pictured here are, from left to right, the following: Sophie Simpson, Tennie Griffitts, Ruby Harris, Bertha Perry, F. E. Russell, Pauline Atkins, and Meta Cardwell. The photograph was taken in 1910 at the twin buildings, which served as an elementary school.

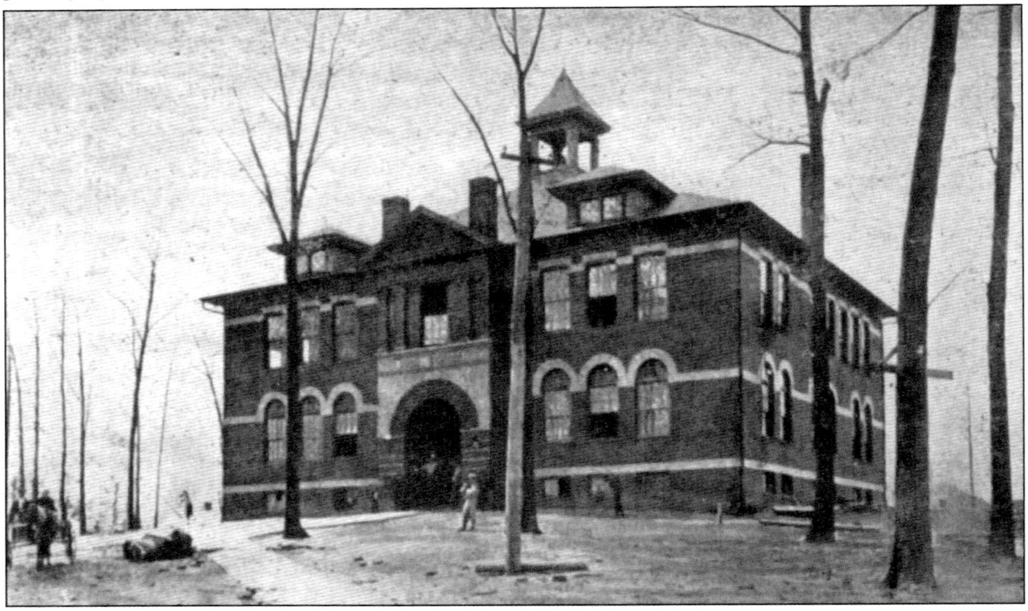

On March 6, 1908, the Lenoir Brick Company and G. W. Stansberry were contracted to erect a high school building in Lenoir City at a cost of $13,092.10. The Lenoir City High School, shown here in 1912, was finished in 1909. Eventually the building became part of a campus complex that consisted of a grammar school built in 1913 and a gymnasium building erected in 1922 by community volunteers. The buildings, located on Fourth Avenue, were razed in 1981.

In 1912, the first Lenoir City High School class consisted of one boy and six girls. They are, from left to right, the following: Frances Bewley, Lou Anderson, Jane Morton, Clyde Hackney, Effie Harrison Jones, Ethel Thompson, and Lola Alexander. Clyde, in his black suit, made a nice contrast to the ladies all dressed in white.

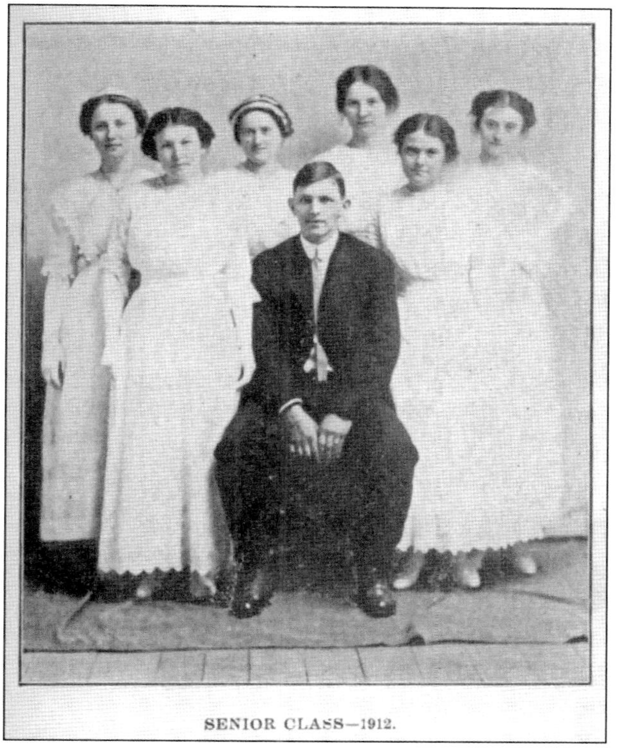

Students stand on the back porch of the Lenoir City High School in the early 1910s. The only two identified are Hazel Foute (standing to the right of the pole) and Pearl Fisher (second from right).

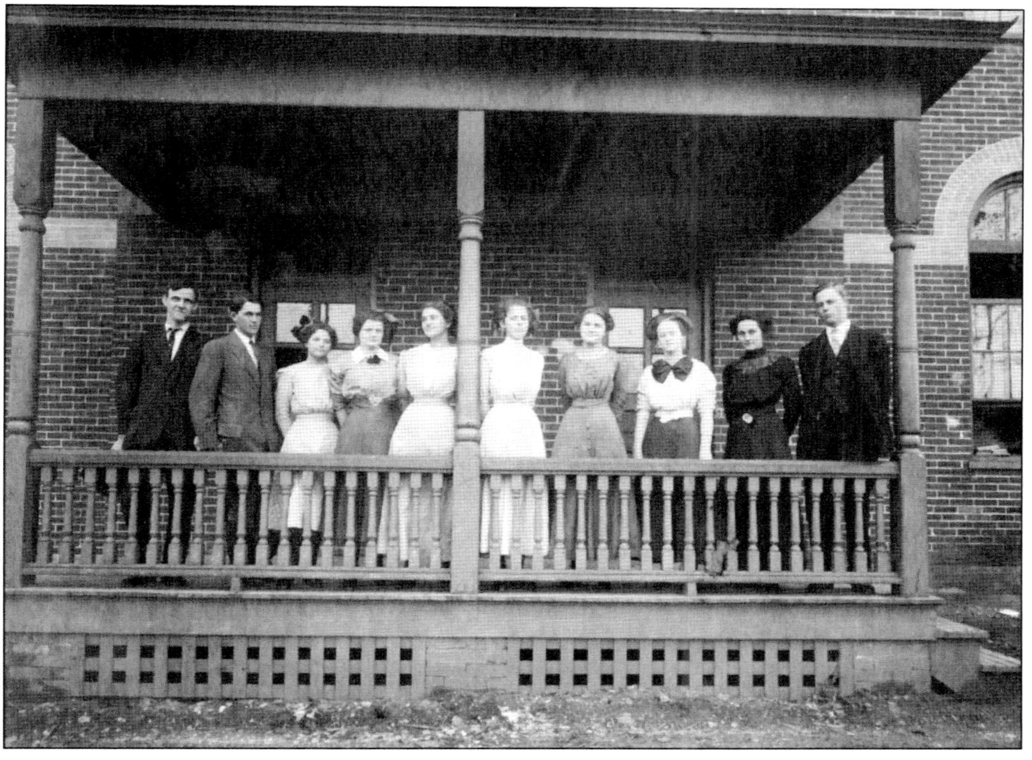

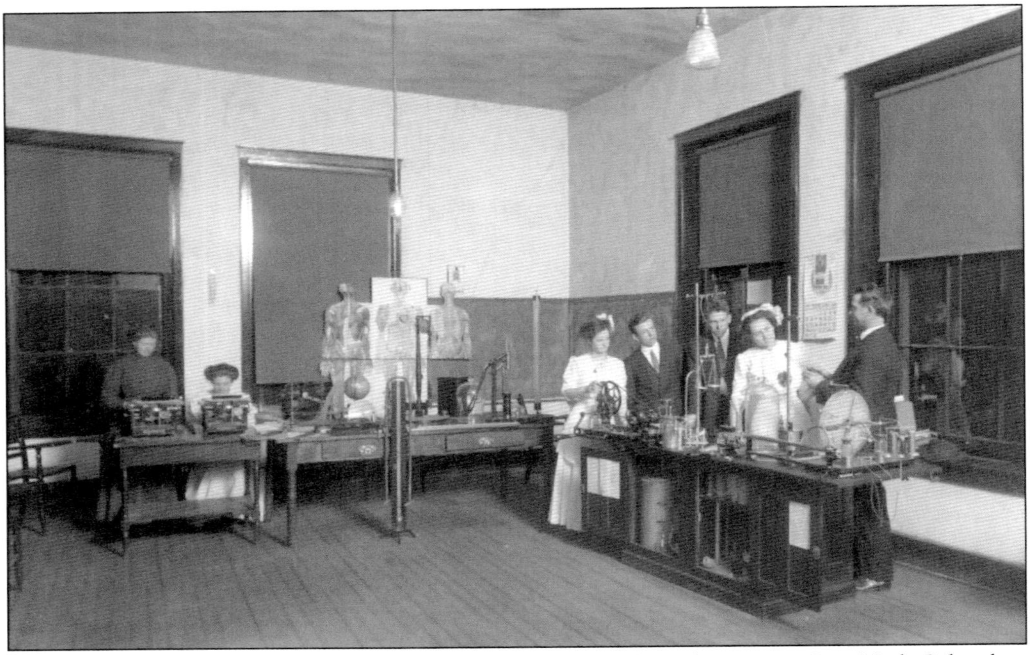

Students worked at different tables in this early science lab at the Lenoir City High School in the early 1910s: the girls type up their findings at the far left table, anatomy charts are hung behind the middle table, and the students watch attentively as the teacher performs a scientific demonstration at the table on the right. The only person identified in this photograph is Anna Mae Fisher (second from right).

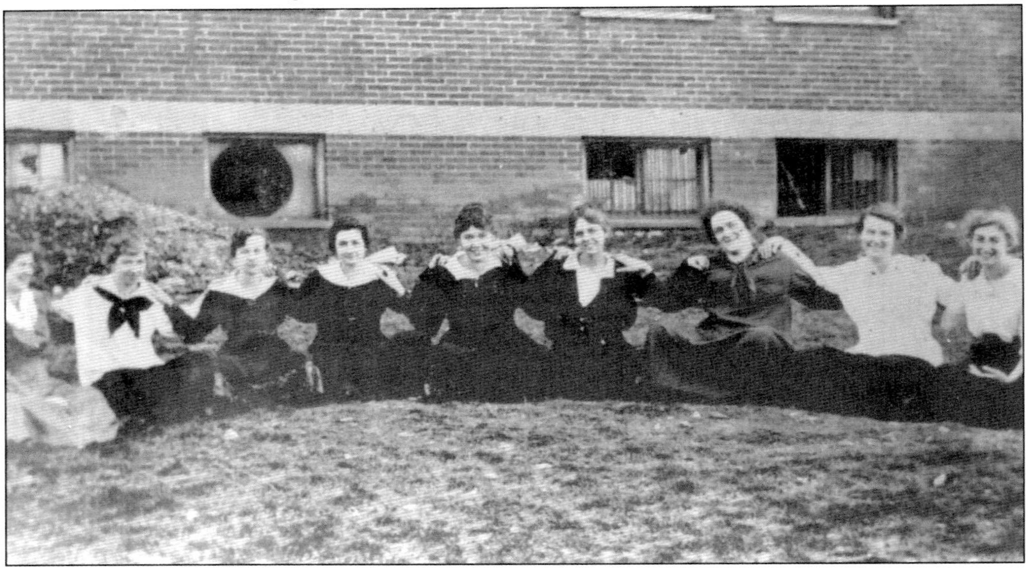

Members of the 1917 Lenoir City High School sewing club were, from left to right, Lillie Hodge, Eva Morrison, Lissie Brown, Flora Soward, Beulah Wesson, Eileen Long, Gladys Jones, Estelle Pair, and Una Winchester. These students, like others in high school sewing clubs across the country at the time, may have contributed to efforts in World War I by providing hospital nightshirts and khaki handkerchiefs, among other items.

These lovely ladies were members of the 1917 Lenoir City High School cooking club. The members pictured here are, from left to right, the following: Daisy Duff, Lillie Hodge, Beulah Wesson, Eileen Long, and Ezerine McAllister. The girls would have learned the latest in cookery and kitchen sciences. Note the pristine white aprons that constituted the club's uniforms.

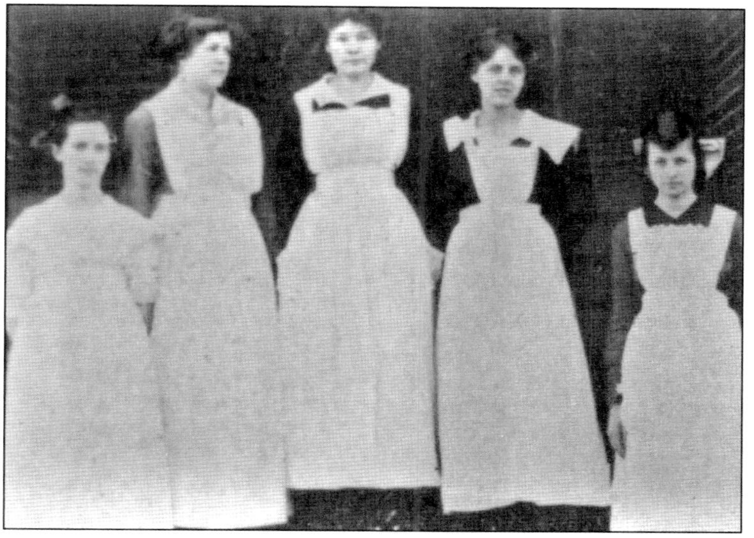

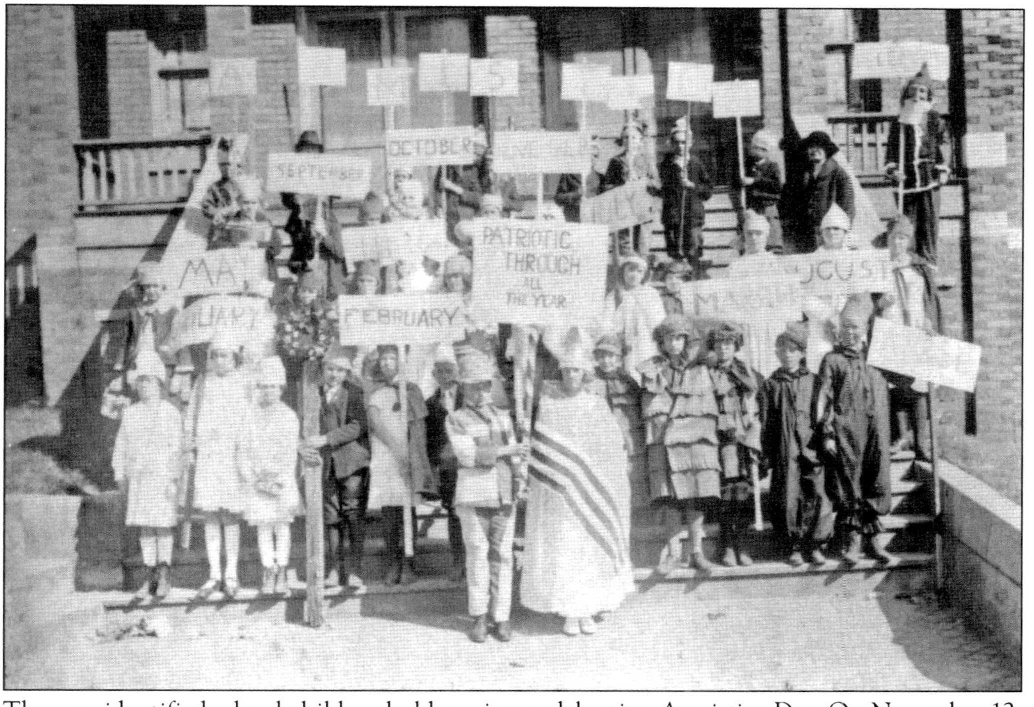

These unidentified school children hold up signs celebrating Armistice Day. On November 12, 1919, Pres. Woodrow Wilson proclaimed the first Armistice Day, "a day dedicated to the cause of world peace" and commemorating the end of World War I. The holiday was renamed Veteran's Day in 1954 to honor all veterans and is celebrated on November 11 to denote the signing of the armistice that ended the First World War, as major hostilities were formally ended on the 11th hour of the 11th day of the 11th month in 1918.

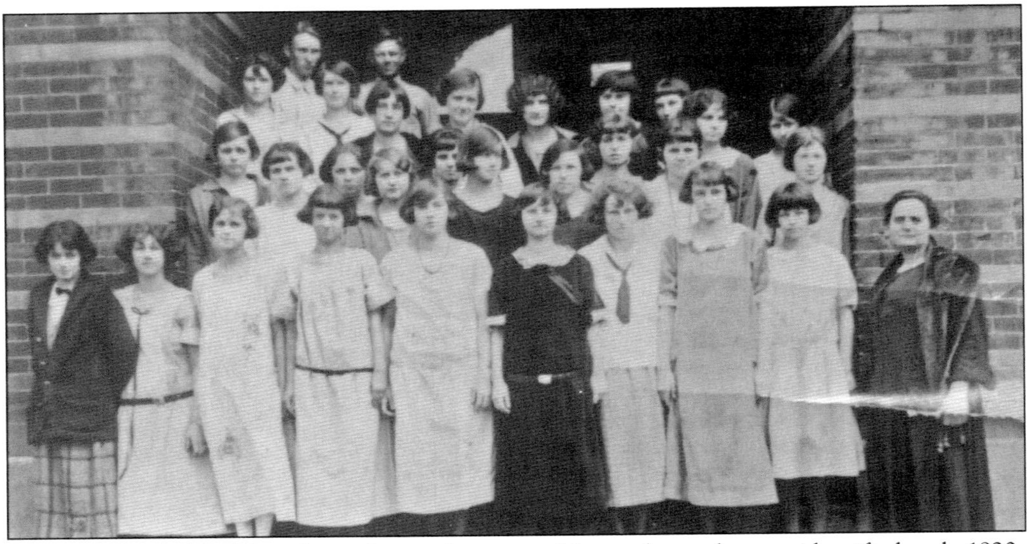

Sporting chic bobbed hair, loose fitting dresses, and fancy shoes, these unidentified early 1920s Lenoir City High School students were certainly dressed for success. The Roaring Twenties was a time of prosperity and new opportunities for young women. In 1928, women would earn 39 percent of the college degrees given in the United States, up from 19 percent at the beginning of the 20th century.

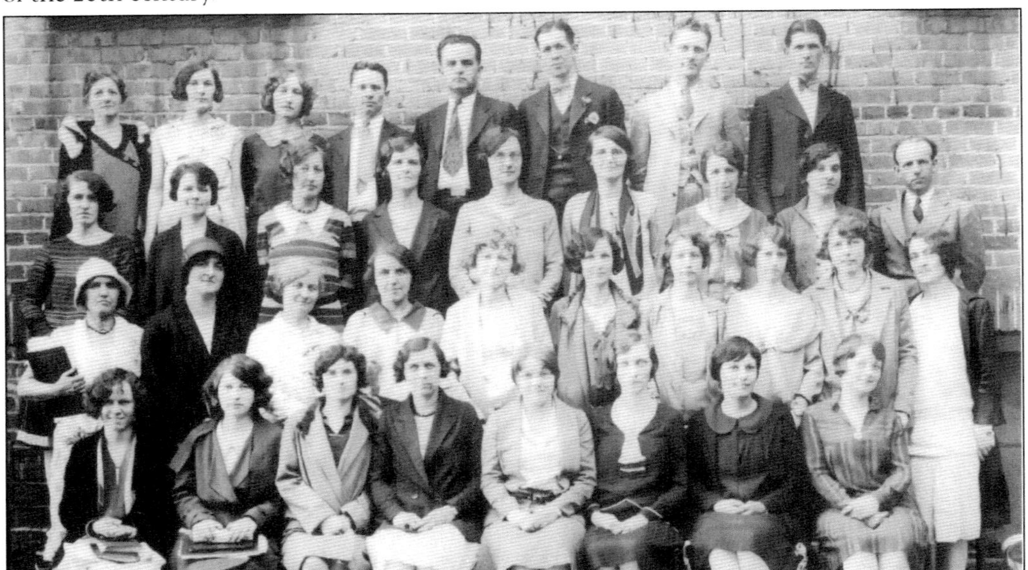

In 1930, the combined faculties of the Lenoir City Schools posed for this photograph. From left to right are the following: (first row) Leila Quenelle, Helen Cates, Ila McSpadden, Florence Rutherford, ? Wallace, Hazel Foute, Stella Taylor, and ? McReynolds; (second row) Nina May, Emma Fritts, Lou Breazeale, Miriam Byrum, Merrill Davis, Nora Bailey, Myra Cobb, Nell Duff, Josephine Foute, and Lois Breazeale; (third row) Laura Glover, Margaret Grubb, Blanche Gill, Alice Kizer, Ruth Riggle, ? Barnett, Mary Isaacs, Gertrude Hart, and ? Anderson; (fourth row) Tennie Bacon, Ruth Gwatlney, Opal Hill, Frank Mullandore, Dewey Humphrey, Andy Bebb, John Hicks, and Robert Reel Keathley.

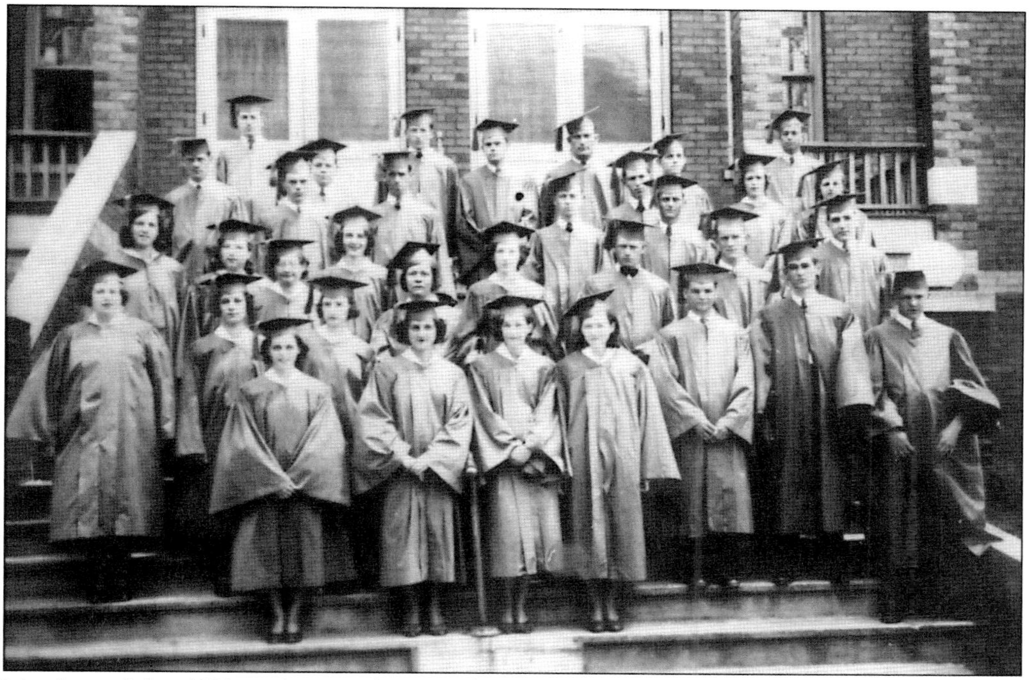

Members of this 1932 graduating class are, from left to right, the following: (front row) Frances Worthey, Eula Clark, Nell Babb, and Maurine Britton; (second row) Elizabeth Weaver, Thelma Jenkins, Zelma Watson, Roy DeRieux, Walter Babb, and Ed Gray; (third row) Rachel Coleman, Merrill Griffits, Frances Spraker, Alma Maples, Juanita Short, Mildred Nipper, Charles Scott, and Porter Campbell; (fourth row) Harry Lynn Scott, Kenneth Phelps, Hayden Hickman, Howard Campbell, Leland Monger, Edley McCown, Louise Hines, and Maxine Hoskins; (fifth row) Preston Harrison, Ronald Grubb, Ralph Waller, Avery Norwood, Noble Williams, Jason Lewis, and Jack Babb.

What better way to exude high school spirit than with a marching band? These unidentified band members were ready to take the field during half-time in their matching capes and hats. Percussion, brass, and woodwinds are all present. Painted on the drum is "Lenoir City High School, presented by class of '33."

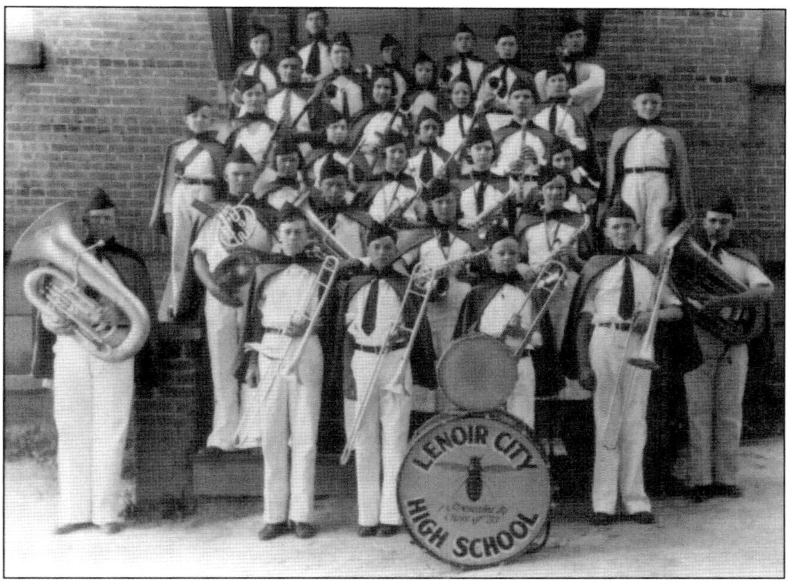

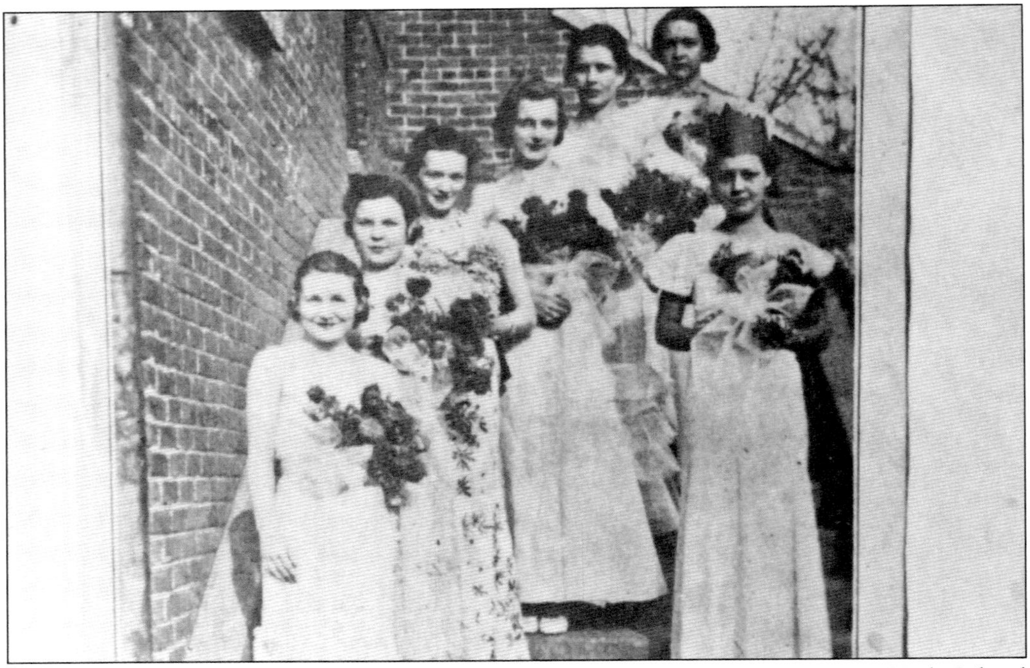

Helen Vaughn (right, wearing crown) was elected carnival queen at Lenoir City High School in 1933. Her court maids included, from left to right, the following: Tommie Lou Lane, Agnes Kerley, Nellie Blackburn, Edith Sewell, Hazel Crouch, and June Smith.

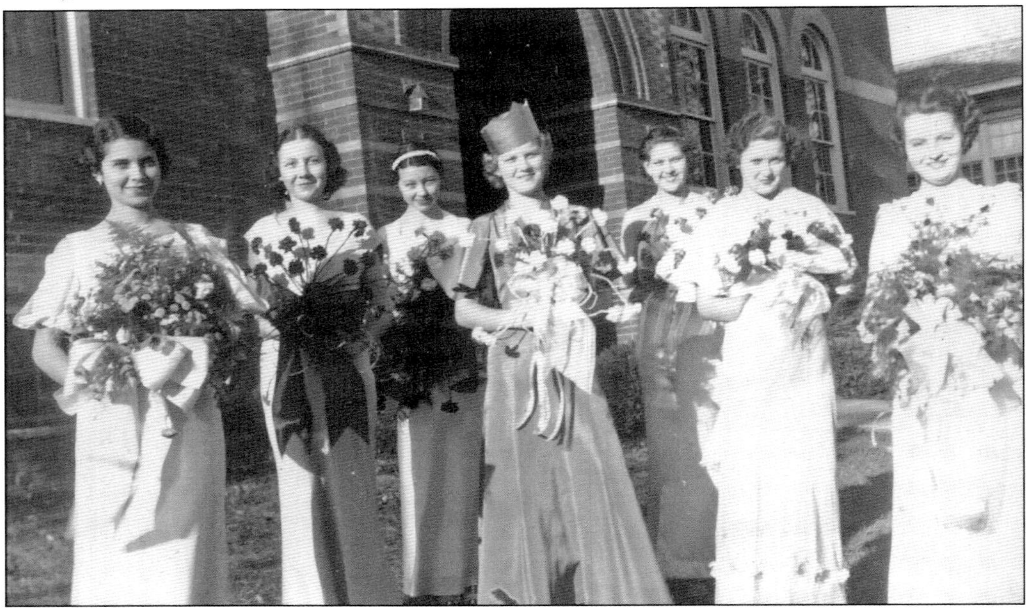

Queen Charlotte Armstrong and her maids of honor pose at the annual Lenoir City High School Carnival in 1935. The carnival was held the day after the Lenoir City and Loudon High Schools played each other in football. Lenoir City won the game 14 to 6. Pictured, from left to right, are the following: Mildred Reno, Virginia Waller, Mildred Ingram, Charlotte Armstrong, Margaret Keener, Inez Buck, and Florence Hair.

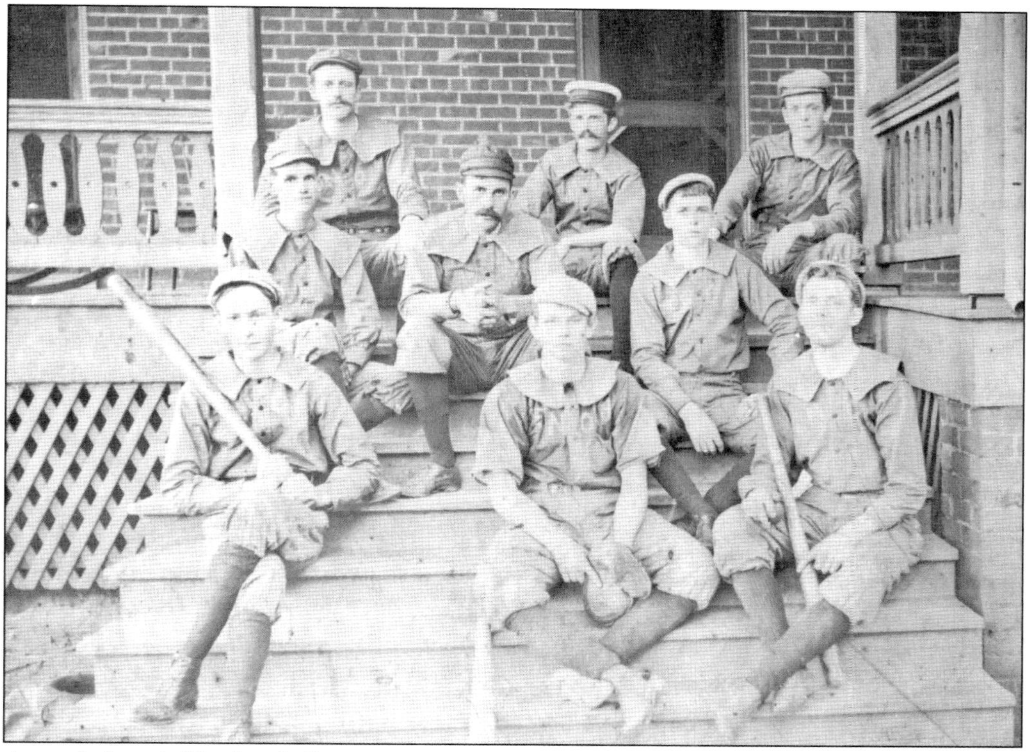

An early Lenoir City baseball team poses on the front steps of the William Ballard Lenoir home. None of the players have been identified, but the year 1880 is written on the back of the photograph. The team was formed even before Lenoir City became an actual town. In addition to local farm boys, team members may have been employees of the cotton and grist mills started by the Lenoir family. The name "LENOIR" is printed on the front of the uniforms; note the wide collars.

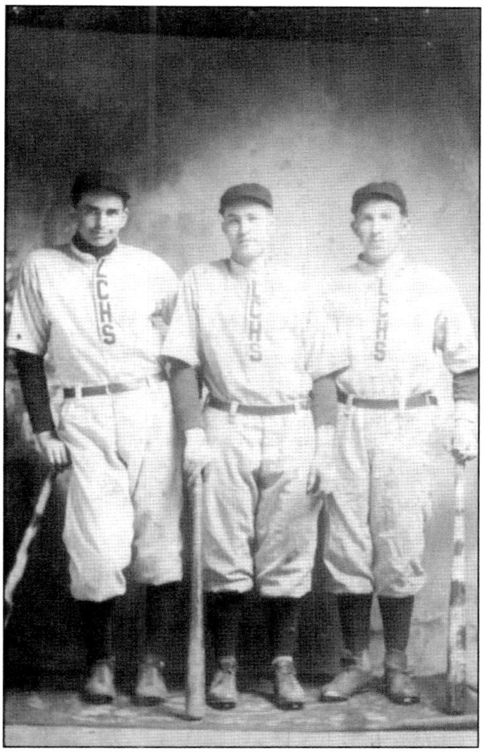

These three Lenoir City High School baseball players were dressed and ready to play ball. From left to right they are Vaughn Browder, unidentified, and Roy Bussell. Touted as America's favorite pastime, baseball's early mid-19th century origins are vague, but there is no doubt as to its popularity. In 1866, Charles A. Peverelly wrote of the sport, "The pastime suits the people, and the people suit the pastime."

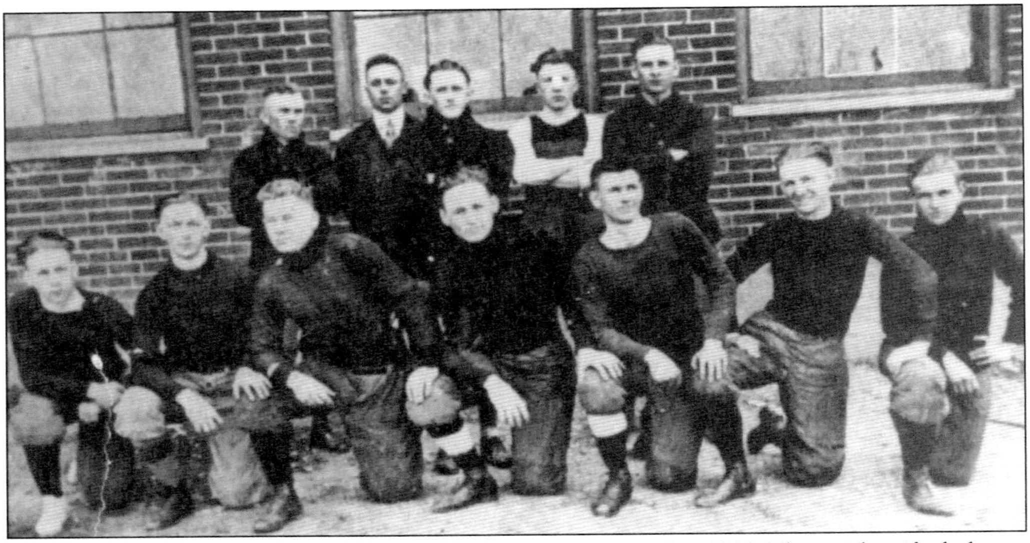

The first Lenoir City High School football team was organized in 1916. The unidentified players in this photograph looked ready to take on their first opponent. Modern day football grew out of a combination of a sport resembling rugby, played at the time in Canada and Europe, and an earlier version of soccer. High schools and colleges across the country adopted the sport with enthusiasm.

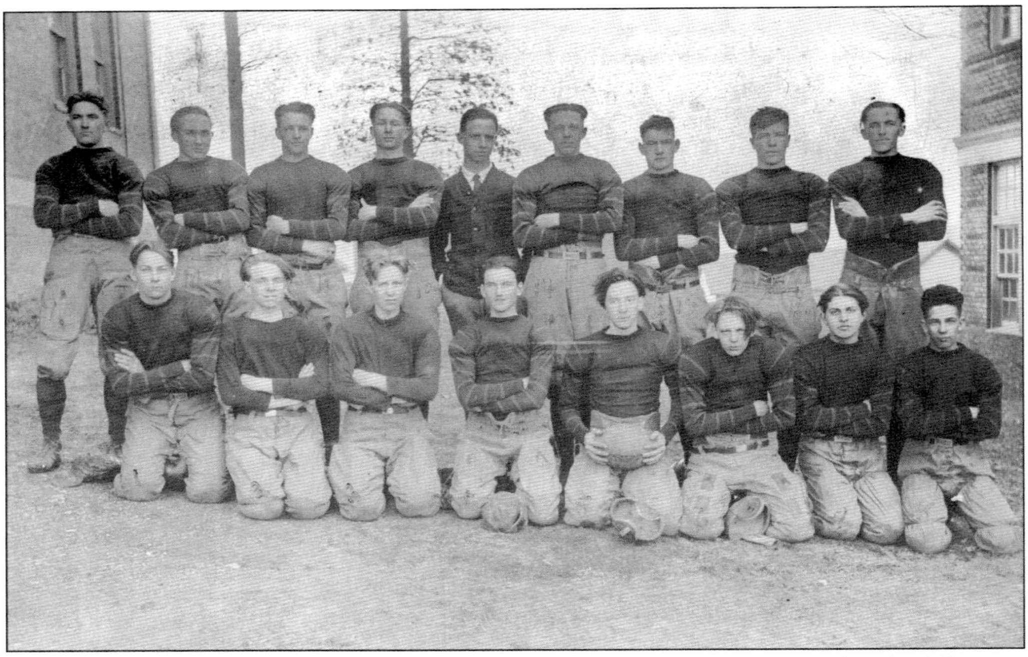

In this *c.* 1925 photograph of the Lenoir City football team are, from left to right, the following: (front row) James Eldridge, Raymond Tutterow, Clarence Simpson, Ralph McAmis, Paul Yearout, Clarence Burdette, James B. Fine, and Floyd Mitchell; (second row) Paul Matlock, Beecher Clark, Jerry Evans, Ben McGuffee, Coach Bob Stapleton, John Smallen, Ed Turnbill, Cecil Thomas, and Jack Breazeale.

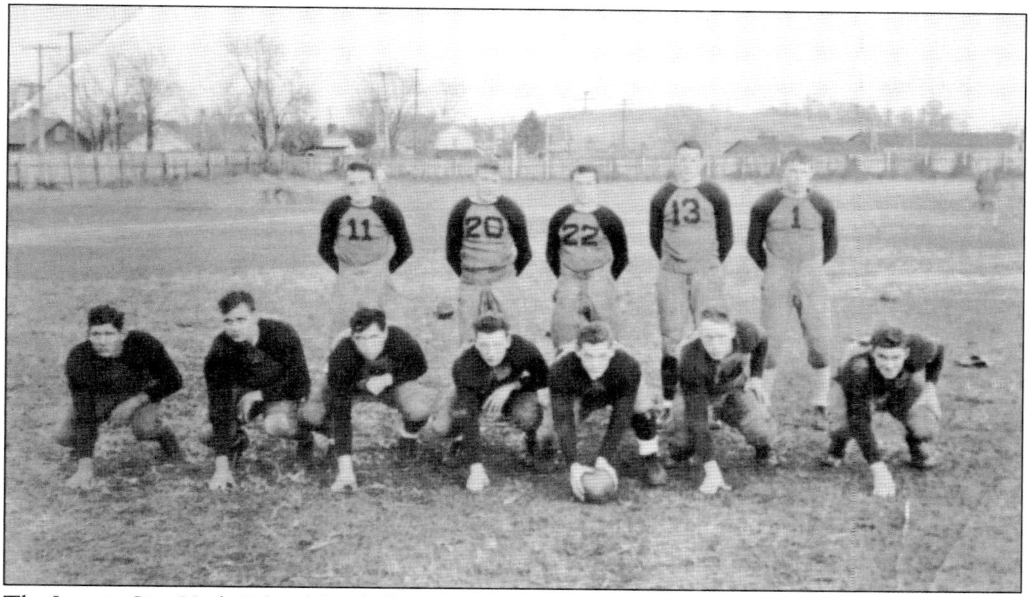

The Lenoir City High School football team went undefeated in 1936. The team, coached by Dean Bailey (not pictured), consisted of the players, from left to right, as follows: (first row) Ed Osborn, Ed Littleton, George Fritts, Gene Armstrong Jr., Paul Davis, Jack Nichols, and Bud Waller; (second row) Conrad Strader, Neville Price, Babe Conner, Bill Yearout, and team captain Ray Schubert. The current Lenoir City football team's mascot is a panther.

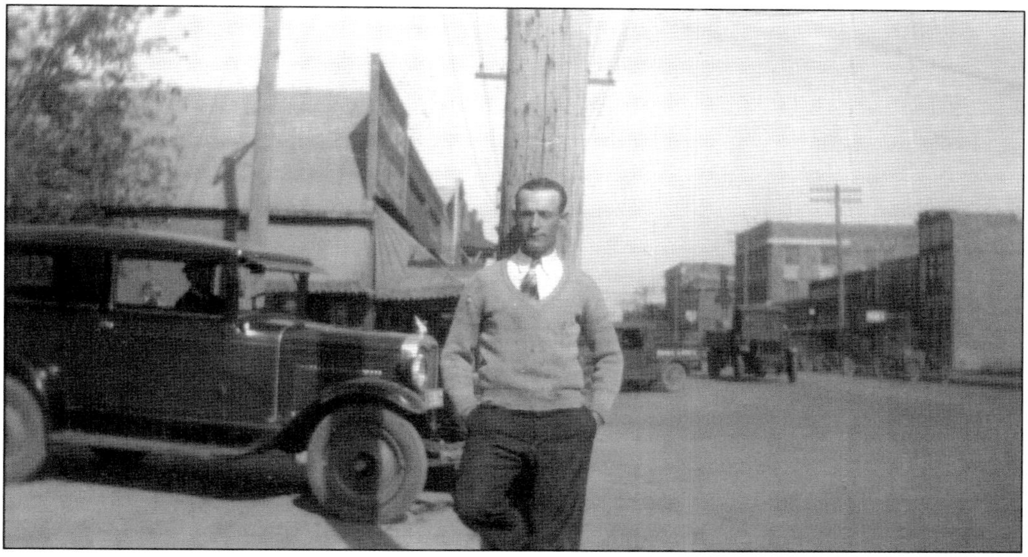

This photograph, taken in the early 1930s, is of Paul "Goat" Ellison. Written on the back it says, "This guy deserves a lot of credit for his 'Tornado Teams,' giving kids lots of game experience before going onto high school programs. 'Sky-scraper' on right in background is the Hotel General Lenoir."

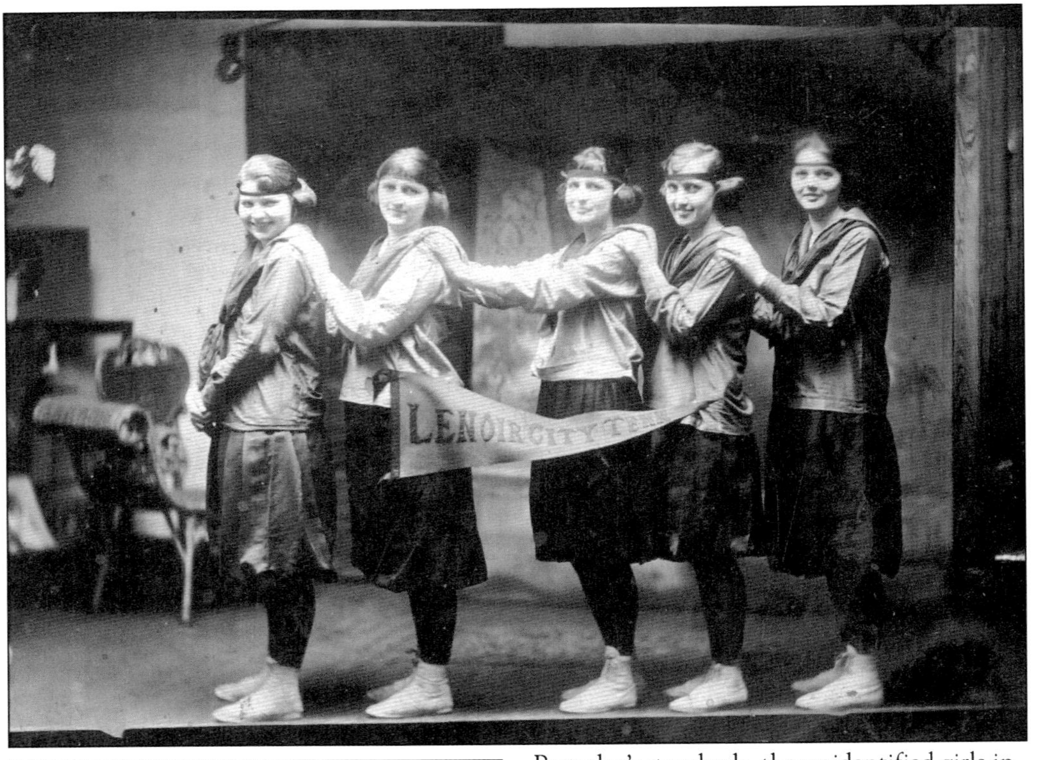

By today's standards, the unidentified girls in this 1923 photograph seem a little overdressed for sports in their pleated skirts and sailor collared blouses, but their tennis shoes suggest their status as a serious basketball team. A Lenoir City banner was pinned across them in support of their school.

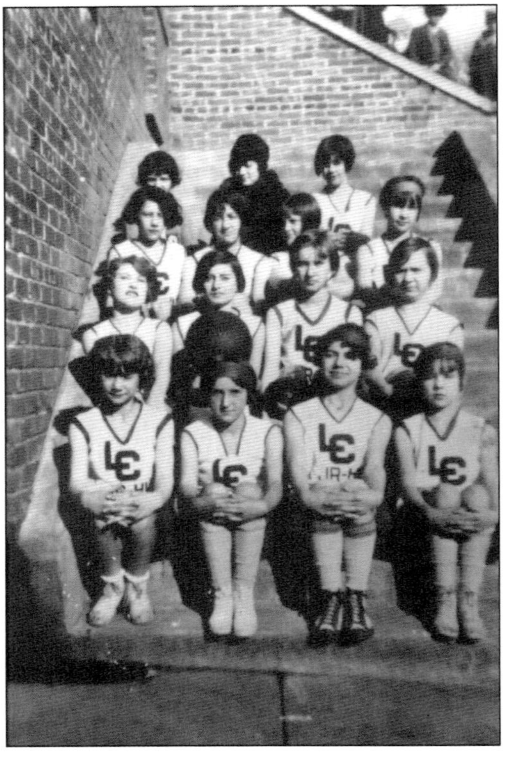

The Lenoir City Junior High girls' basketball team posed on the school steps for this 1928 photograph. From left to right are the following: (first row) Irene Yearout, Eula Clark, Grace Law, and Louise Hines; (second row) Alverine Smith, Fleta Duggan, Evelyn Johnson, and Ossie Gray; (third row) Catherine Thomas, Grace Gossage, Ernestine Harris, and Geneva Keith; (fourth row) Edna Lee Hope, Miss Lilian McReynolds, and Sue Crookshanks.

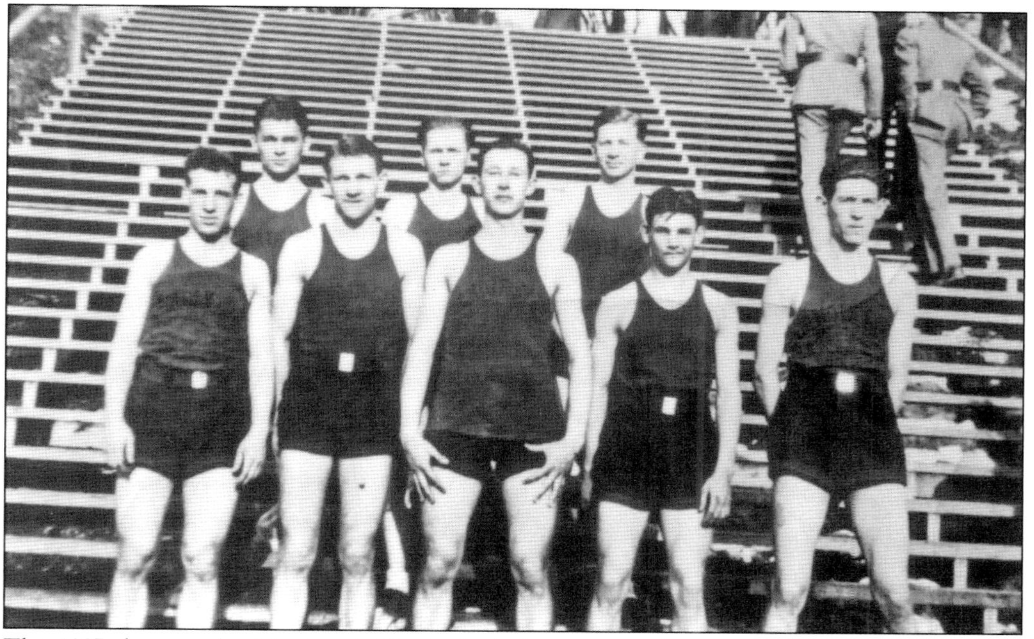

This 1927 photograph of the Lenoir City basketball team was taken at the University of Tennessee. From left to right are the following: (first row) Leonard Smith, Thomas Foster, Maurice Littlefield, Richard Baskett, and Ralph Huffman; (second row) Ed Baskett, Gilbert Johnson, and J. K. Ward.

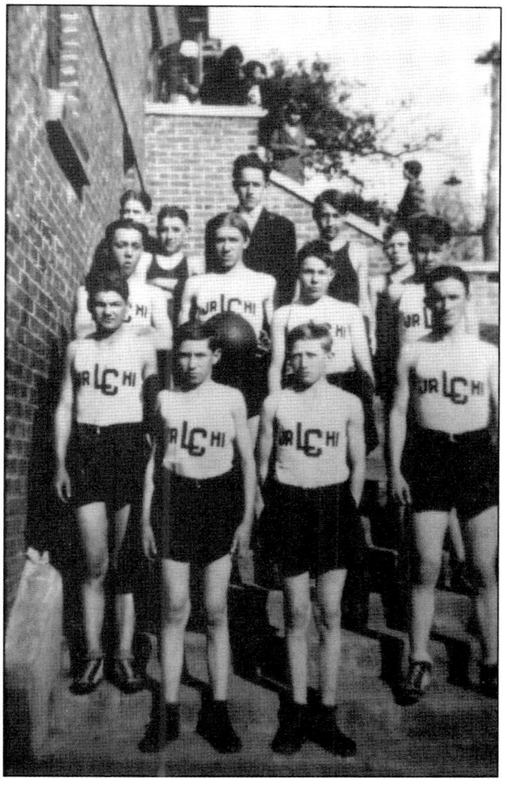

The 1928 Lenoir City Junior High basketball team is pictured, from left to right, as follows: (first row) Leland Monger and Ralph Waller; (second row) Roy DeRieux, Ernest Barron, and James Griffitts; (third row) G. H. Long, B. J. Burns, and Cletus Cooper; (fourth row) Paul Stewart, Porter Campbell, coach Ben Duff, Bob Morrison, and Ronald Grubb.

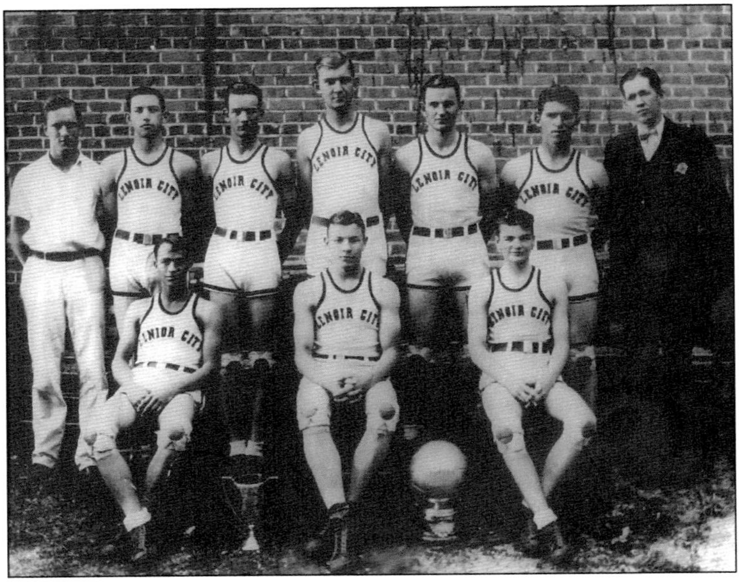

The Lenoir City basketball team won the Tennessee State Championship in 1930, beating Memphis Central 26 to 19. From left to right are the following: (first row) Jack Babb, Charles "Tootie" William, and Roy "Snookie" DeRieux; (second row) Manager Charles Scott, Pete Littleton, Clarence Littleton, Avery Burdette, Henry Foster, Gene Conner, and Coach Andy Bebb.

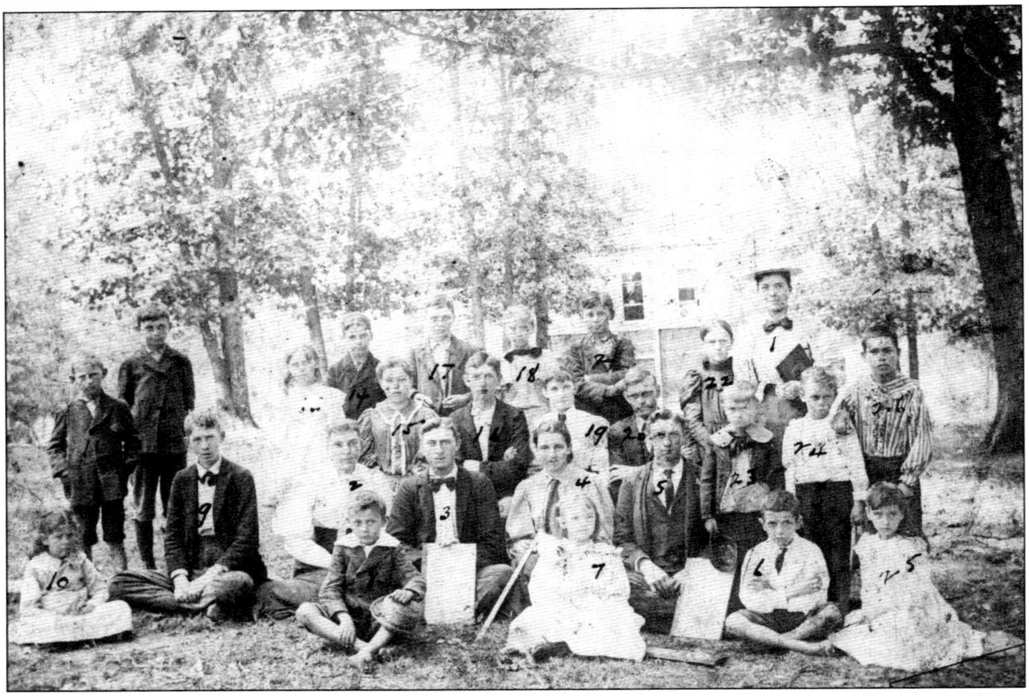

This photograph, taken in 1900, shows students who attended a private school held at Dr. William Taylor Foute's office building. Although the numbers written on the photograph could be a distraction, they are helpful in identifying the subjects. In order from 1 to 26 are the following: Miss ? Petree, Kate Wilkerson, Warham Fine, Nancy Leeper, Jim Foster, Fred Wilkerson, Annie Foster, unidentified, Avery Burdette, ? McCrary, unidentified, Lester Johnson, unidentified, Hodge Stanfield, Carrie Lee Jones, Henry Foster, Winfield Belton, Louise Golling, Jessie Stanfield, Charley Monger, Gus Johnson, Louise Reed, Ben Standfield, Luther Nelson, Stella Wilkerson, and Walter Garrigus.

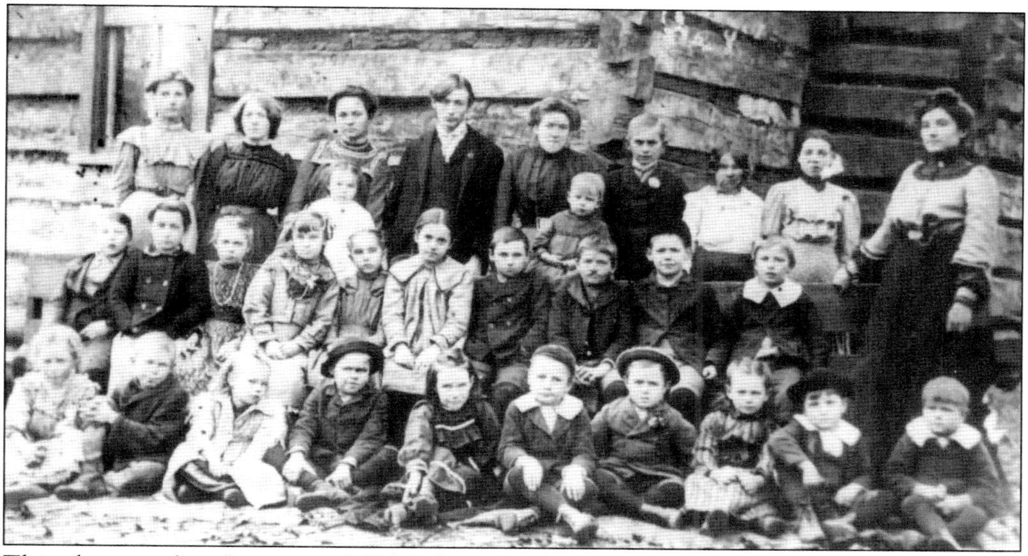

This photograph, taken around 1900, shows students at the Busselltown School, one of the many small schools that existed in the early years of Loudon County. The teacher, Mrs. ? Schultz (standing to the far right in the back row), and student Louise (Stinnett) Vincil (standing to the left of Mrs. Shultz) are the only ones identified.

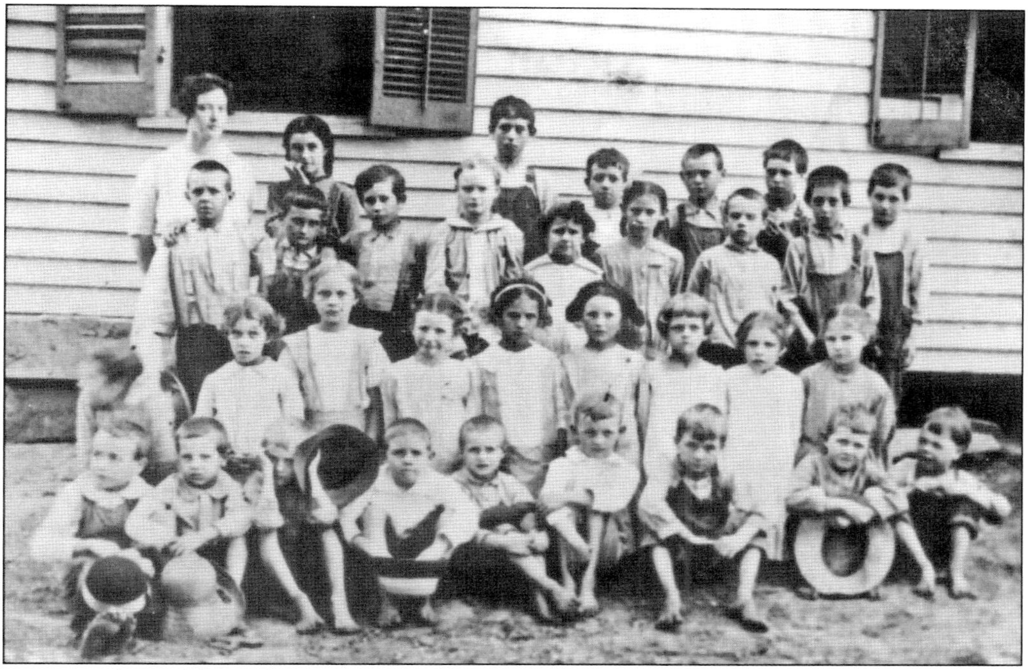

Miss May (Crouch) Smith is shown here about 1910 with her first class at the Providence School near Lenoir City. The unidentified children would have come from surrounding farms. Before the Civil War, only about 20 percent of teachers were women. That number rose dramatically to more than 65 percent after the war.

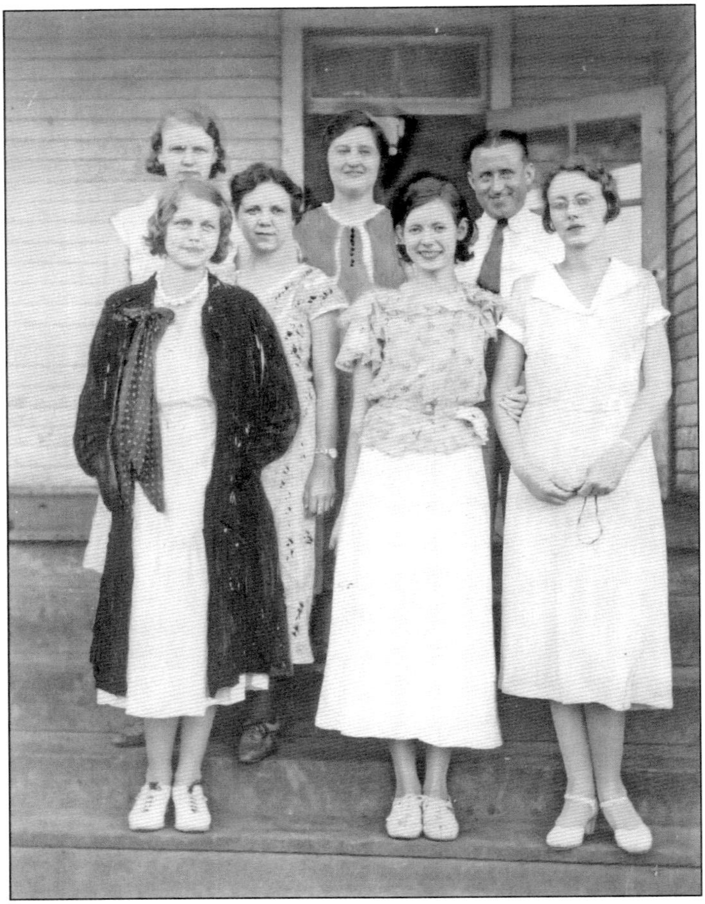

The Eaton Elementary School staff members seen on the steps of the school in 1933 are, from left to right, the following: (first row) Frances Williamson Garner, unidentified, and Lavona Simpson; (second row) unidentified; (third row) Alma Williams Hedrick, Kate Hope Galbraith, and unidentified.

The Nichols School, at the corner of C Street and Second Avenue in Lenoir City, was built in 1924 by Barber-McMurray. The original building contained an auditorium and classrooms. In 1936, an addition was built to house the school offices, library, cafeteria, and classroom space with the aid of the Works Progress Administration (WPA).

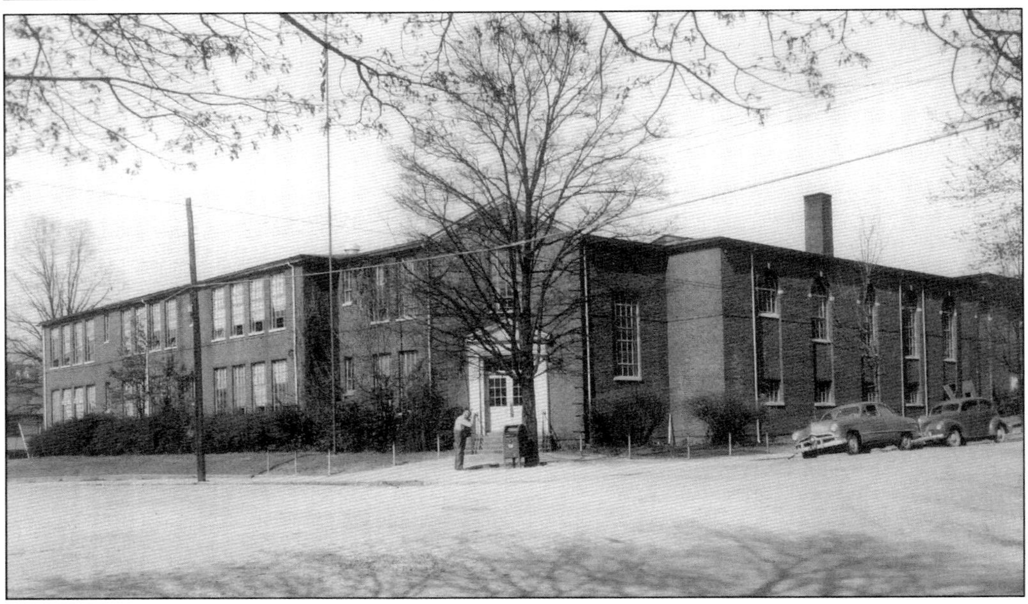

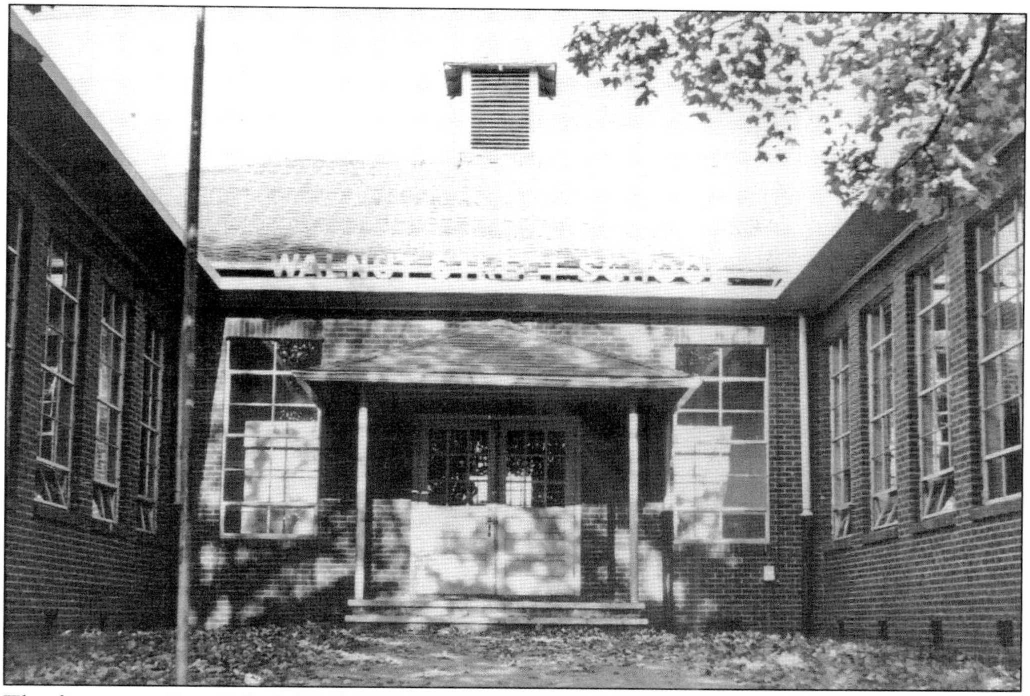

The four-room East Side School was completed in 1924. Ross Bohannon was the principal and fourth grade teacher. Working with him were Emma Fritts, Evelyn Monger, and Elizabeth Limburg. Four more classrooms were added in 1952, and it became the Walnut Street School.

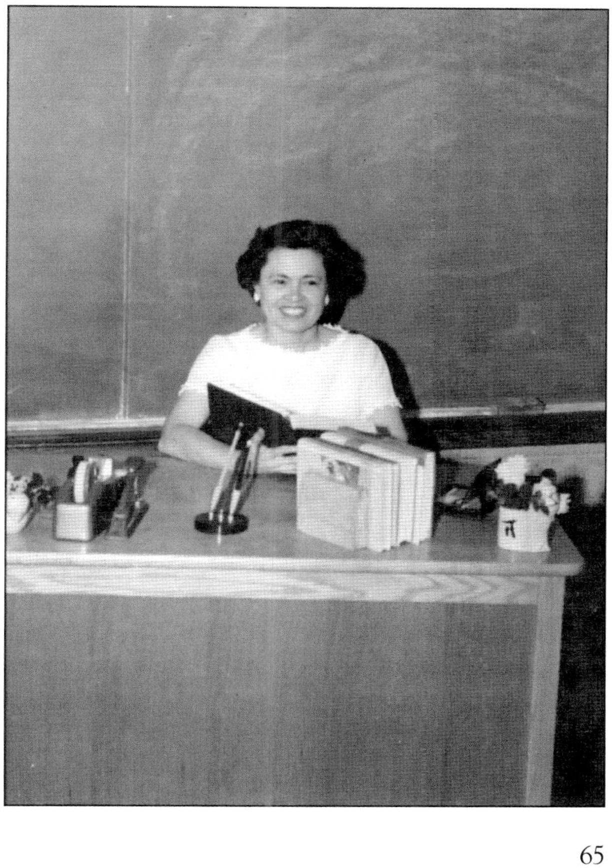

In addition to being a teacher, Mrs. Freeman Littlefield was principal of the Walnut Street School. In a photo album featuring pictures of the school in 1959 is written, "Walnut Street is a small neighborhood school which retains many traditions such as the ringing of the bell by the pulling of a rope . . . this school strives to keep that which is good and constantly experiments with new ideas which seem feasible."

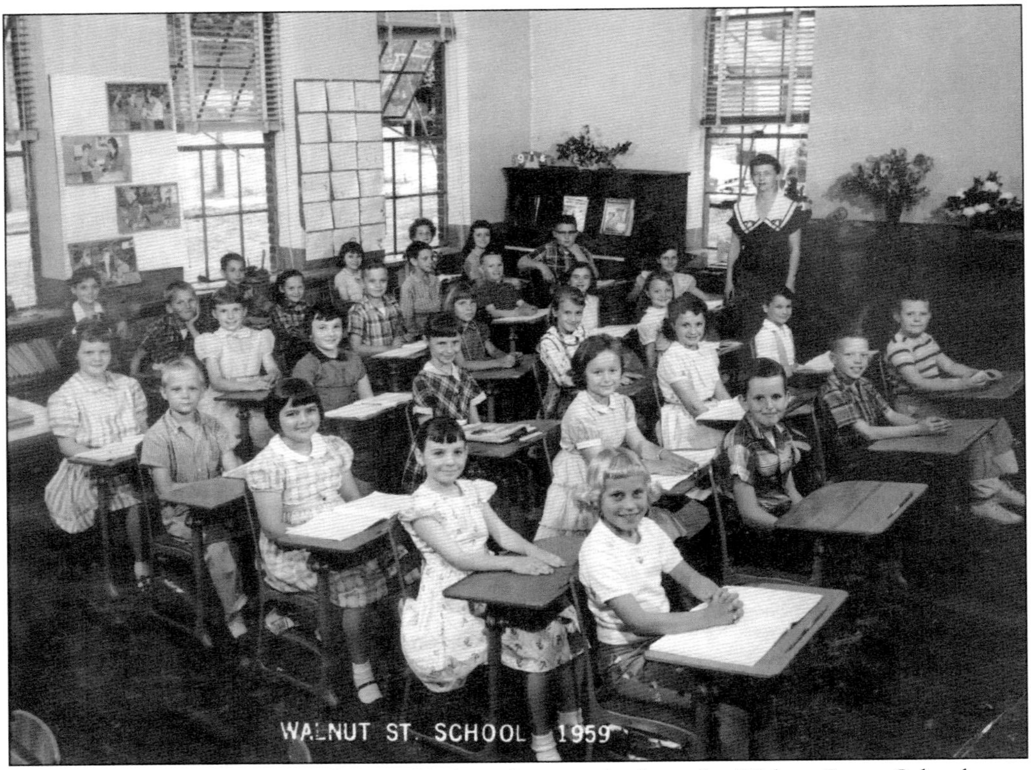

The unidentified children in these 1959 class photographs from the Walnut Street School seem to be saying, "We're all in our places with bright shiny faces." In the top photograph, Mrs. Betty Bell's class benefited from a piano in their classroom. The sixth grade class of Mrs. Freeman Littlefield read from the book *Success in Spelling.* Originally built in 1924 as a four-room brick building known as East Side School, the structure was doubled in 1952 and renamed the Walnut Street School. According to a 1959 souvenir program published during the town's golden jubilee celebration, the school hosted five grades and 200 students in that year.

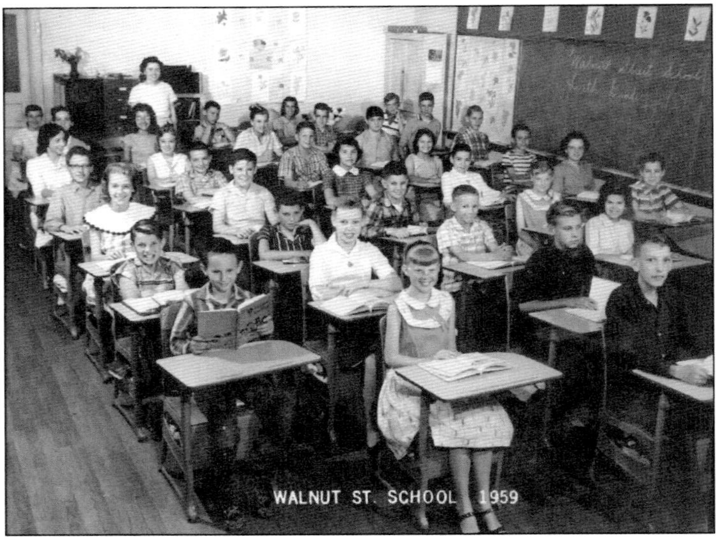

Five

Religion

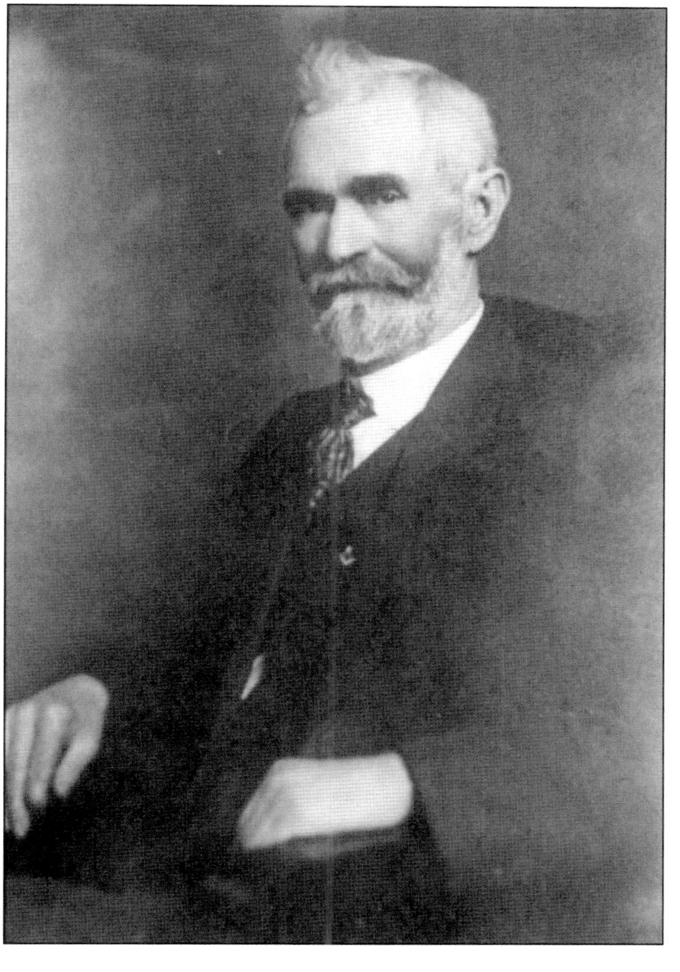

Rev. David H. Gibson was a farmer, justice of the peace, and circuit-riding preacher. He married Alice Caledonia "Callie" Scarbrough. The family home, prior to moving to a home on Third Avenue in Lenoir City, was located on what is now known as White Wing Bridge over the Clinch River on Highway 95. Callie had a twin sister named Alice California Scarbrough.

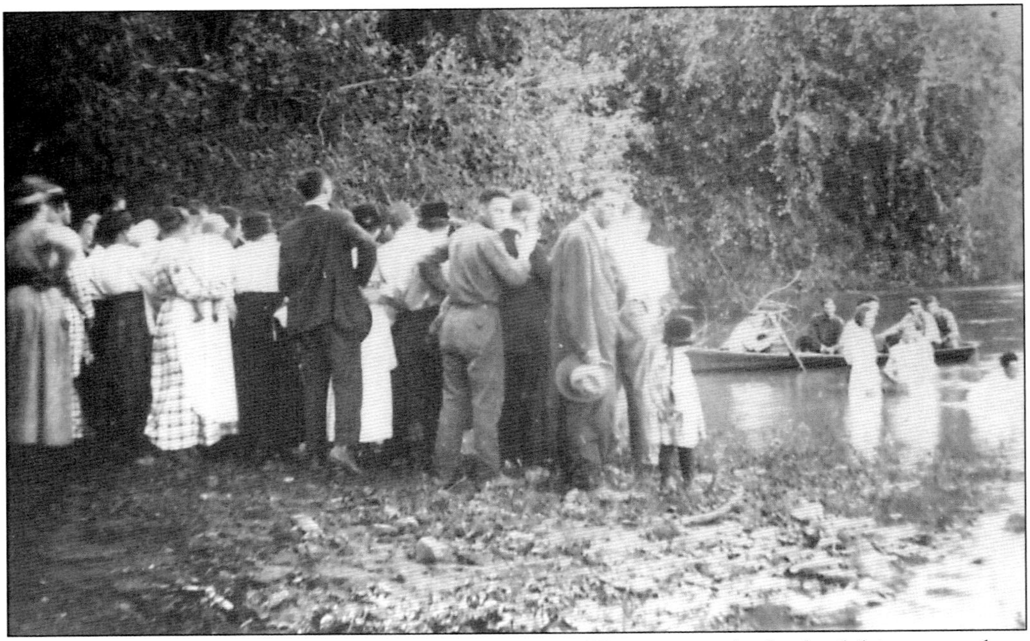

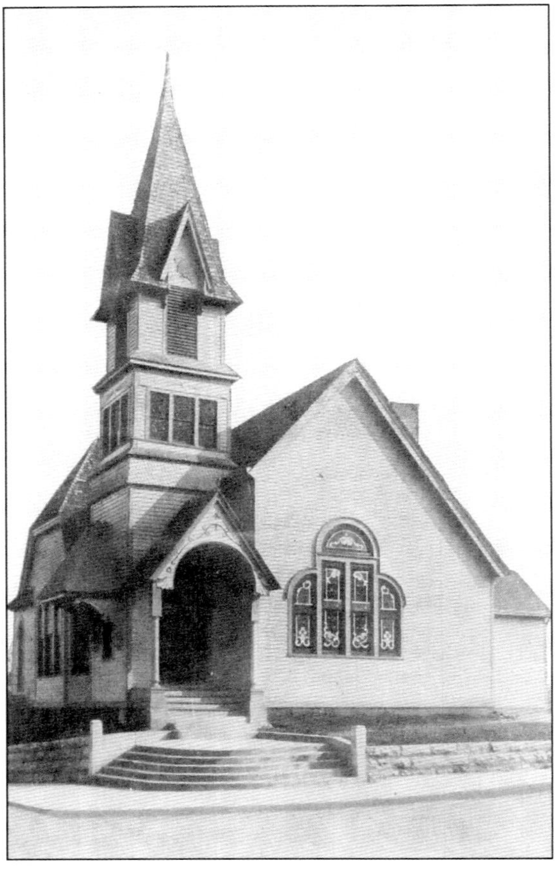

The note on the back of this postcard reads, "Dear Aunt Annie [Quillen Tallent] I am sending you a picture of myself when I was baptized. It's not very good, but I wanted to send you one. I am sending Papa one. It is a little better than this one. Rev. Rainwater has Gracie French under the water, and I am standing behind Minnie Johnson. Roy and Irene Vineyard are waiting to be baptized. Minnie and I have been baptized. The little girl at the edge is Elizabeth French." The card is signed by Lillie Quillen.

This photograph of the Methodist Episcopal Church South was taken in the early 1900s, when it was called the Southern Methodist Church. Over the years, the building has undergone many renovations, including a drastic reduction in the height of the steeple. The church is located at the corner of Second Avenue and C Street and is now known as the Trinity United Methodist Church.

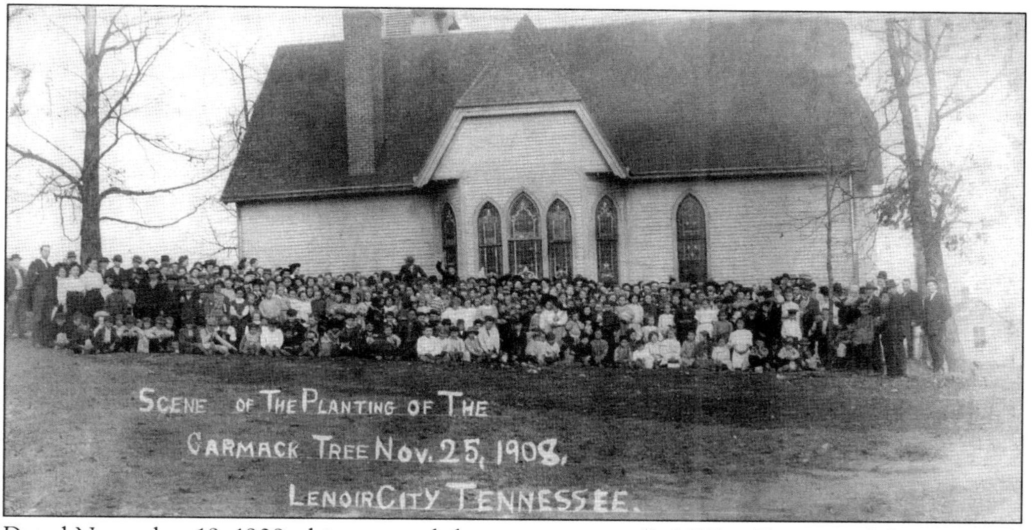

Dated November 19, 1908, this postcard shows an event called "The Planting of the Carmack Tree" at the Trinity Methodist Church in Lenoir City. Evidently the congregation turned out in its entirety for this momentous occasion. Note the beautiful arched stained glass windows on the side of the building.

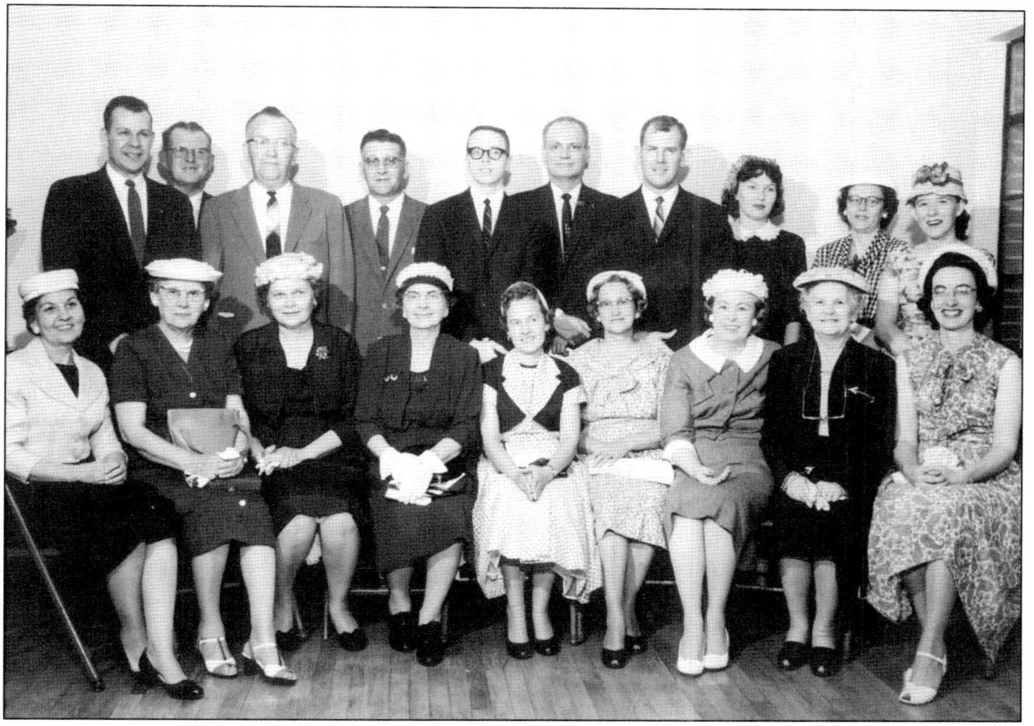

Seen in this c. 1959 photograph of the Trinity United Methodist Church, Sunday school teachers from left to right are the following: (first row) Itha Fine, Lena Mitchell, Anne Avery Bailey, Willie Rice Wilson, Hazel Maples, Edith Smalley, Mary Louise Davis, Dollie Hair, and Delene Hargis; (second row) Nelson Wilkins, Mixon Williams, John Ballentine, Ted Trevarthan, Joe Spence, Claude Wilson, unidentified, Emily Rose Stephenson, Anna Dykes, and Betty Burnette.

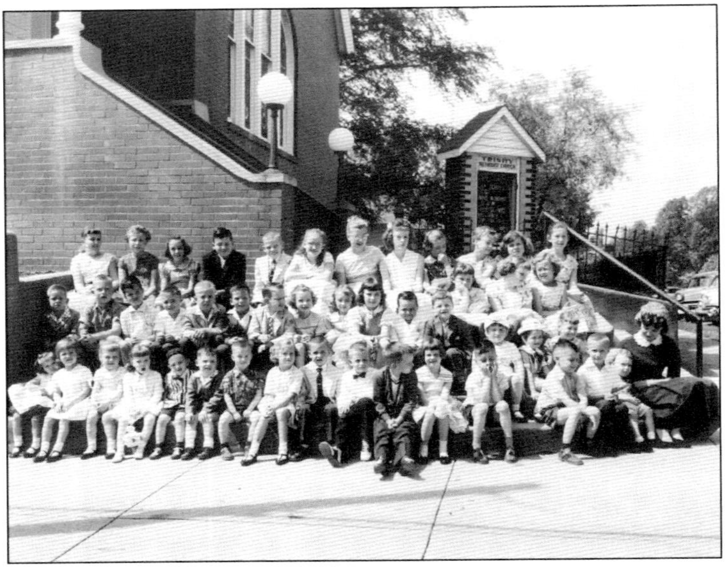

The unidentified members of the Trinity United Methodist Church children and youth departments, looking adorable in their Sunday best, posed for this photograph in the summer 1958. Emily Rose Stevenson (first row, far right) was in charge of the youth.

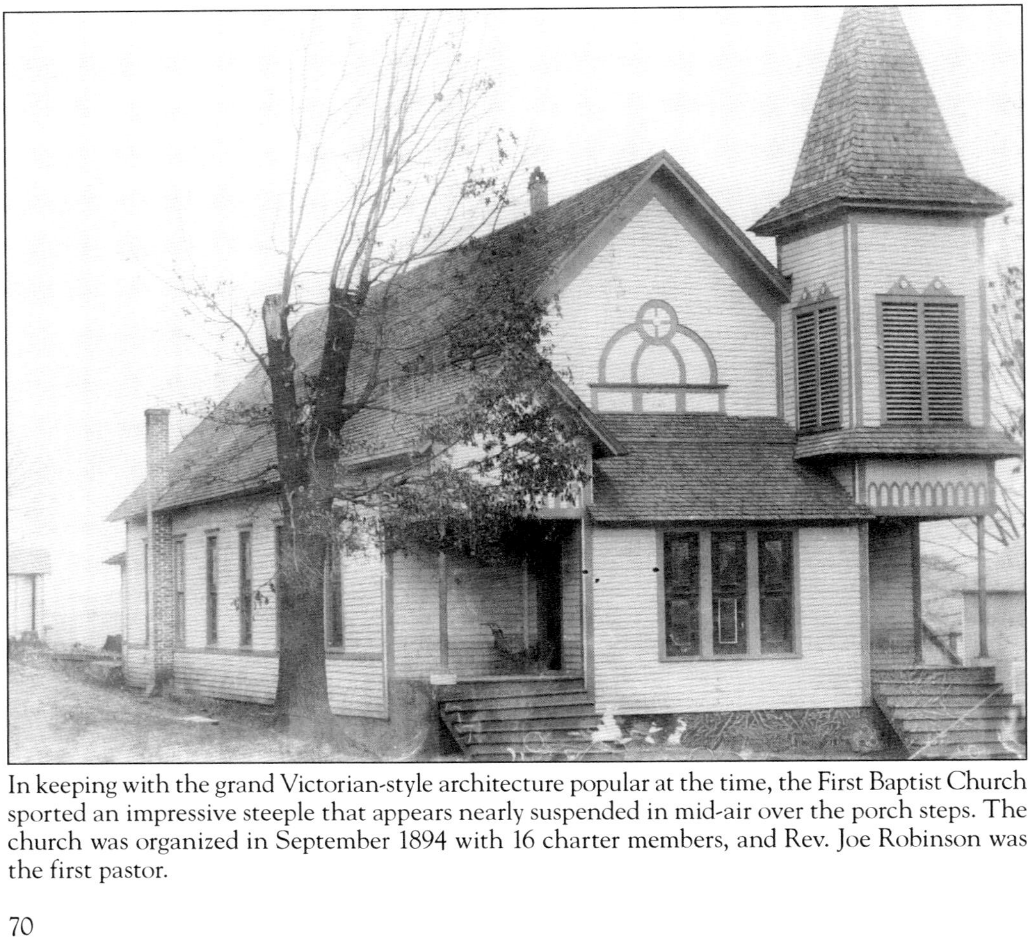

In keeping with the grand Victorian-style architecture popular at the time, the First Baptist Church sported an impressive steeple that appears nearly suspended in mid-air over the porch steps. The church was organized in September 1894 with 16 charter members, and Rev. Joe Robinson was the first pastor.

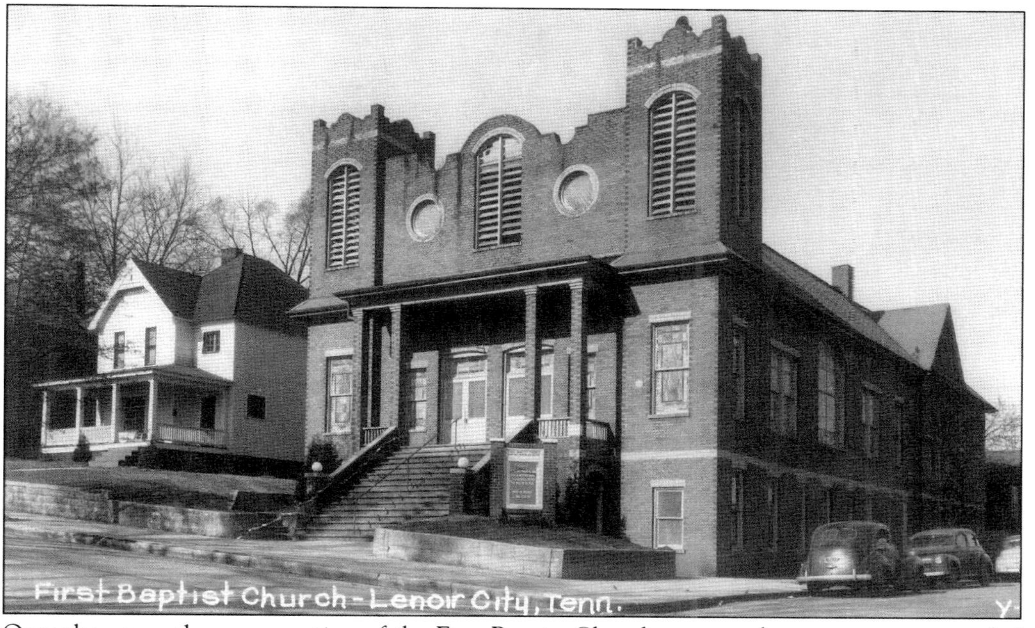

Over the years, the congregation of the First Baptist Church grew, and more room was needed to accommodate their needs. The church was rebuilt from a modest frame structure into an impressive brick edifice, as shown here in the 1940s. To the left of the church is the original manse or parsonage.

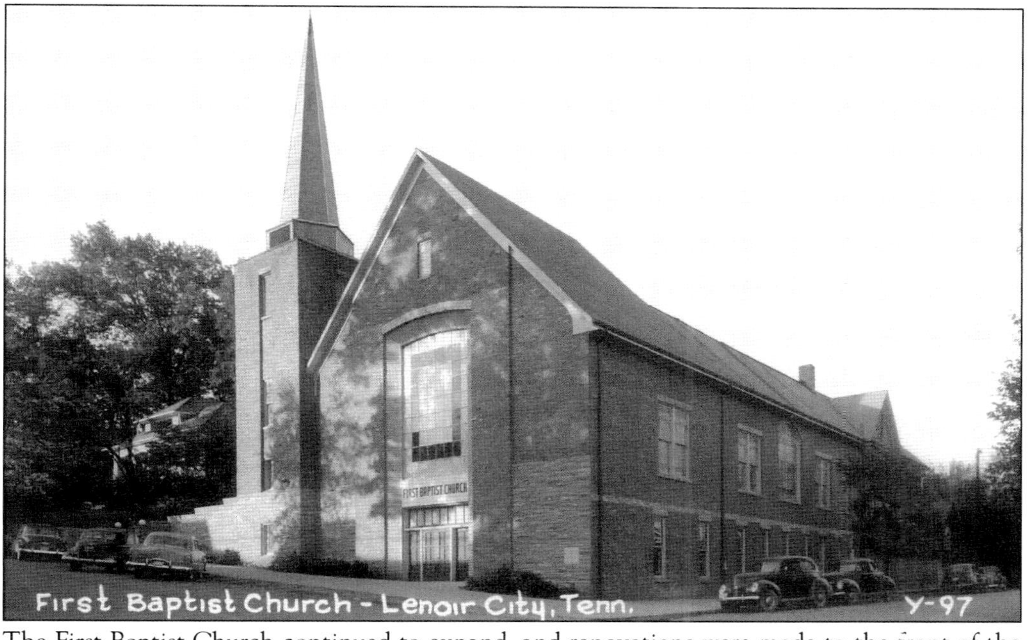

The First Baptist Church continued to expand, and renovations were made to the front of the building. The church served its congregation at this downtown location for more than 100 years. Eventually the church moved into a new 34-acre facility on Simpson Road, where the current congregation continues to meet regularly for the purposes of worship, evangelism, discipleship, missions, and fellowship.

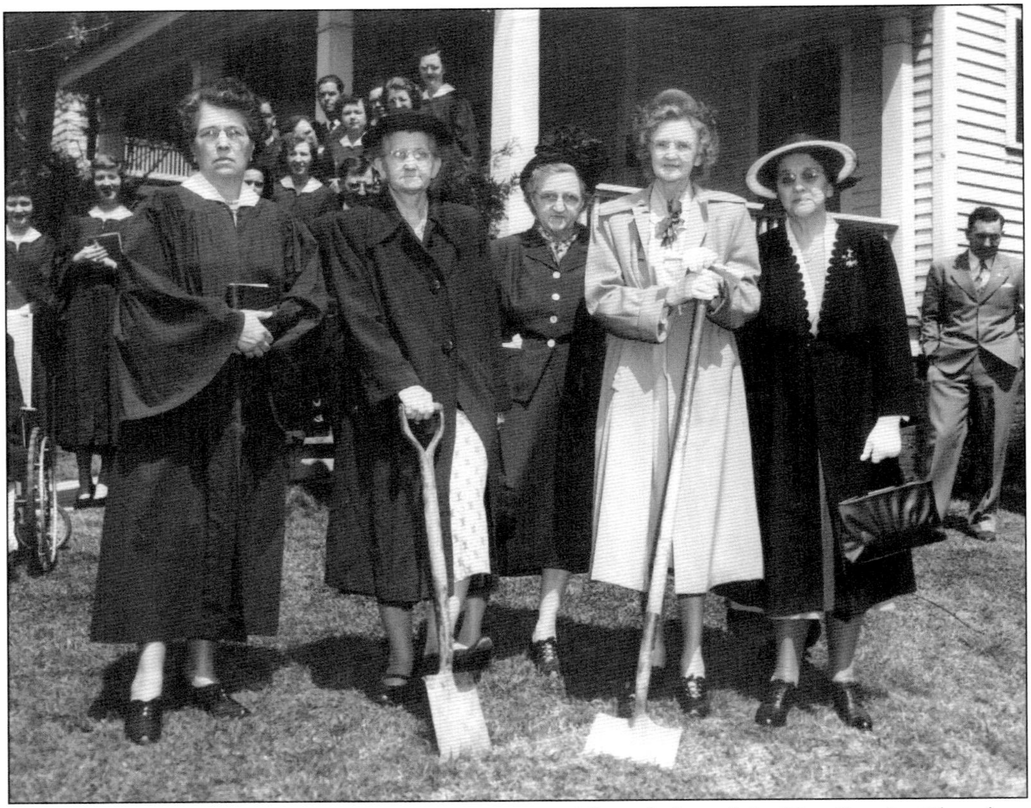

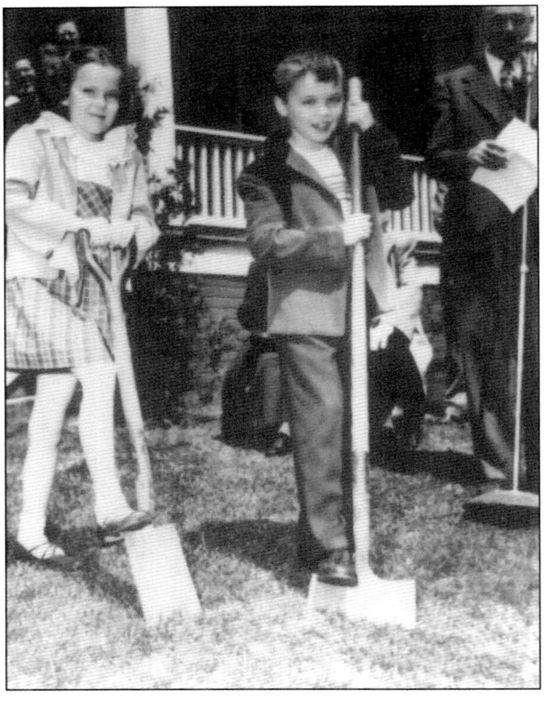

These ladies of the First Baptist Church, located at A Street and First Avenue, gathered to break ground for a new addition to the front of the church in 1951. They are, from left to right, Lola Hulin, Elizabeth Waller, Jodie Scarbrough, Addie Byrum, and Kate Alford.

The festivities for the 1951 groundbreaking ceremony for the new addition at the First Baptist Church was not limited just to adults, children were allowed to participate as well. JoAnn (Hall) Luckett and Tom Collins take a turn with the shovel as Thomas D. Pickell (on right behind microphone) looks on.

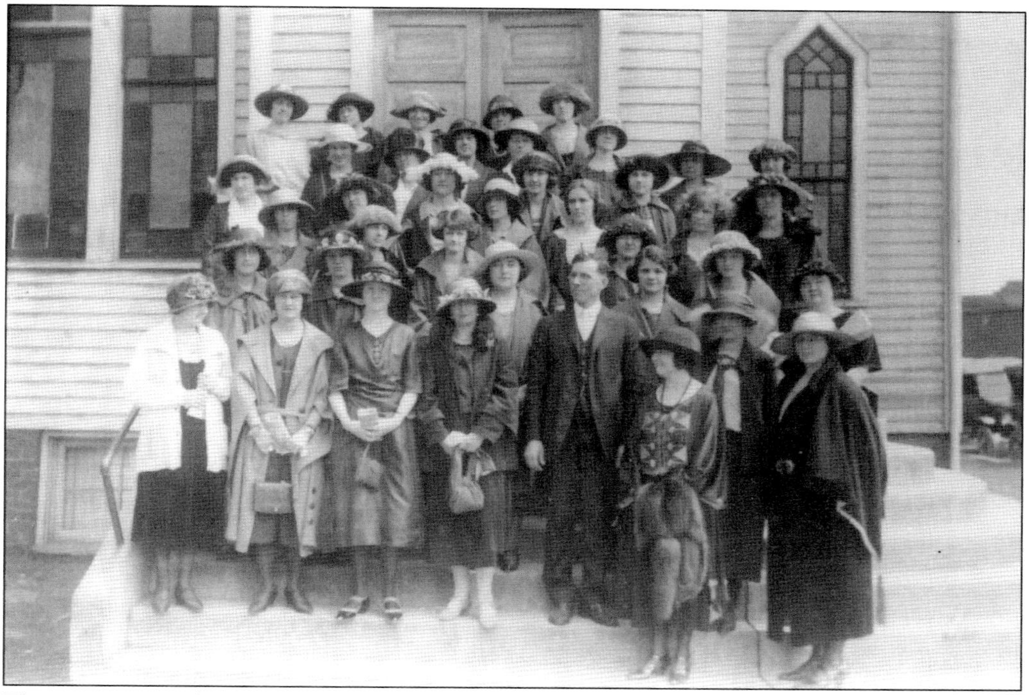

These women in their lovely hats made up the matrons Sunday school class at Central Methodist Church in Lenoir City during the early 1920s. The names on the back of the photograph begin with the notation "top row, left to right." However, the rest of the rows are not noted, so some guesswork is involved in identification. The names as they appear are the following: Beulah Baker, Mell Valentine Walker, Verna Blackburn, Winifred Janis, Grace Simpson, Mary McKinney, ? Bice, Pearle Hutsell, Cliffie Williamson, Zula Corum, Edna Pickle, Mrs. Hobart Heary, Hazel Wright, Lora Goforth, Mary Eblen, Essie Clark, Viola Spraker, Nona Clark, Jorea Littleton, Verna Ghormley, Nora Bailey, Dora Grubb, Mary Lynn Griffitts, Bessie Walker, Alberta Keener, Lucile Kinzer, Evelyn Peters, Roena Edmondson, Mamie Derieux, Ruth Irvin Lucille Grubb, Edna Byrley, Ruth Bird, Lily Lowery, Leo Holdridge, Thelma Hall, ? Hayes, Mattie Gregory, and Ollie Jenkins.

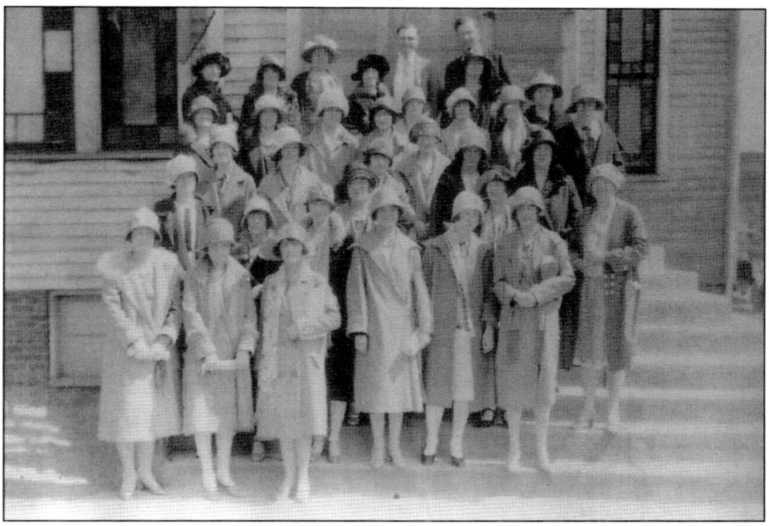

The matron's class at the Central Methodist Church posed for this photograph taken in the early 1920s. Many of the smartly dressed women sported fashionable cloche hats that fit closely over their freshly bobbed flapper hairstyles. All looked chic and sophisticated and ready for Sunday church services.

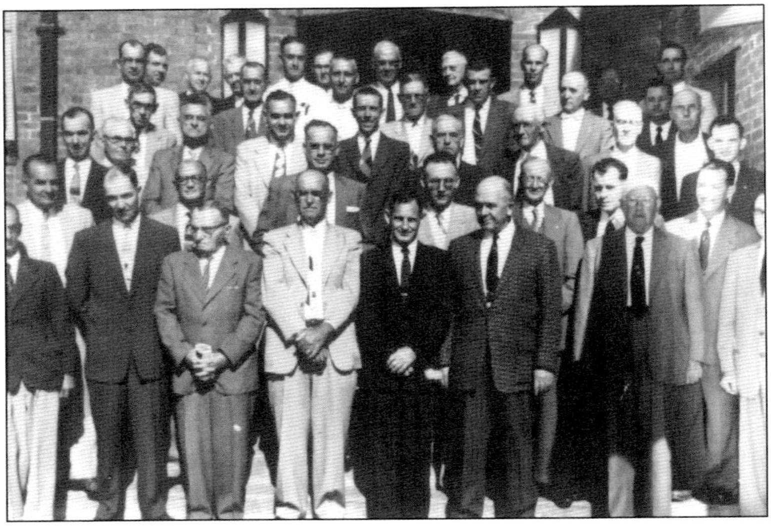

These unidentified men, photographed in the early 1950s, were members of the volunteer Sunday school class at the Central United Methodist Church in Lenoir City. The group is standing on the steps of the church, which was located at the corner of First Avenue and B Street. The church was originally established in 1901.

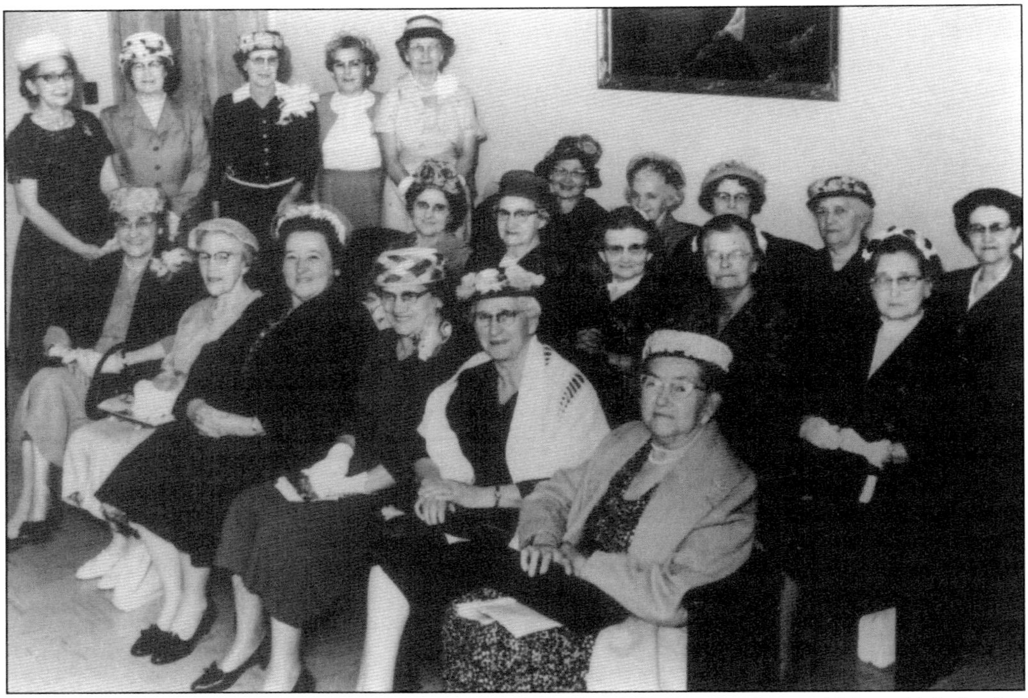

These unidentified members of the matron's Sunday school class at the Central United Methodist Church in Lenoir City show off their finest 1950s pillbox hats. The church, which began as the Methodist Episcopal, became a part of the United Methodist Church when the Methodist Church and the Evangelical United Brethren Church merged in July 1968.

Six

Celebrations

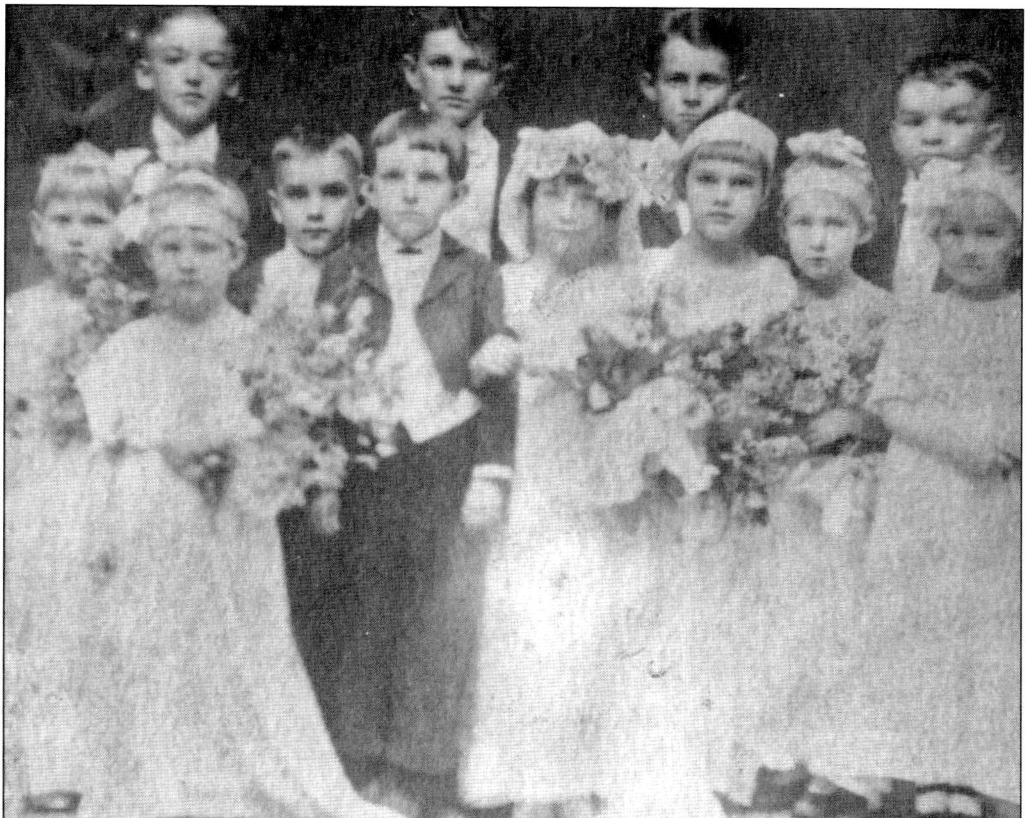

A Tom Thumb Wedding was held about 1920 in Lenoir City. The children were, from left to right, the following: (first row) Mildred Richey, Mary Frances Stanfield, Porter Campbell, Jason Lewis, Laverne Morrell, Marian Remine, unidentified, and Nell Babb; (second row) Ed Calloway, Henry Foster, James Jarvis, and Randy Leeper. These weddings were an American fad based on the real marriage in 1863 of little people Gen. Tom Thumb (born Charles Stratton) and Lavinia Warren.

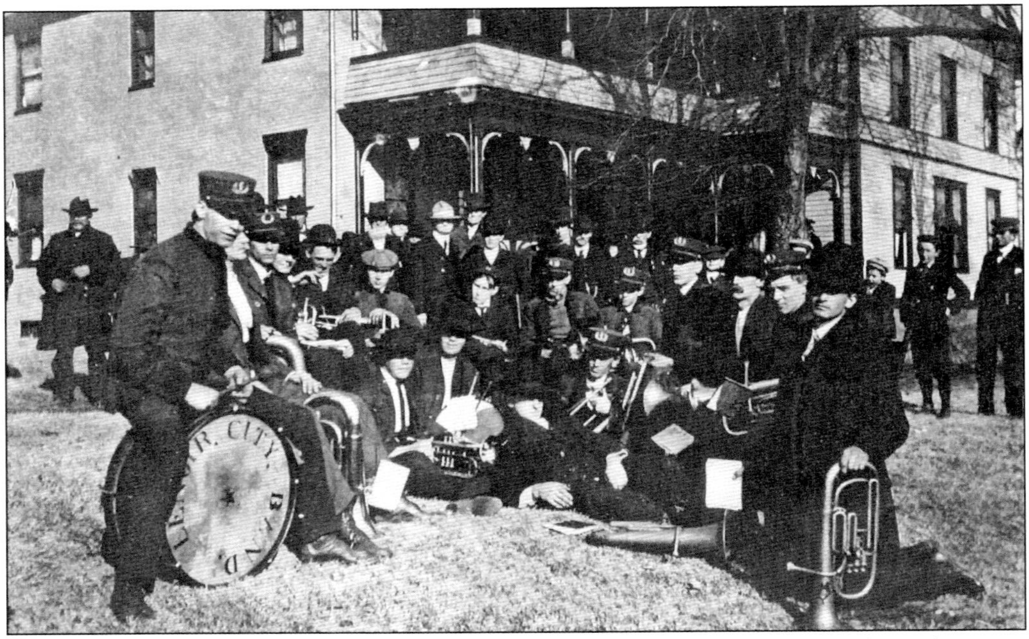

Marching bands in one form or another have been around for hundreds of years. This early Lenoir City community band gathered in front of the Lenoir Inn, possibly in anticipation of a parade or other local event. The members probably provided their own instruments, but they do not seem to be wearing a consistent uniform.

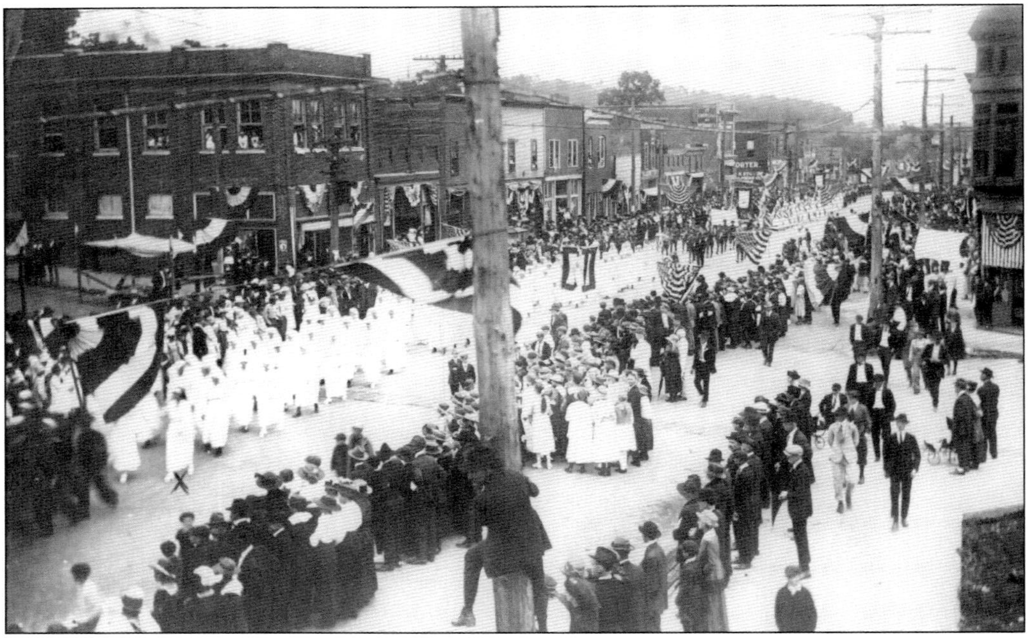

A parade was held on Broadway Street in downtown Lenoir City celebrating the return of World War I soldiers, often called doughboys. Doughboy was a term used during the Great War to refer to American soldiers who were sent to France. A man scales a power pole in order to get a good look at the returning heroes.

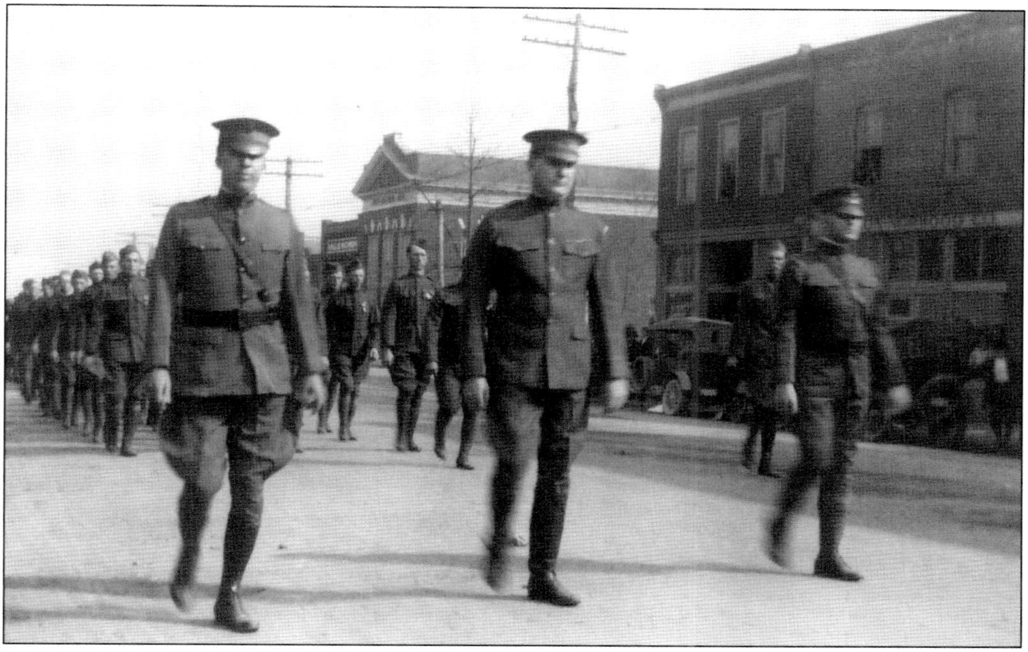

Lenoir City resident Roy G. Cardwell Sr. (right) is shown here marching with two unidentified World War I soldiers in a parade given in honor of returning servicemen. The war lasted from 1914 to 1918. The United States got involved in the spring of 1917 after the sinking of the RMS *Lusitania* by a German submarine.

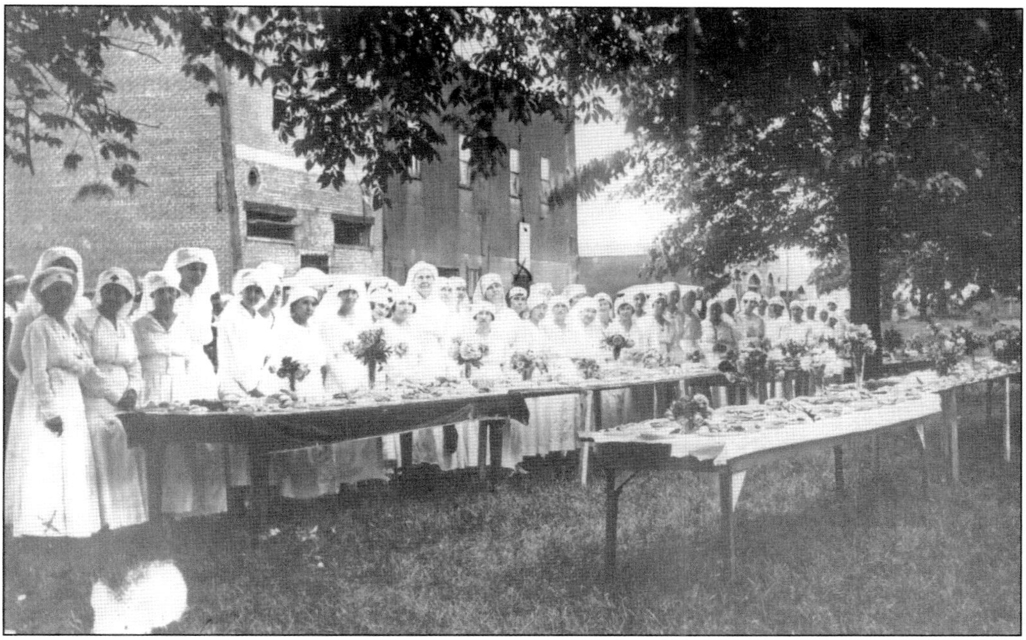

Red Cross volunteers of Lenoir City hosted a luncheon for the returning World War I veterans at the present site of the Lenoir City Museum. In 1914, there were 16,708 Red Cross volunteers, and by 1918, the number had climbed to 20,390,173, most of whom were women.

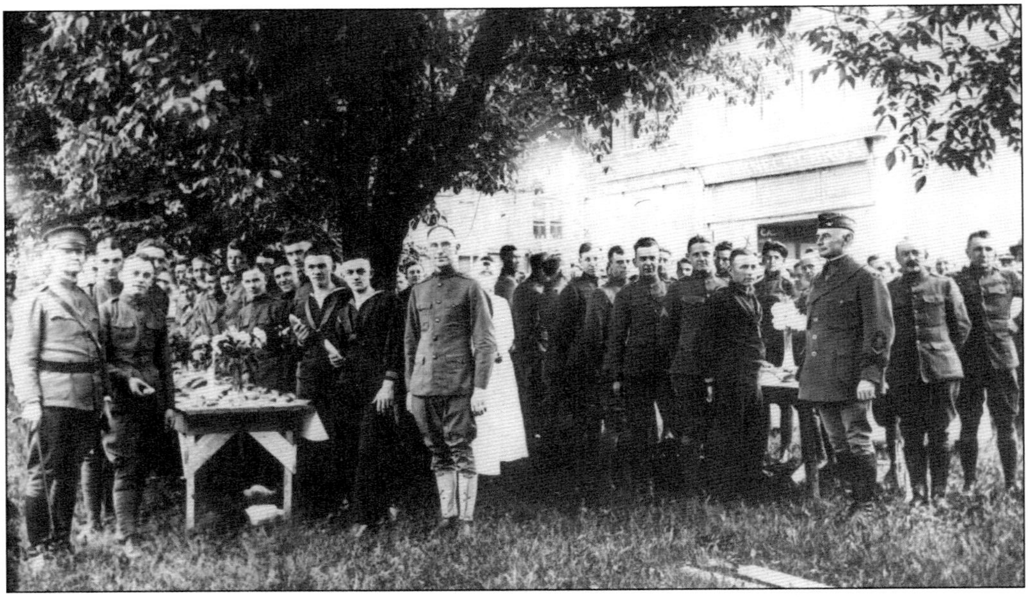

After a parade celebrating their return, the 30th Army Division from Loudon County was given a luncheon in honor of their services during World War I. Gen. Lawrence D. Tyson is at far left, and Gene Rudd is the first soldier on the left side of the table. John Bussell is in the center, and behind and to the left of Mr. Bussell are John Browder, George McCrosky, and Clyde Robinson, all in naval uniforms. Col. Cary F. Spence, who led the 30th Division in Europe, is standing in the foreground at the right.

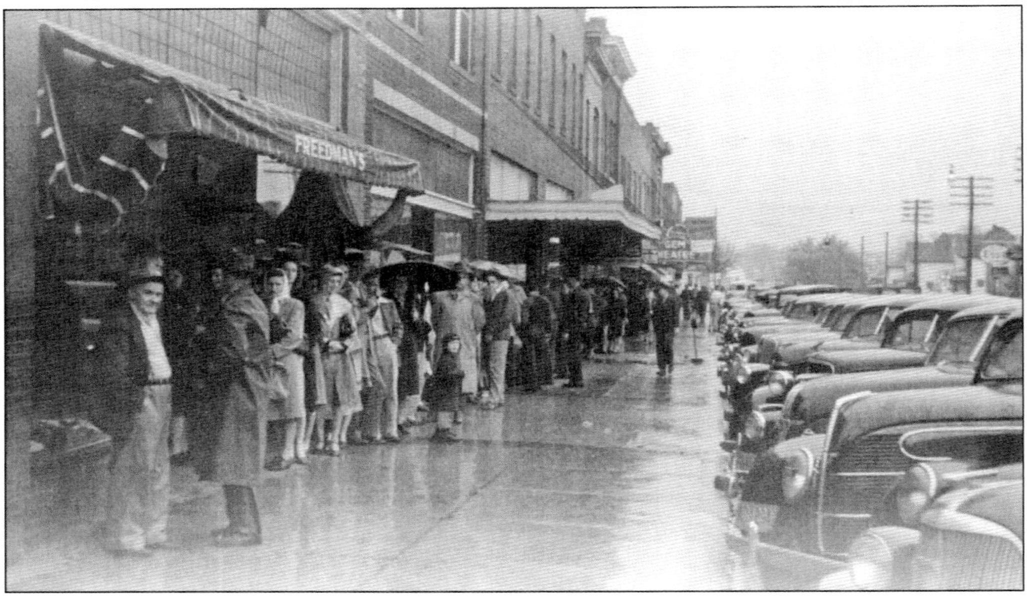

In 1941, manufacturers stopped making women's nylons in order to produce items such as parachutes, nylon rope, and tents, creating a shortage of women's nylons. After World War II ended in 1945, nylon stockings were once again sold in stores, and thousands of women stood in line to buy the first ones available, like these women at the Hub, owned by the Freedman family, in downtown Lenoir City.

Lenoir City celebrated its Golden Jubilee with a series of events during the week of August 11–17, 1957. The week started off with Parade Day, and the program boasted a "Gigantic Parade, 4 miles long" to be held starting at 2:30 p.m. Residents lined up along Broadway Street to watch the festivities. Other events that week included "Dance with your Dolly," the "Legend of Lenoir," fireworks, a magic show, and more.

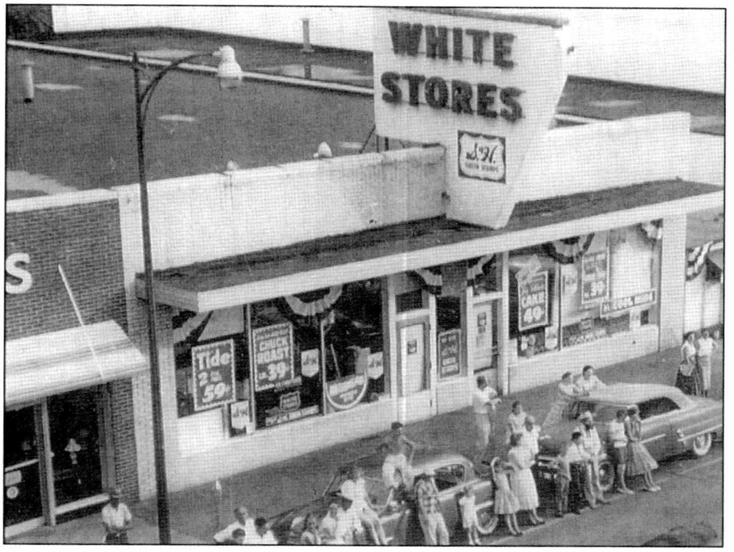

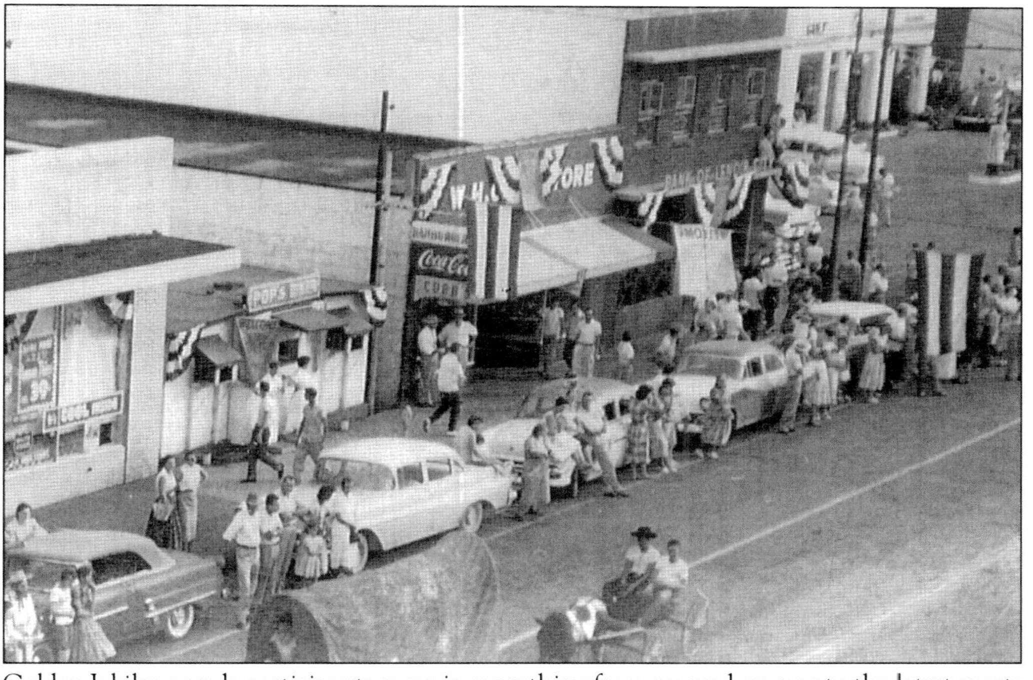

Golden Jubilee parade participants came in everything from covered wagons to the latest sports cars. Flags hung over the street heralding the fun of Parade Day; Governor's Day; Civic, Service and Fraternal Day; Old Fashioned Bargain Days; Industrial Day; and Salute to Youth Day. Everybody got into the spirit of things and turned out in full force to celebrate the town's birthday.

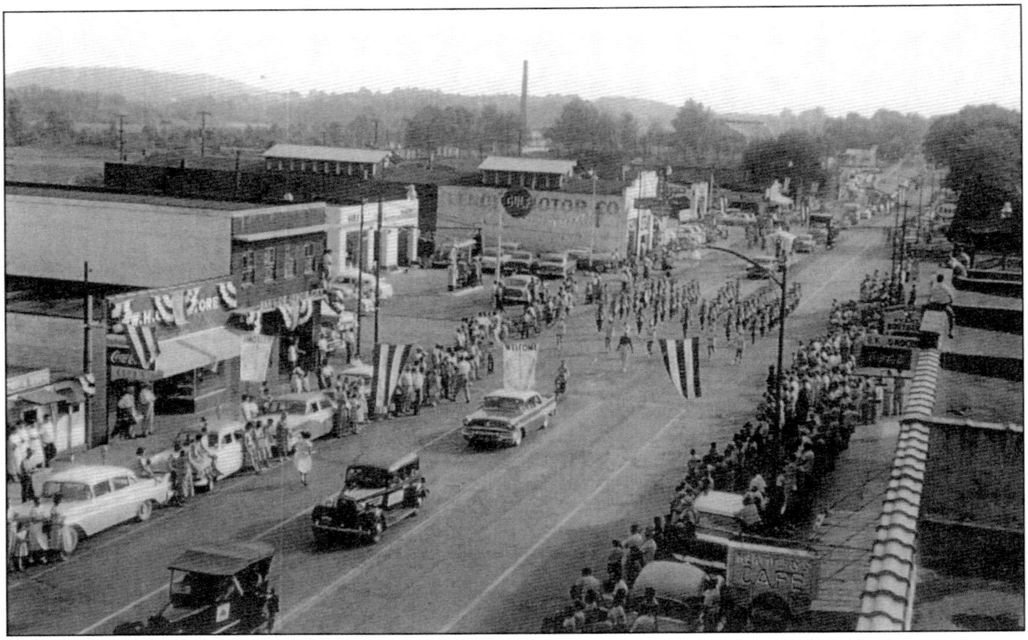

Cars of all eras, marching bands, and floats made up the participants of the 1957 Lenoir City Golden Jubilee. Stores decorated their facades for the event, and the town assumed a festive air with flags, banners, and festoons. Mayor W. J. Hamilton offered a "welcome to one and all" in the souvenir program available during the week's events.

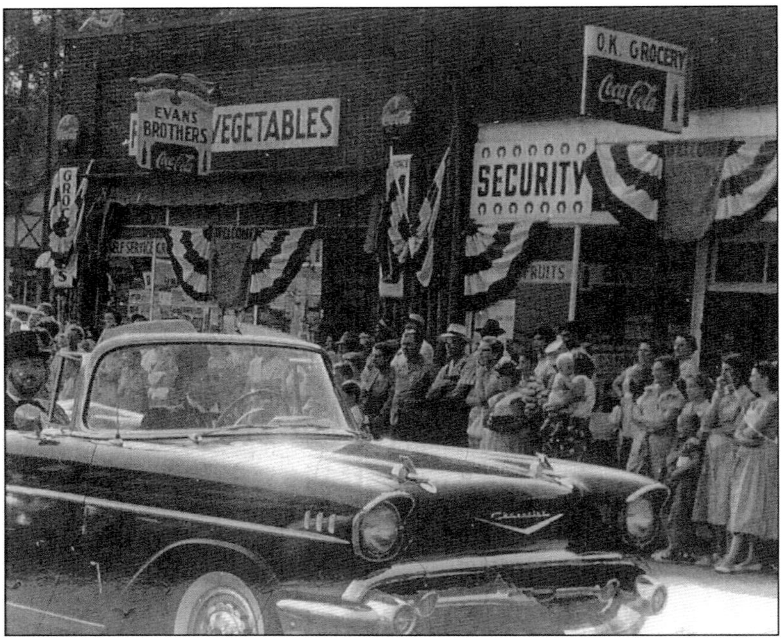

Attendees standing along the parade route may have read Mayor W. J. Hamilton's words in the souvenir program. He wrote, "I am proud to be the Mayor of such a fine progressive city as our Lenoir City. This Golden Jubilee Celebration is an expression of the unity and spirit of our wonderful citizens."

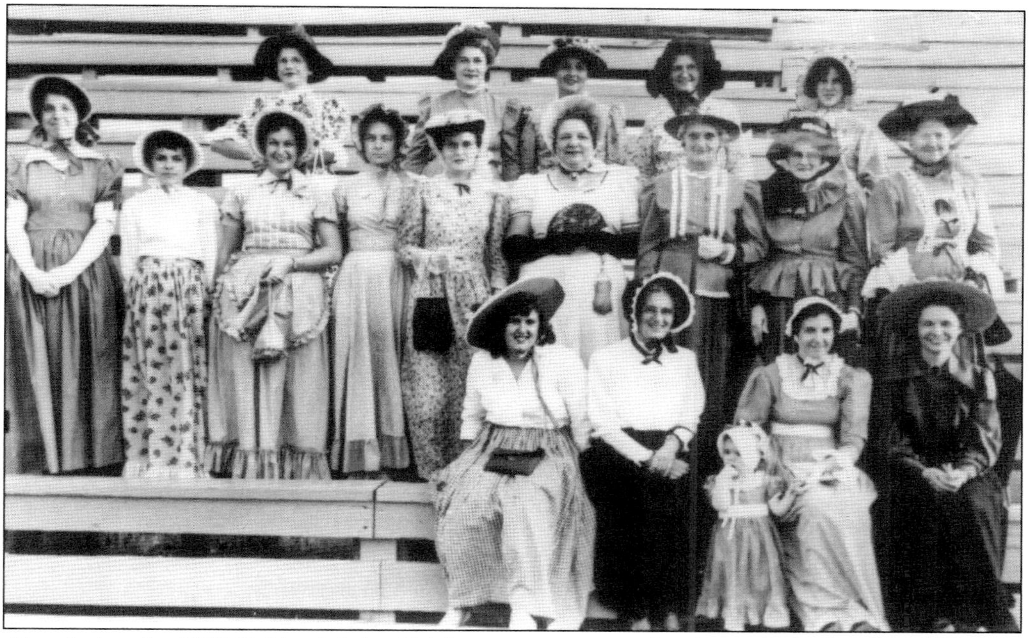

Also during the 1957 Golden Jubilee Celebration, women and girls were asked to dress like their ancestors. This photograph shows a group of unidentified "Sisters of the Swish" in dresses and bonnets of an earlier Lenoir City era. A women's old-fashioned style show was held on Governor's Day, Tuesday, August 13, so participants could show off their costumes.

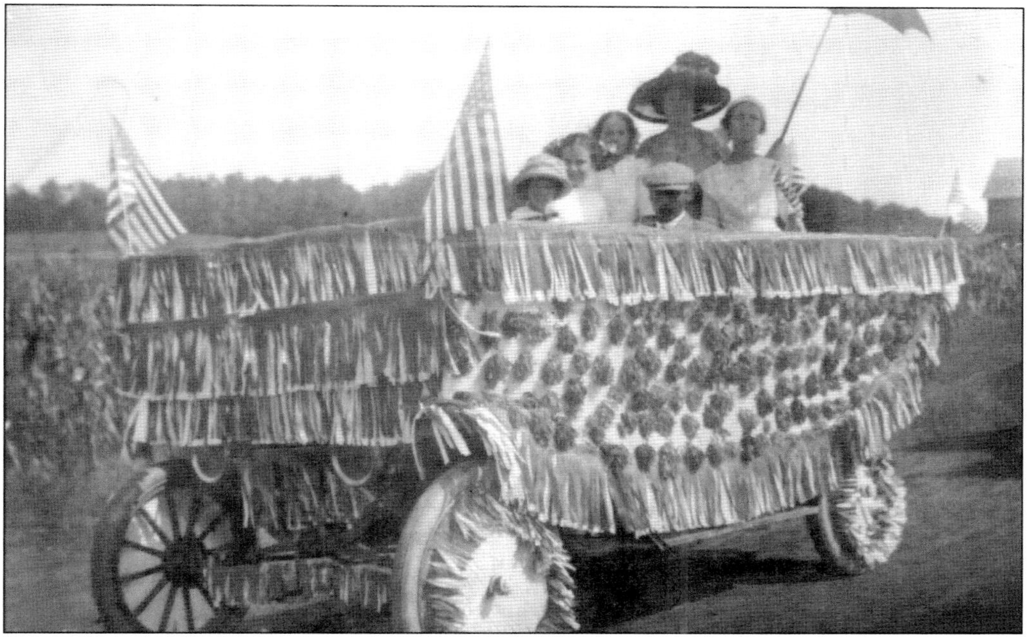

Thomas Edgar Ghormley, who owned a local garage, drives this unique float at the July 4, 1916 parade event. Dixie (Ghormley) Morrison rides in the back under a shaded parasol. The children are unidentified. Before her marriage to Benjamin Morrison, a preacher from McMinn County, Dixie worked at the knitting mill.

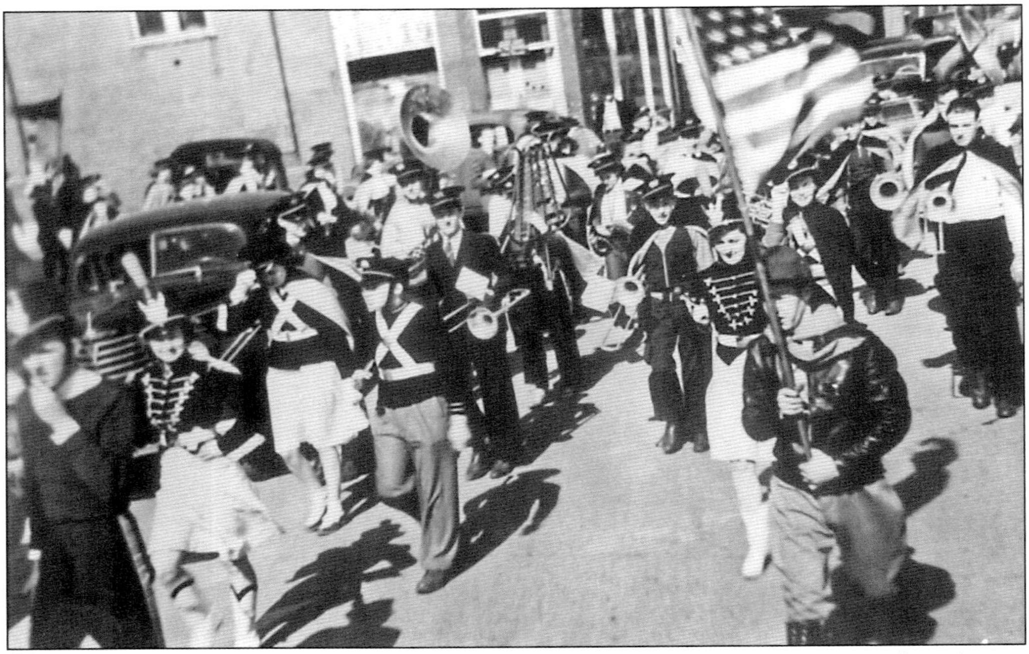

In the 1940s, the Lenoir City High School Band participated in a parade on Broadway Street. Those identified in this photograph are the following: Jesse Hope, drum major; Mabel Marshall, majorette; David Ghormely, sousaphone; Ralph Dial, with trombone at left; and Jason Baker, hatless with trombone at right.

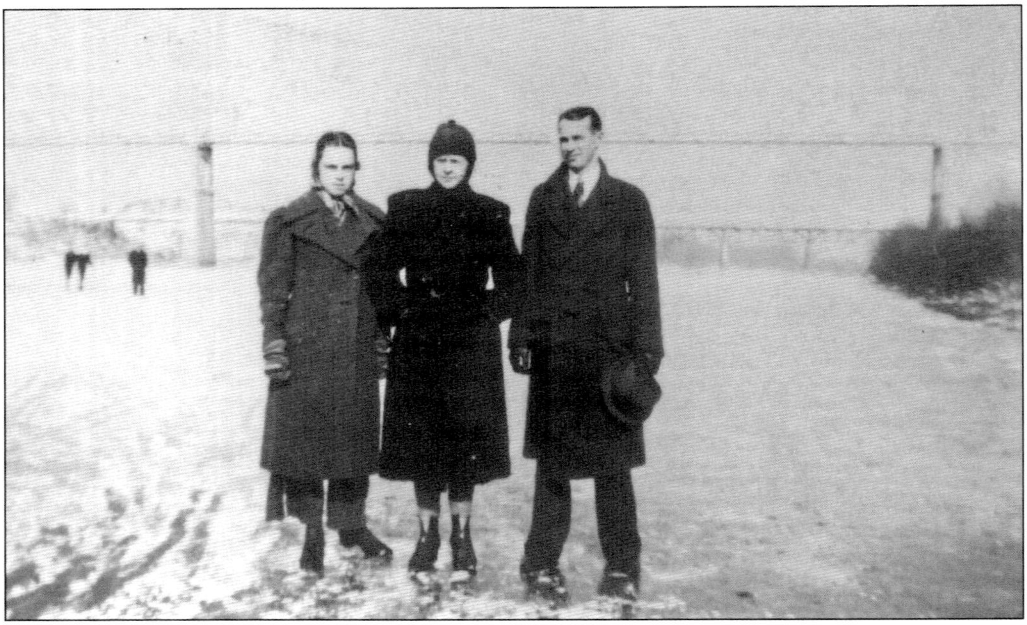

Although a frozen river may not seem like a big deal in northern states, when the Tennessee River froze on January 14, 1940, it was downright newsworthy. Many area residents risked the chance of falling through the ice as they made their way across the river. Three such daredevils were, from left to right, Rachel Blair, Kate Blair, and Gillus Purdy.

Seven

TRANSPORTATION

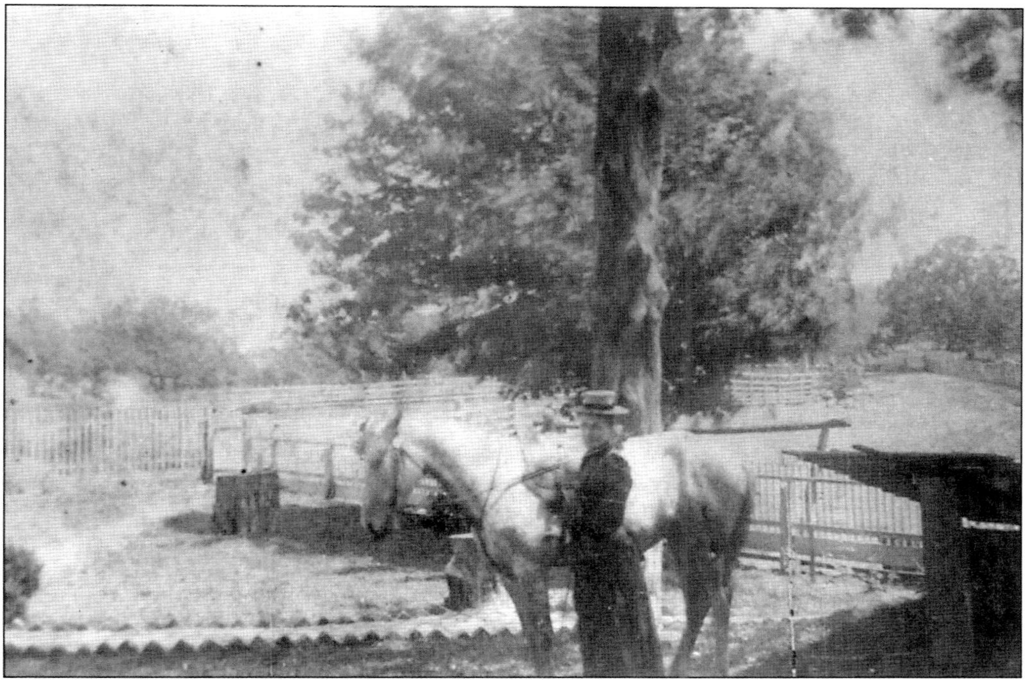

This woman may be unidentified, but there are many who can identify with her. Long before cars were readily available, horses were the best choice for transportation, especially for lengthy trips. This type of horsepower could also be used to pull a wagon, help yank out a stump, or plow a field.

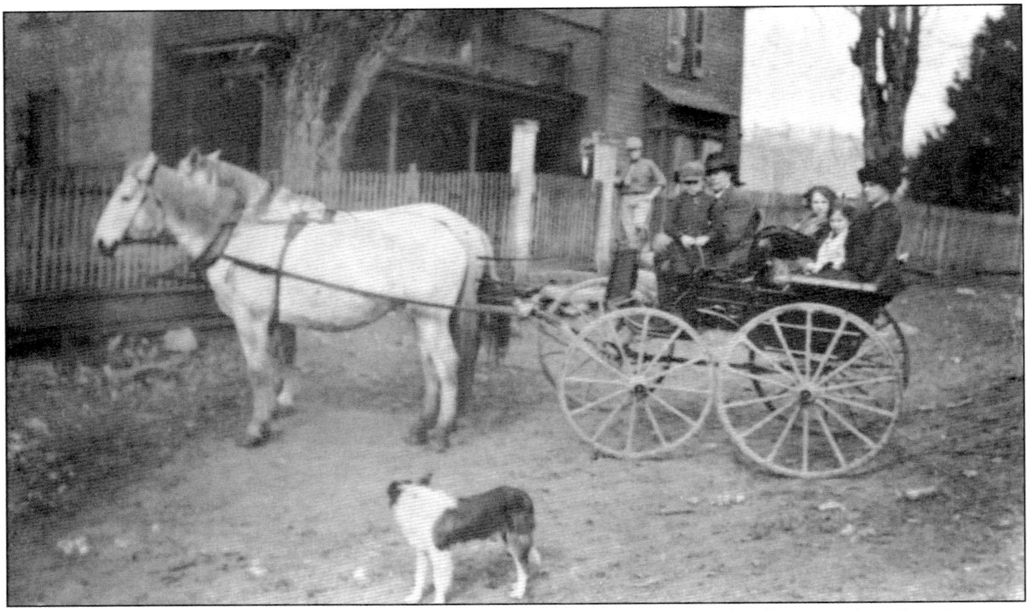

This unidentified family of five appears to be dressed in their Sunday best as they head out in their beautiful black horse drawn buggy. The family dog and two men in the background watch as they leave on their unknown journey. The photograph was taken in 1912 in front of the James Hope home located on Hickory Creek Road.

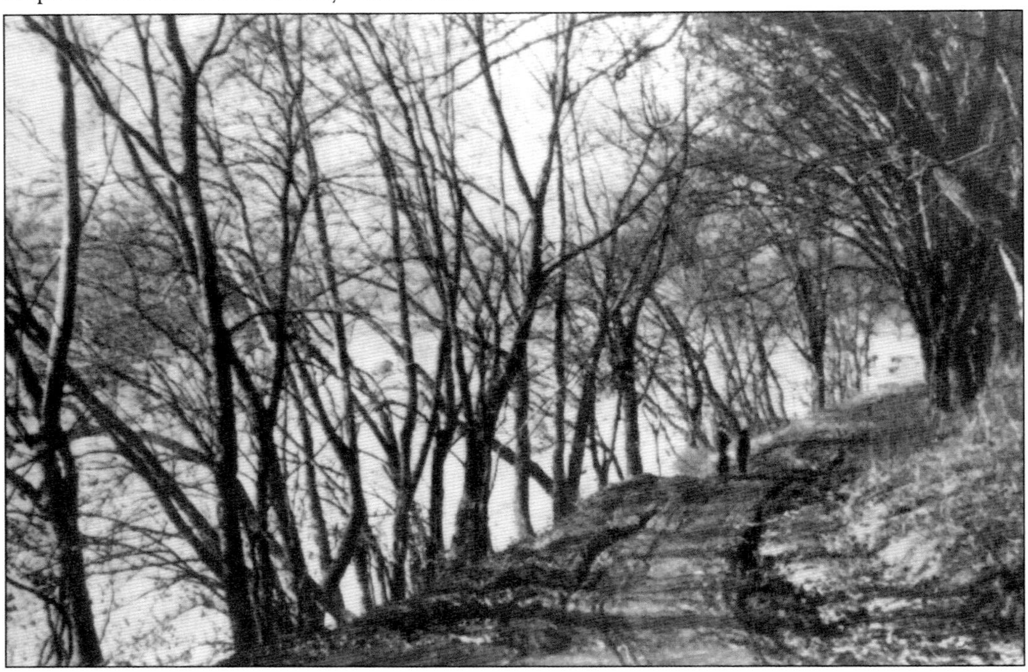

There were probably plenty of folks who went "sparking" over the years on Lover's Lane, the old road to Bussell's Ferry. It was located at Town Creek near Nelson Street (just before the junction with the Tennessee River). The canopy of trees would have provided some privacy on the deeply rutted dirt road.

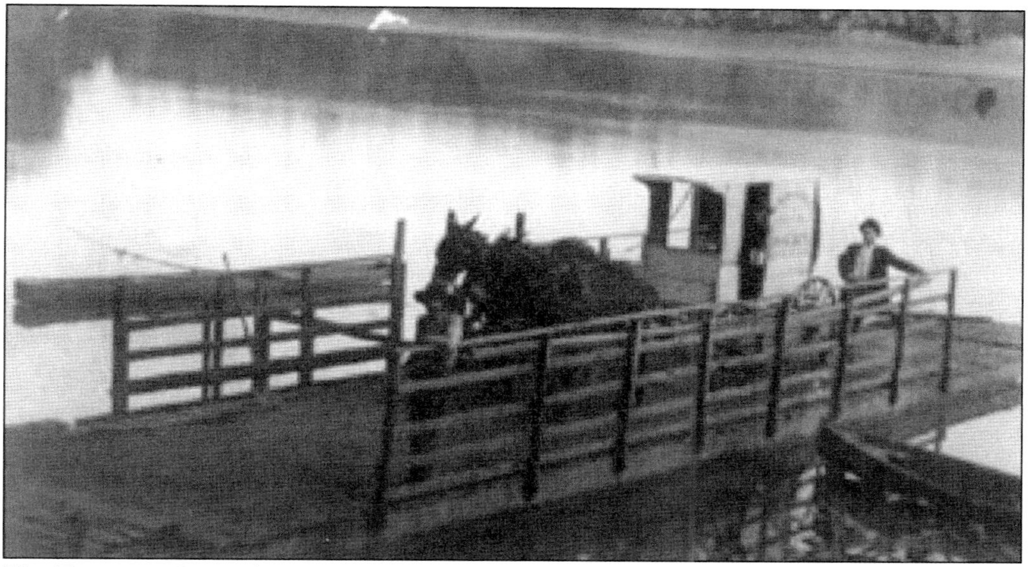

The Tennessee River, formerly the Holston, wraps itself around East Tennessee like a coiled snake. A simple journey of a few miles as the crow flies could take days if a traveler had to go around the abundant waterways. Enterprising businessmen built ferries, like this one known as Bussell's Ferry at Lenoir City, to provide a way to efficiently transport people and goods safely from one side to the other.

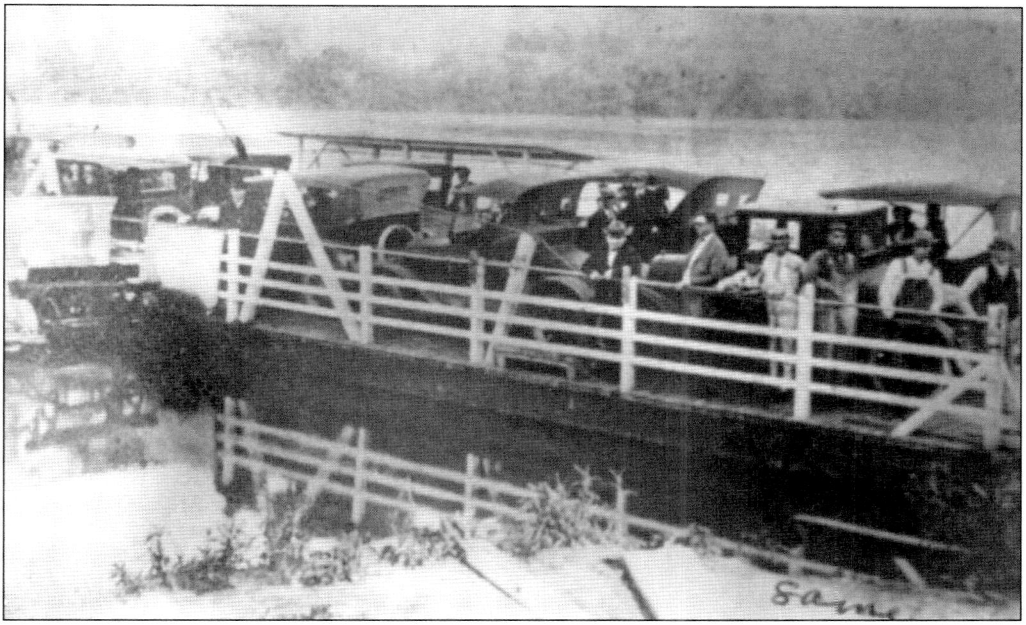

First powered by overhead cables, and later by steam and gasoline engines, the many ferries on East Tennessee waterways made it easy for drivers to cross the Tennessee River before bridges were built. This photograph taken in the early 1920s shows a full load on Bussell's Ferry.

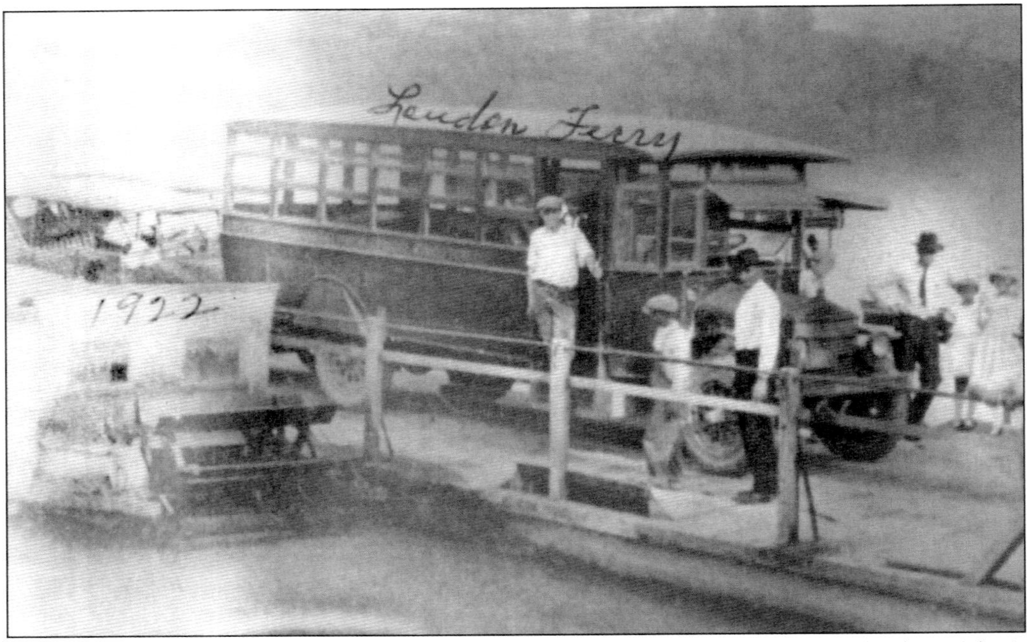

Even passenger buses took advantage of the convenience of crossing the river by ferry. Blair's Ferry ran from Lenoir City to Loudon offering an easy route for travelers heading to and from Knoxville to points south along Highway 11. Construction of a toll bridge to Loudon began in 1927. In 1947, it became a free road, which was the beginning of the end for local ferries.

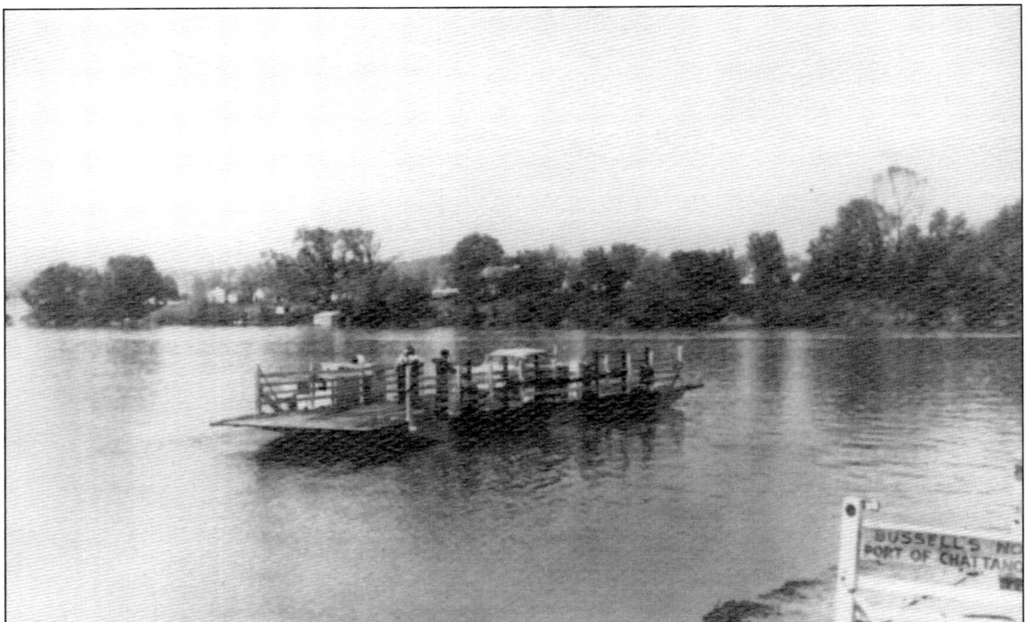

Just imagine if your morning commute included a trip across the river on a ferry, it might make the drive to school more interesting for the kids. Ferries along the Tennessee River played a vital role in the lives of Loudon Countians. The sign in the corner of this photograph taken in the 1950s says, "Bussell's Ferry, Port of Chattanooga."

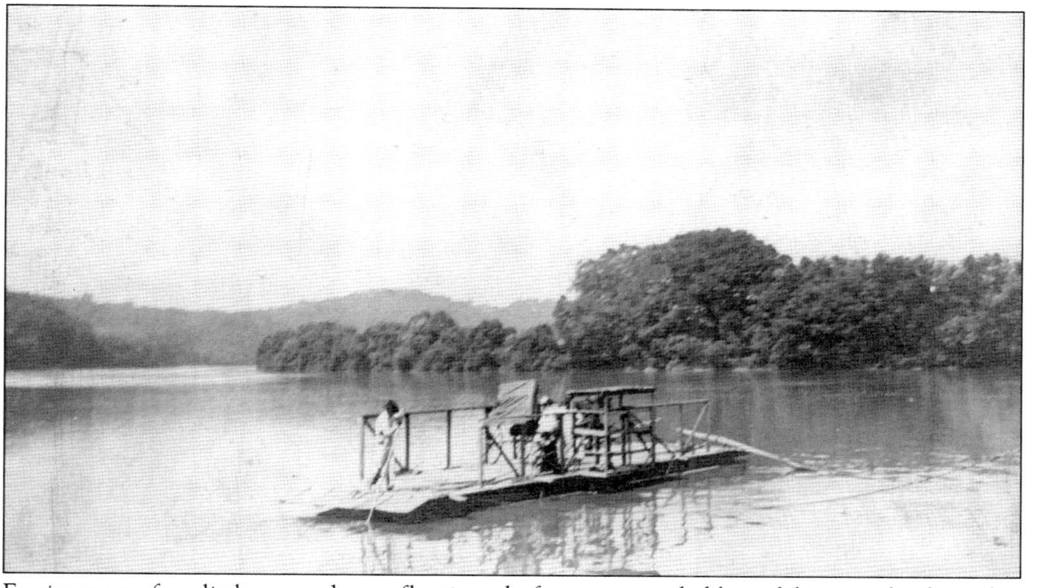

Ferries were often little more than a floating platform surrounded by a delicate web of wooden railings, but they offered a viable alternative to early poorly maintained roads. Goods could be loaded easily on and off of the flat low-slung ferry decks, making them a perfect choice for commercial activity between river and wagon transportation.

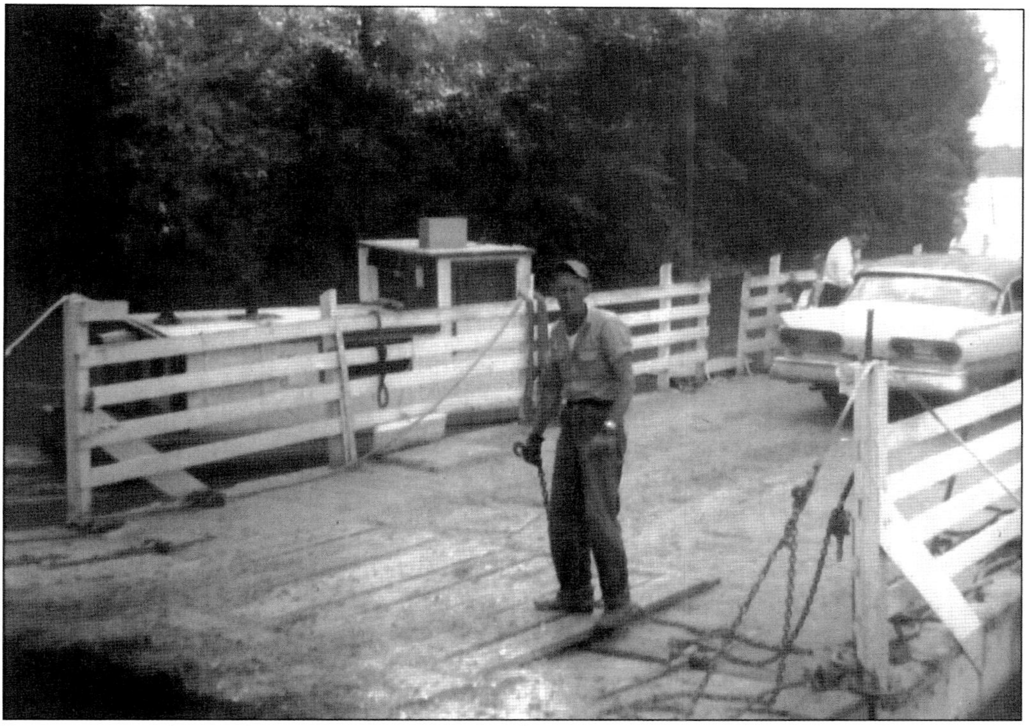

Ferries operated into the 1960s in some parts of East Tennessee. Hi Cheatham, shown in this photograph taken on July 4, 1961, ran Bussell's Ferry at Lenoir City for many years. He ferried people and their cars back and forth across the river several times a day.

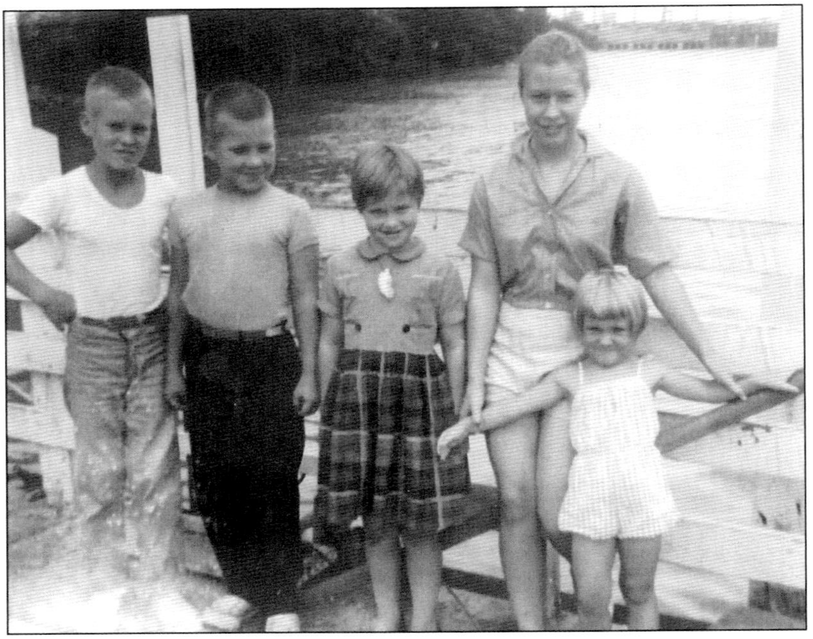

Like many ferries, Bussell's Ferry was a family business. Shown here in this 1961 photograph, the children of ferry operator Clinton Cook are, from left to right, Gary, Ray, Pat, Jane, and Debbie. Pat sports a lucky rabbit's foot on a chain around her neck.

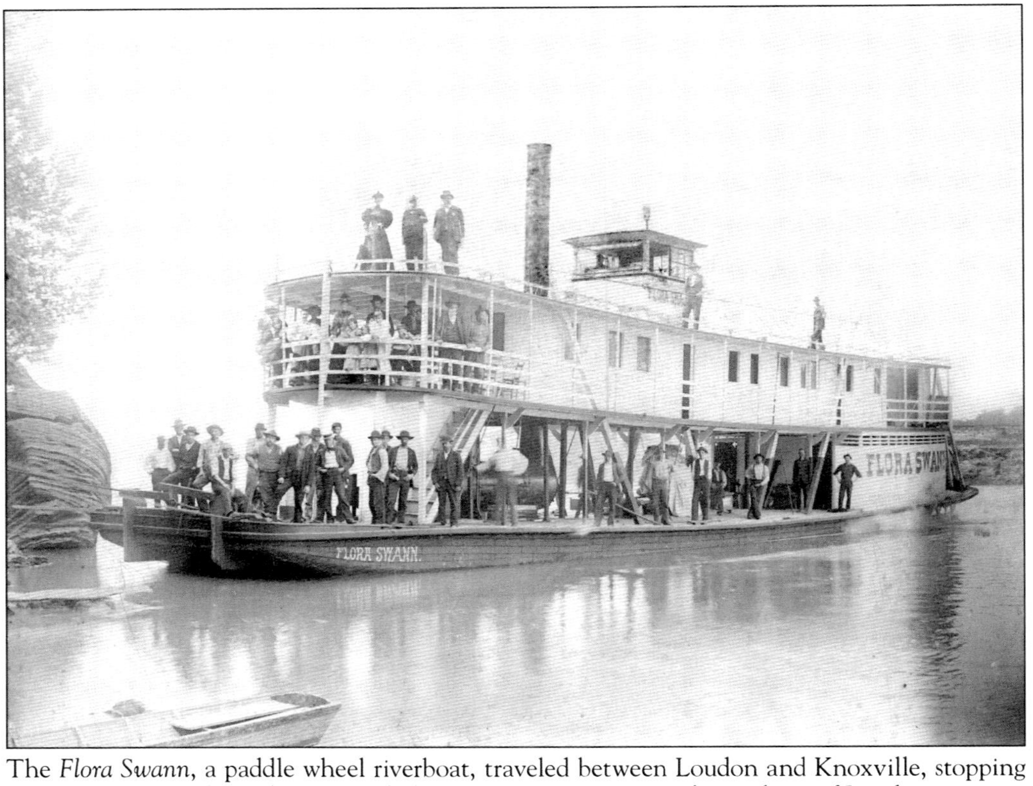

The *Flora Swann*, a paddle wheel riverboat, traveled between Loudon and Knoxville, stopping at various points along the way including Lenoir City. As noted in a diary of Loudon attorney Edward P. McQueen, "The boat stopped at Calloway's Landing at Concord where a delicious dinner was served by Mrs. Calloway."

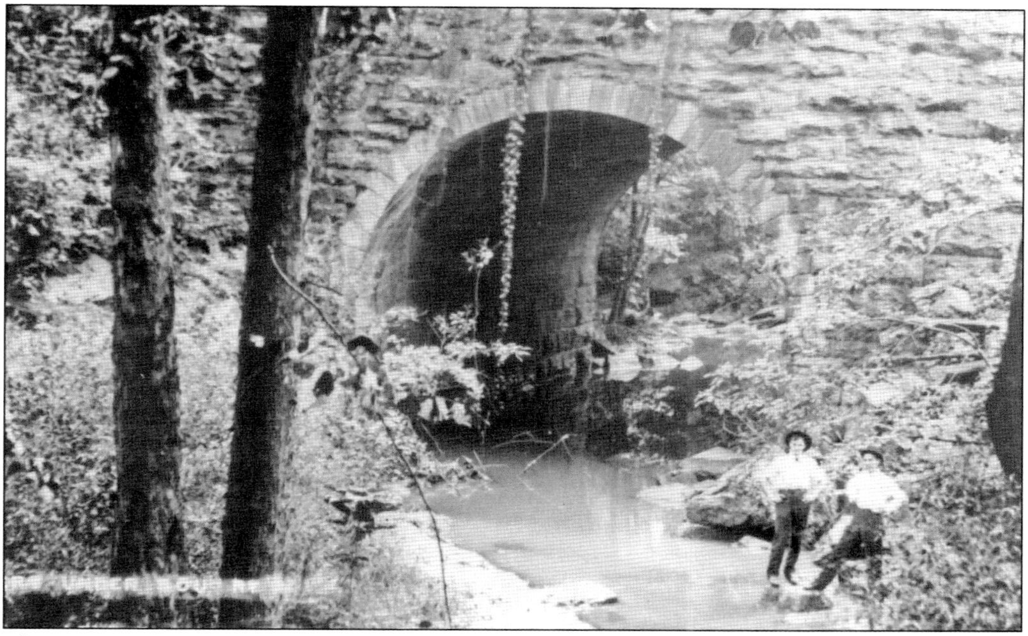

This *c.* 1908 photograph shows a scenic culvert near Lenoir City with two unidentified boys. The Southern Railway ran on tracks high above the stream. Created in 1894 largely from the financially stressed Richmond and Danville system and the East Tennessee, Virginia, and Georgia Railroad, the Southern Railway owned two-thirds of the 4,400 miles of line it operated. The remainder was leased or held through stock options and ownership agreements.

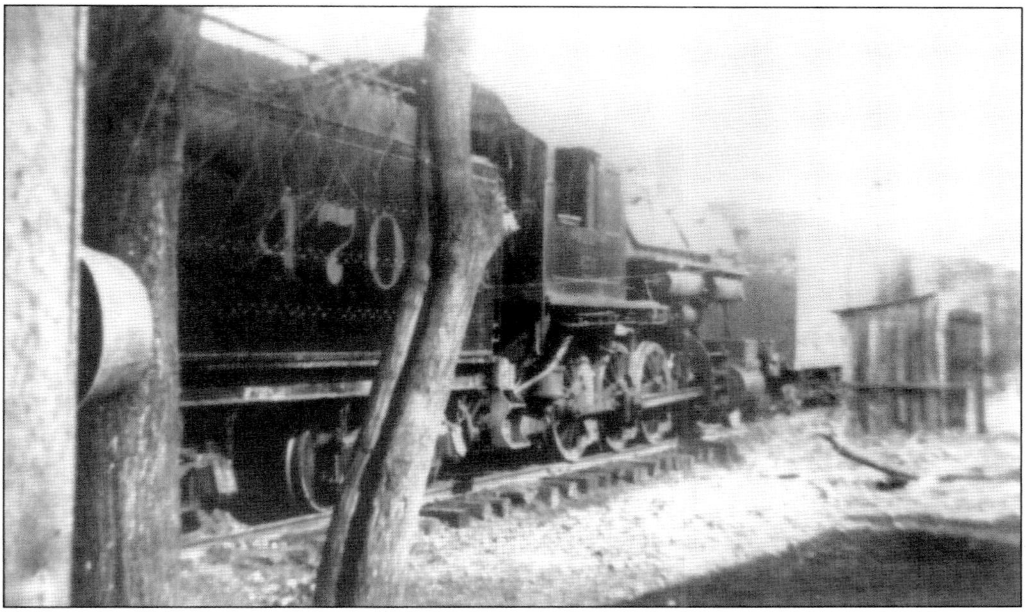

From 1852 to 1854, the railroad bridge at Loudon was built. It opened in 1855 allowing trains pulled by steam-powered engines, such as this one, to run from Atlanta to Chattanooga to Knoxville and back. Lenoir City benefited greatly from the railroad. Not only did the town grow due to the proximity of the tracks, but also from the jobs provided by the Lenoir Car Works.

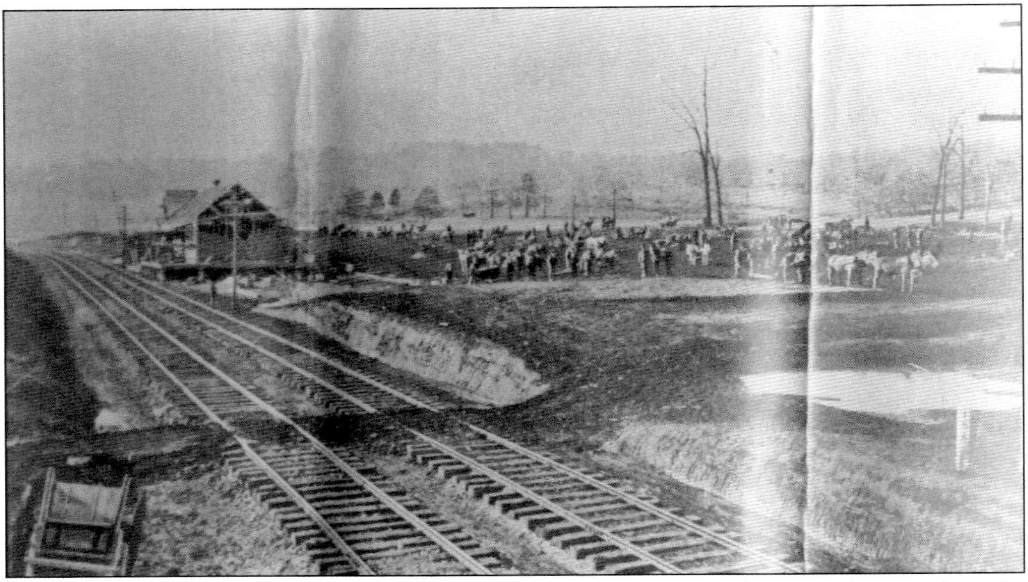

Early Lenoir City's growth was tied to the railroad tracks upon which it sat. The train brought both people and goods into the emerging city. As the town planners began to take the city from paper to land, streets were laid out. A team of road builders with mule and horse drawn machinery prepared to grade the roads in the distance.

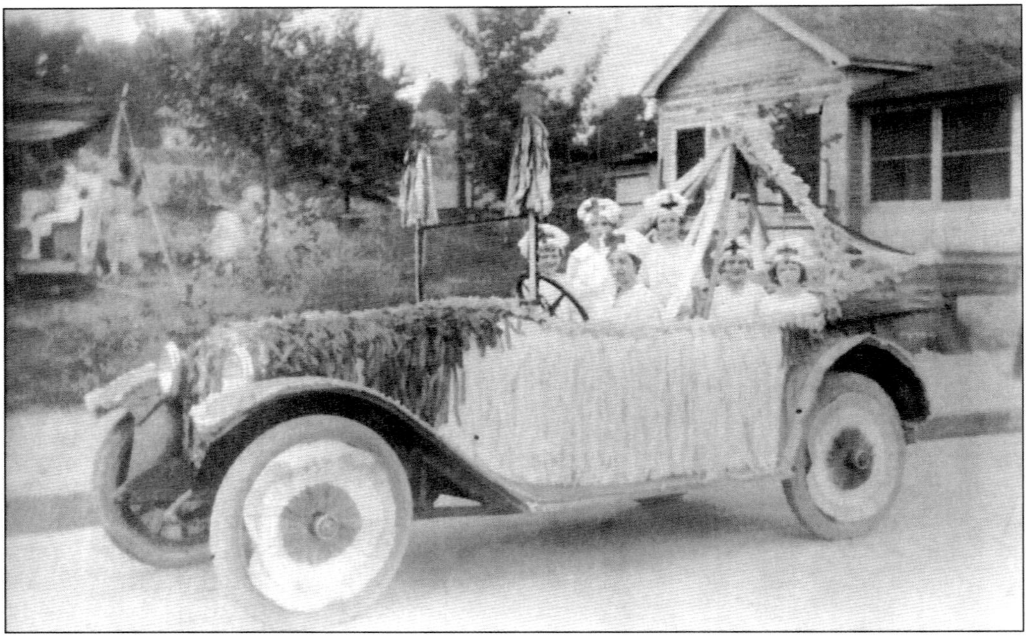

From the minute they became available to the mass market, cars played an important part in the lives of Americans. In addition to making travel more convenient, they offered other less obvious options, such as carrying participants in a parade. Annie Calloway is at the wheel of this float decorated for a parade event held in Lenoir City in the late 1920s. The other riders are, from left to right, Julia Margaret Foster, Edgar Calloway, Mary Lynn Foster, Annie Elizabeth Lacy, and Helen Foster.

Eight

THE DAM

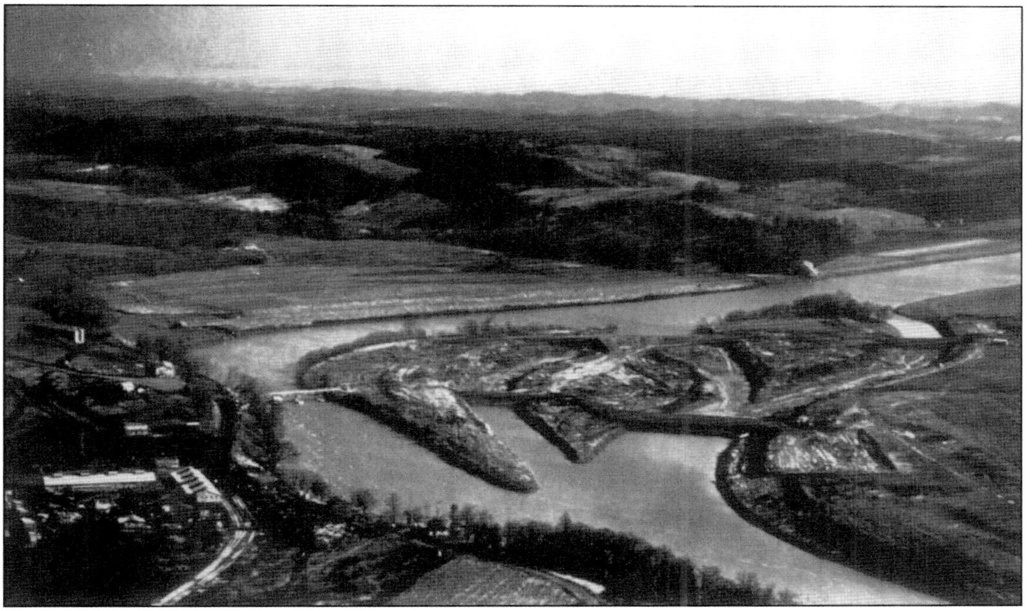

The Tennessee River system that wraps itself around the eastern end of the state has created a lush and fertile valley teeming with abundant flora and fauna. The rivers, lakes, and streams not only provide water for growing food, but also for transportation and power. However, the same waterway that gives so much also takes it away during periods of flooding.

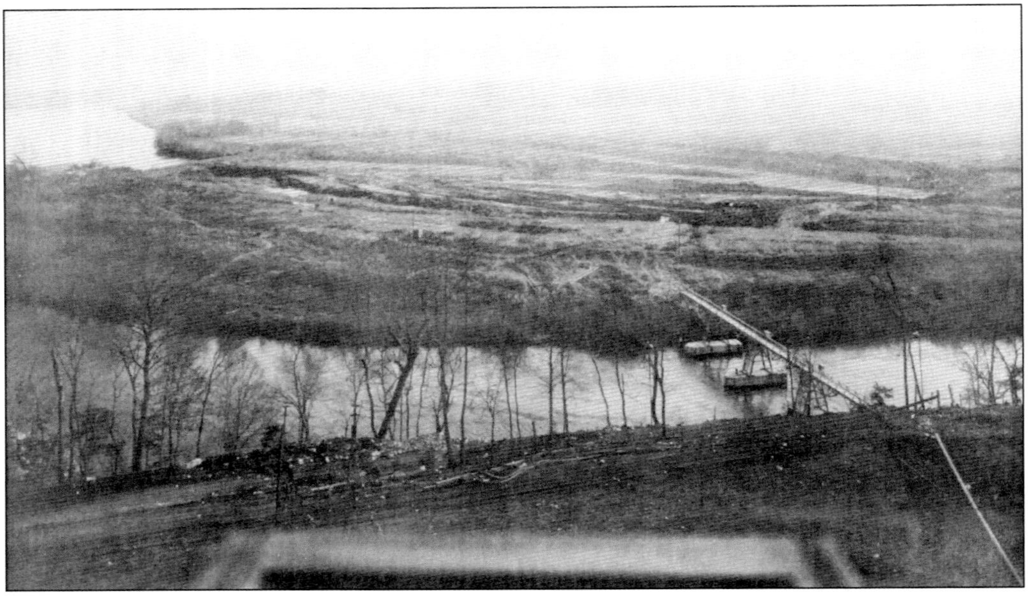

As more and more families settled along the Tennessee River, the need for both flood control and power increased. In 1933, congress passed the TVA Act creating the Tennessee Valley Authority as part of Pres. Franklin D. Roosevelt's New Deal to address resource management in the Tennessee Valley. The river system was accessed for power production, navigation, flood control, malaria prevention, reforestation, and erosion control possibilities.

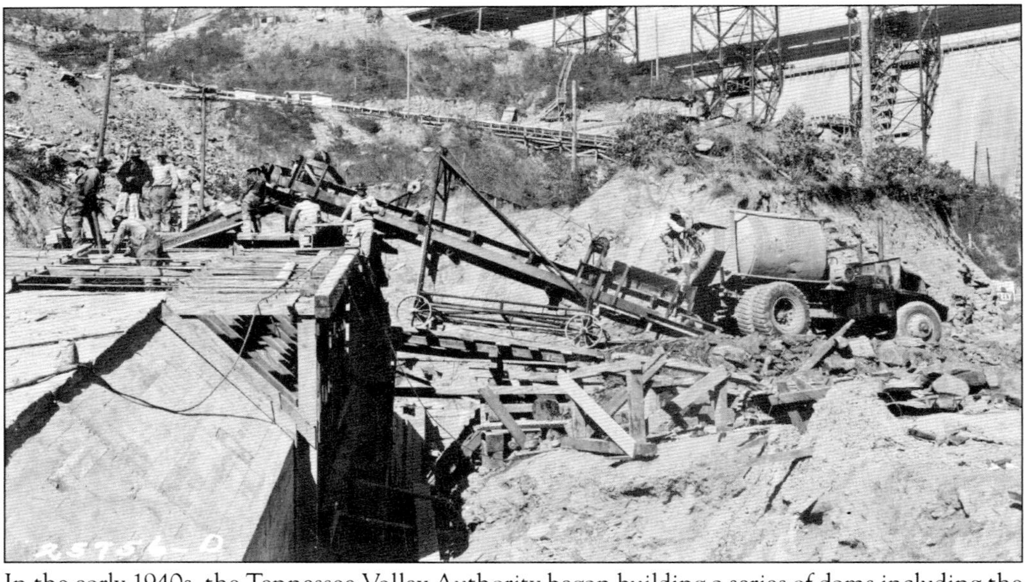

In the early 1940s, the Tennessee Valley Authority began building a series of dams including the Fort Loudon Dam. Construction of a series of more than a dozen hydroelectric projects and a steam plant reached its peak in 1942, providing 28,000 employees with design and construction jobs. By 1945, the Tennessee Valley Authority had completed a 650-mile navigation channel the length of the Tennessee River.

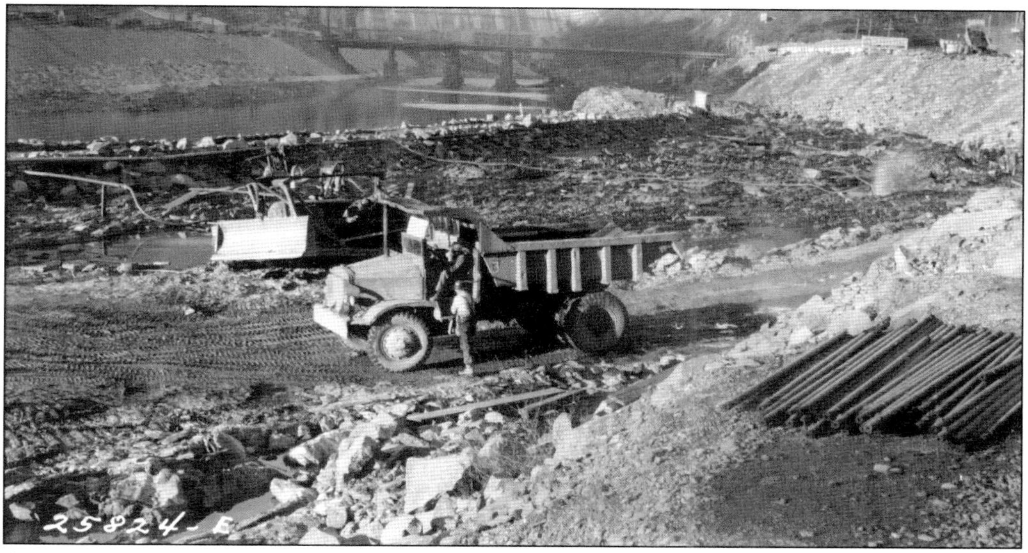

Construction of the Fort Loudon Dam began on July 8, 1940, and ended August 2, 1943, costing $41 million. It started generating power on November 9, 1943. The dam is 4,190 feet long and 122 feet high. A lake extends 55 miles from the dam and offers more than 360 miles of shoreline.

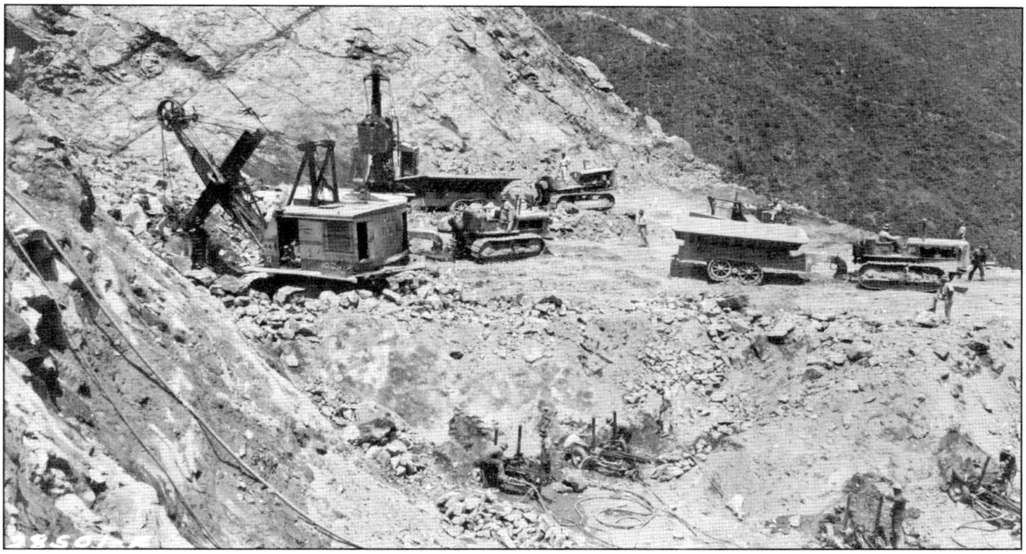

Nearly 90 percent of urban dwellers had electricity in the 1930s. From 1930 to 1939, the percentage of rural homes with electricity had risen from 10 to 25 percent. The need for affordable electric power was increasing, and hydroelectric power, like that provided by the Fort Loudoun Dam, became a viable alternative.

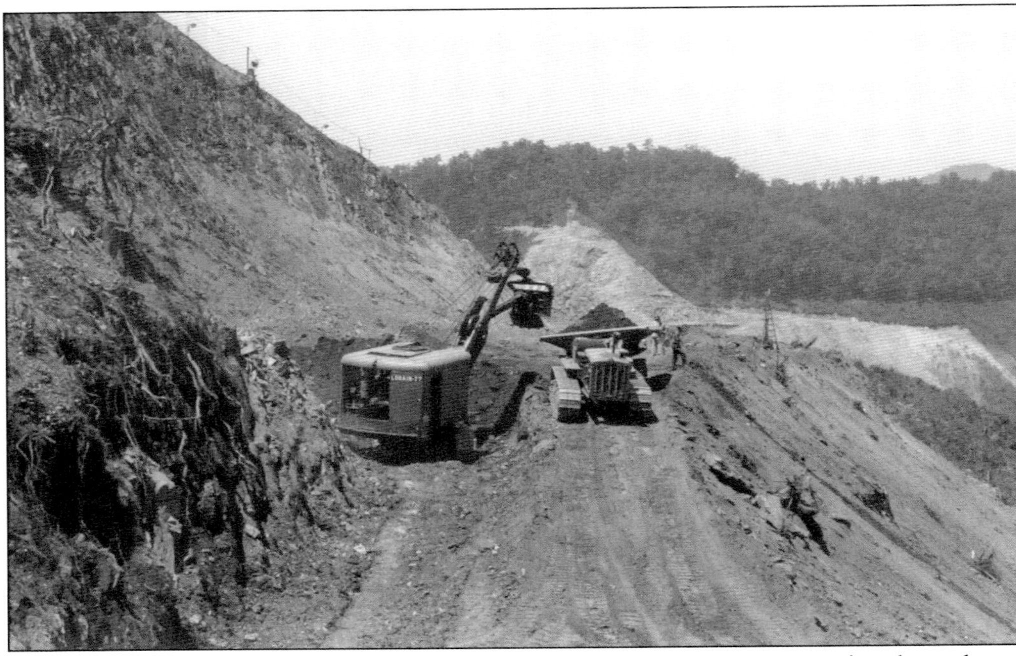

Fort Loudon was the last dam built on the Tennessee River and was constructed in three phases. During phase one, the lock-and-earthen dam was constructed on the south side of the river on Belle Island. The spillway was built during phase two, and the construction of the powerhouse in phase three finished the project. The highway bridge over the dam was not added until 1963.

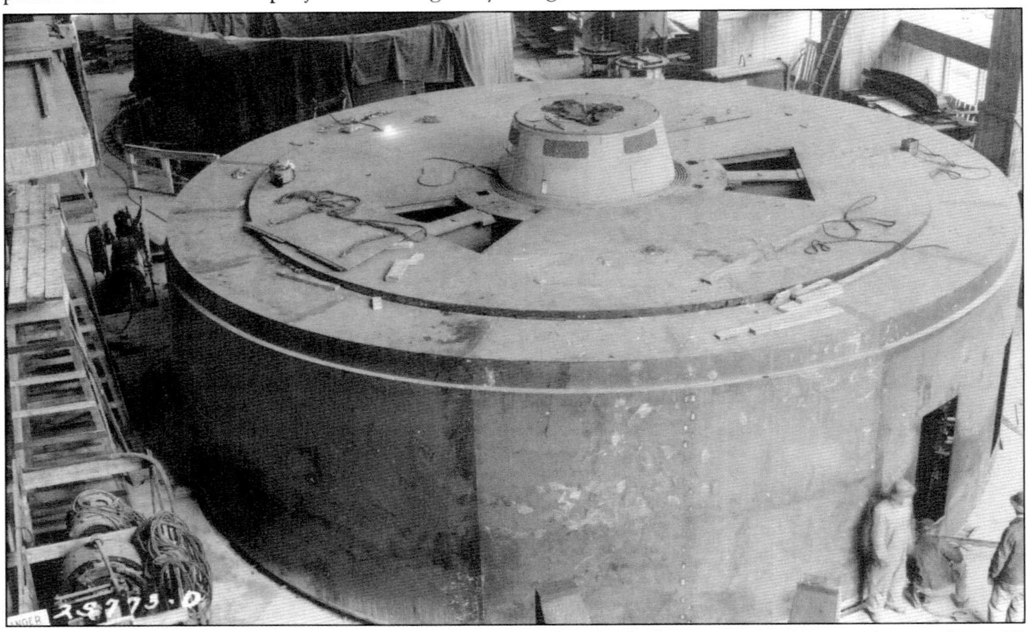

Fort Loudon Dam is equipped with a 60-foot-by-360-foot lock that raises and lowers boats about 70 feet between Fort Loudoun Lake and Watts Bar Lake. There are four hydroelectric generators at the dam with a combined generation capacity of 155.6 megawatts of electricity. The reservoir has 379 miles of shoreline, 14,600 acres of water surface, and a flood storage capacity of 111,000 acre-feet.

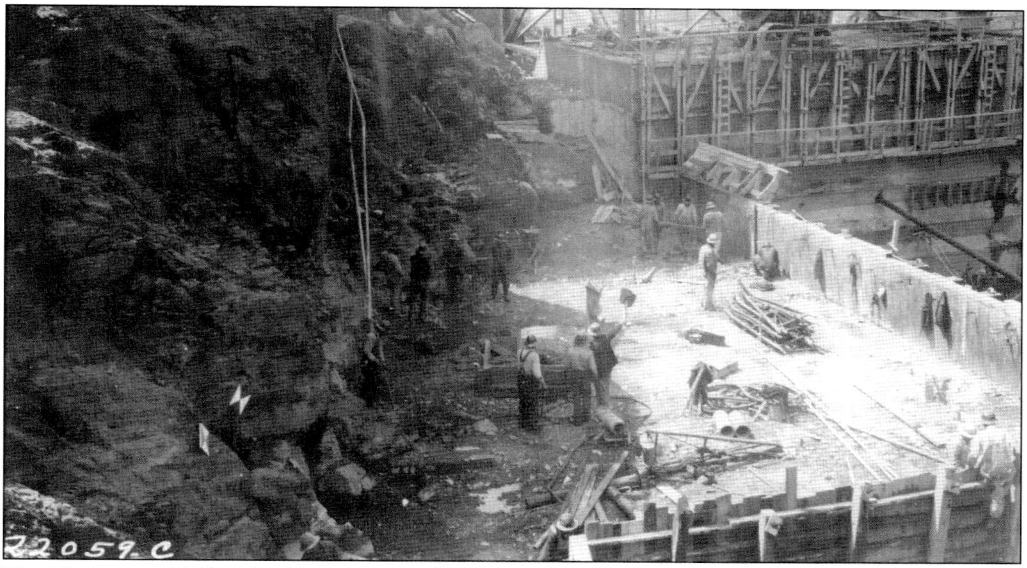

The Tennessee Valley Authority originally planned to complete the Fort Loudon Dam in 1944. However, the outbreak of World War II brought increased funding and urgency, and the dam was completed nearly a year ahead of schedule on August 2, 1943. The first generator went online November 9, 1943, and the second went online January 15, 1944.

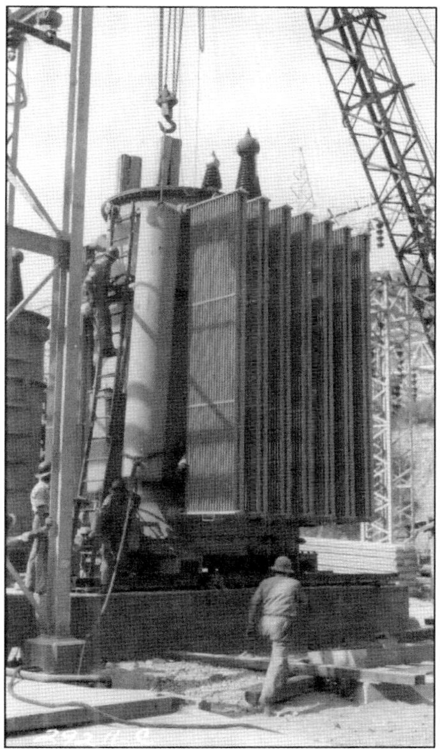

The Fort Loudon Dam project required the purchase of 16,200 acres of land and flowage rights. During the building and flooding process, 317 residents, 6 cemeteries, and over 60 miles of roads had to be relocated. Construction efforts required 582,000 cubic yards of concrete and 122,000 cubic yards of riprap.

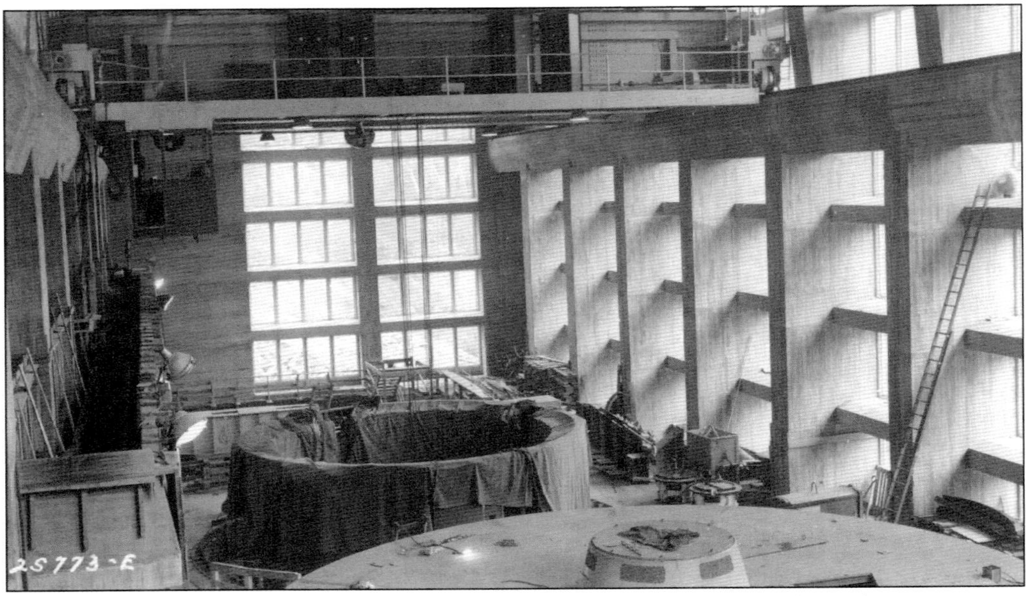

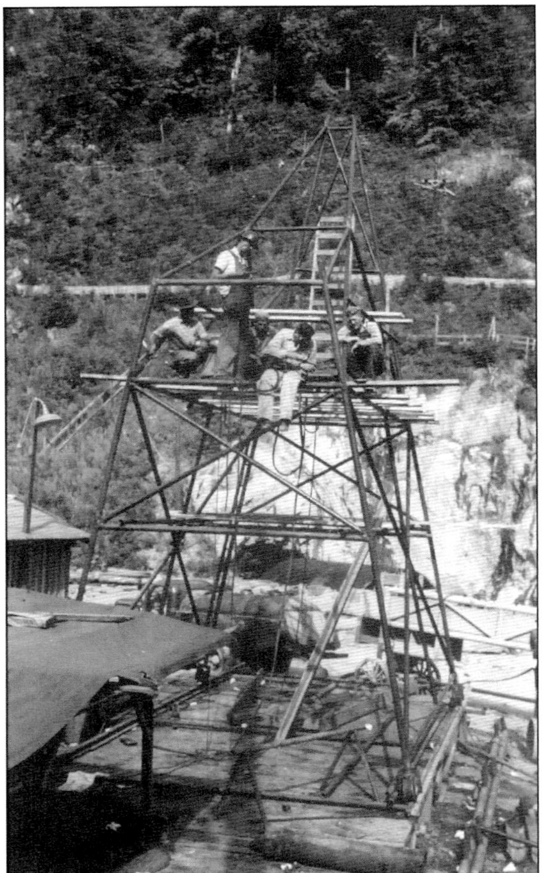

Fort Loudon Dam is located at just over 602 miles upstream from the mouth of the Tennessee River and nearly 50 miles downstream from the river's source, at the confluence of the Holston and French Broad at Knoxville. Lenoir City is located immediately north of Fort Loudon Dam. The reservoir includes parts of Loudon, Blount, and Knox counties.

The Tennessee Valley Authority provided millions of dollars to transform the economies of depressed, rural Southern states along the Tennessee River. The program included dam-building, electric power generation, and flood and erosion control. It provided relatively high-wage jobs in construction throughout a region the president called "the nation's number one economic problem."

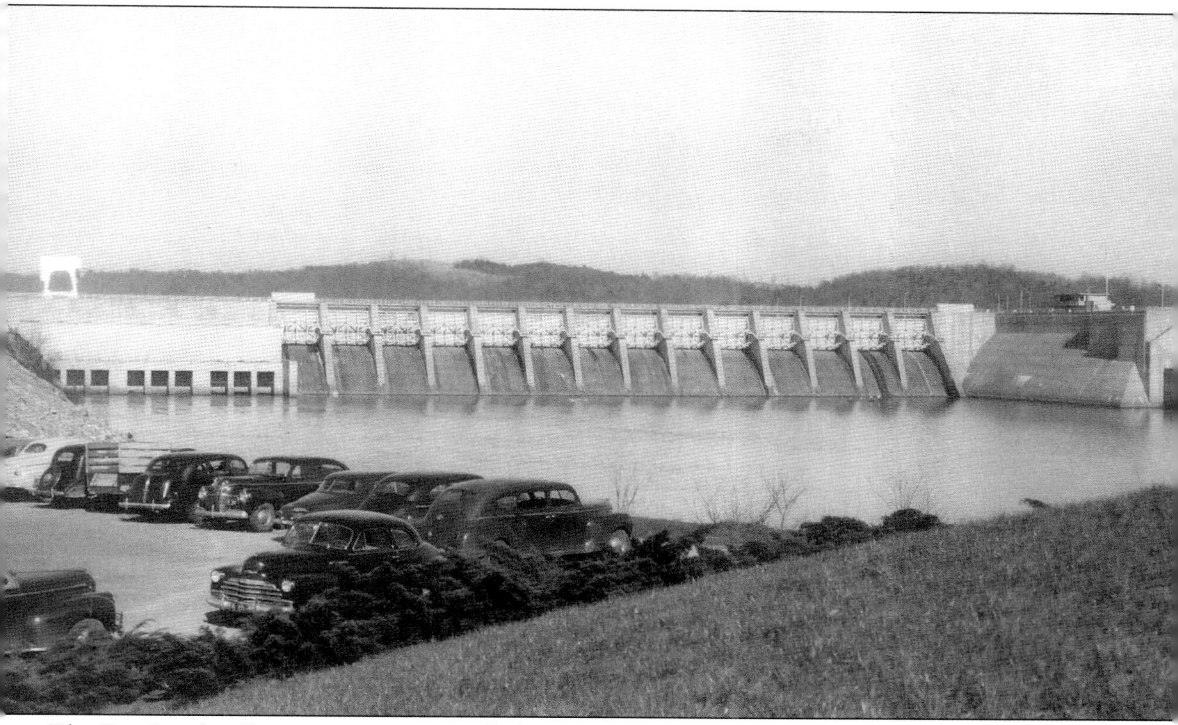

The Fort Loudon Dam project was initially known as a the Coulter Shoals project, named for a site identified by the U.S. Army Corps of Engineers 6 miles upstream from the present dam site. Thousands of men were employed in the building of the dam thanks to Franklin D. Roosevelt's New Deal. The dam is located on Highway 321 on the main channel of the Tennessee River. There are four hydroelectric generators at the dam with a combined generation capacity of 155.6 megawatts of electricity. Although the dam was finished in 1943, it would take 20 more years before a highway bridge was built over the top.

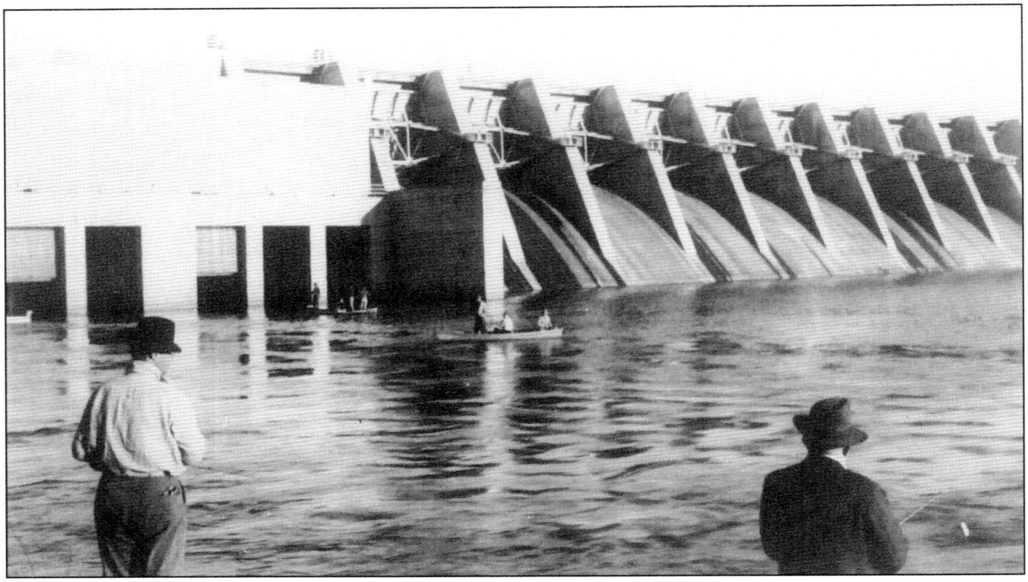

After three years of construction, the reservoir area around Fort Loudon Dam was flooded, and by November 1943, power was being generated. The dam and reservoir not only provide power and flood control, but also offer residents and visitors ample recreational opportunities, including boating, fishing, and other water sports.

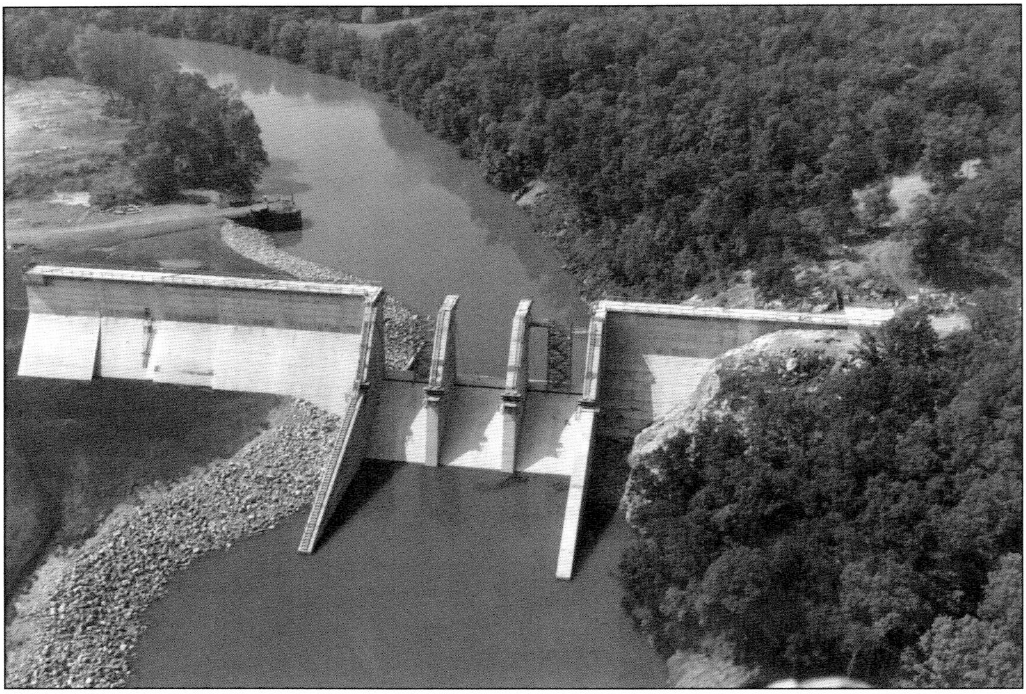

Although there was much opposition to its construction, the Tellico Dam was built at a cost of more than $110 million, after years of lawsuits reaching all the way to the U.S. Supreme Court. Despite the controversy swirling around the negative impact of the dam's construction on a little fish called the snail darter, the structure was finished on November 29, 1979.

Nine

HOUSES

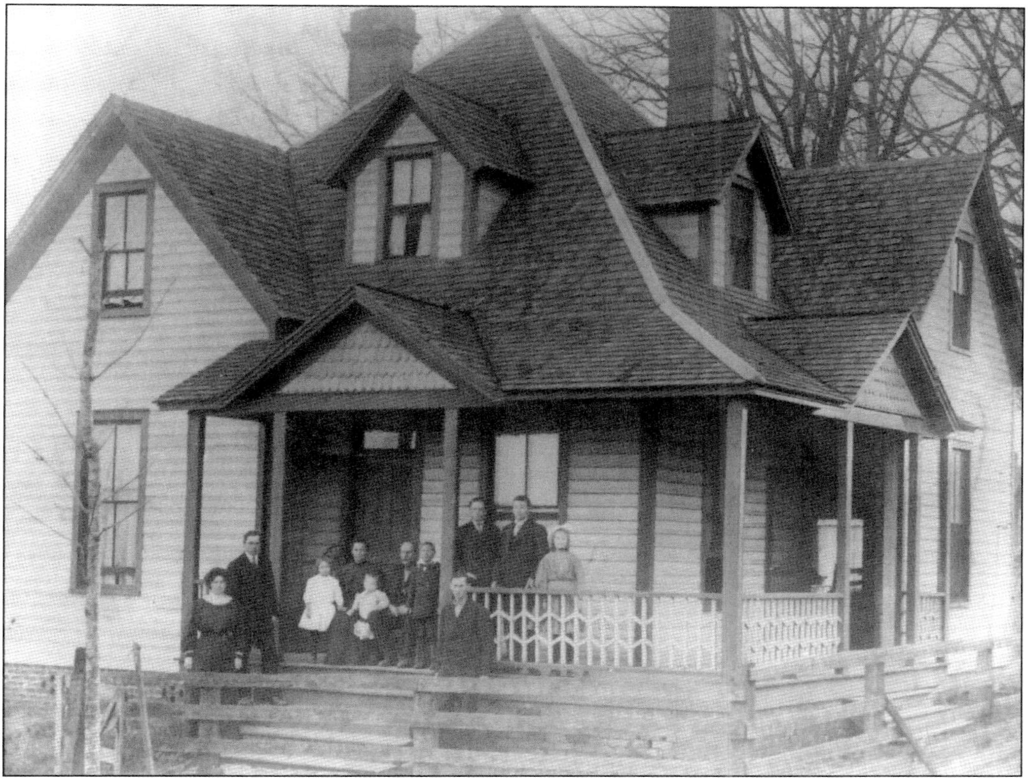

The William H. Ghormley house was located at 110 B Street in Lenoir City. This photograph, taken around 1910, shows three generations of the Ghormley family enjoying the spacious front porch. Curiously, a wooden fence is built nearly up against the bottom porch step. The Ghormleys owned the first Lenoir City Ford dealership.

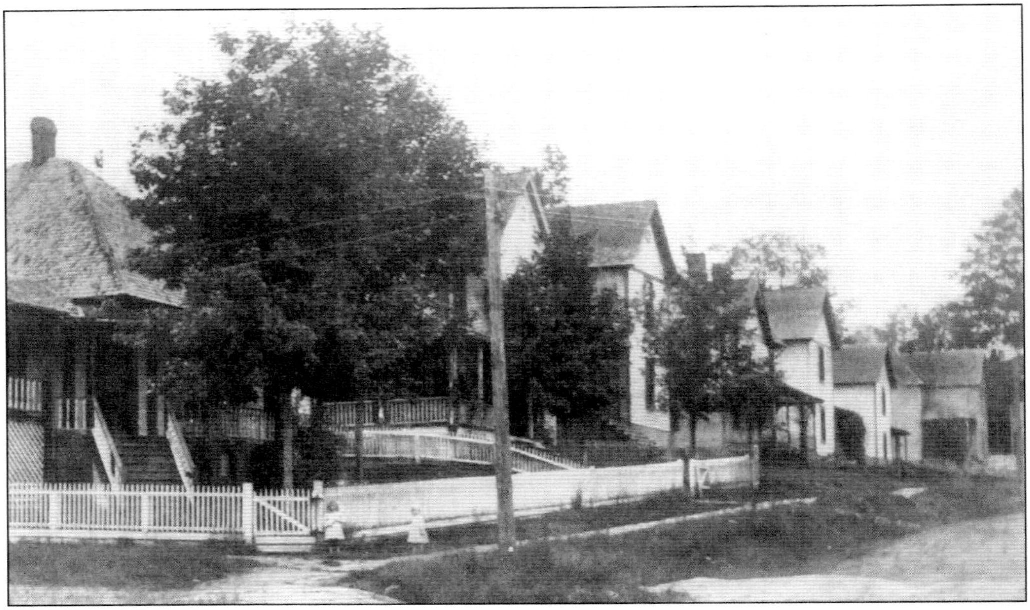

This *c.* 1910 photograph shows two unidentified children playing in front of a picket fence that surrounds one of the beautiful clapboard houses on B Street in Lenoir City. Many of the homes along this street have been renovated and restored in recent years but still retain the charm of an earlier era.

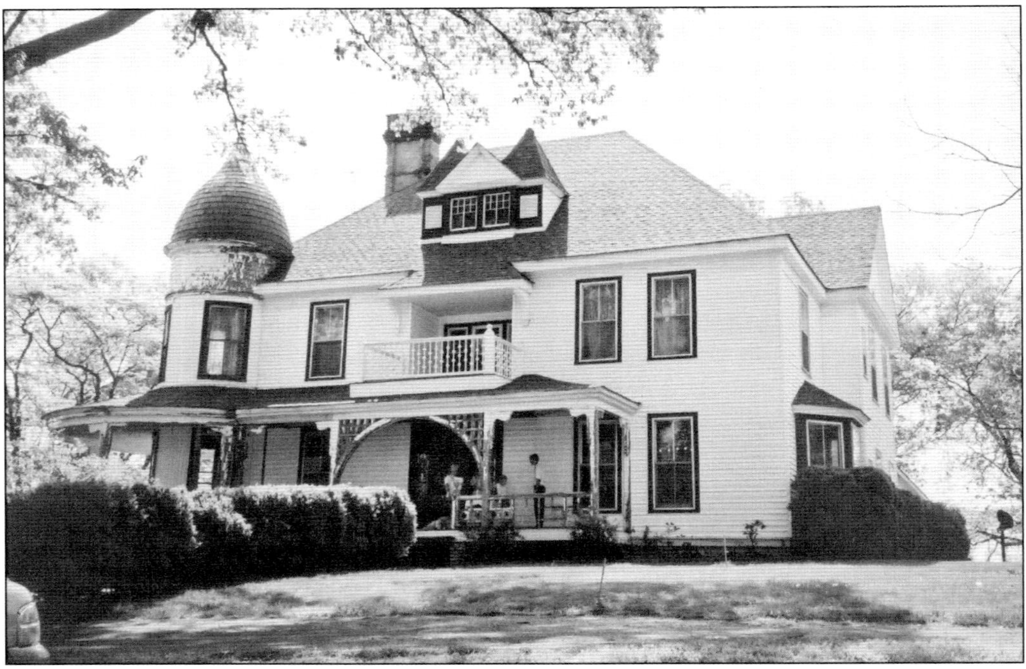

With its domed turret, round porch, and delicate details, the George Madre Burdette home is a beautiful example of Queen Anne architecture. The home was designed by the Bristol, Virginia, architectural firm of Beaver and Hoffmeister and built in 1888 and 1889. The interior features elaborate oak, walnut, cherry, dogwood, and maple woodwork.

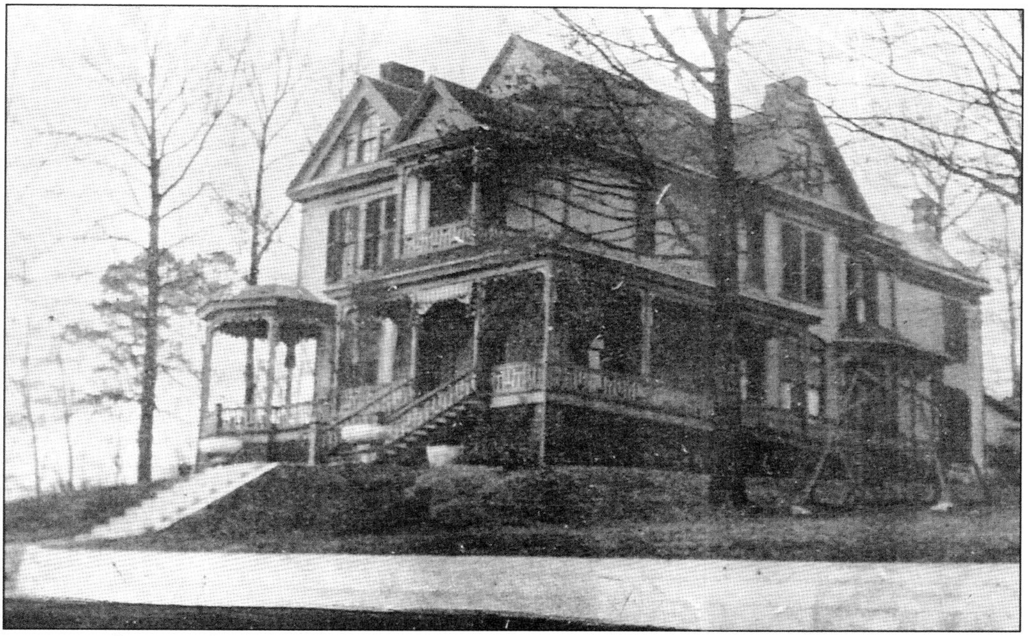

West Heights was the name given to the Charles H. Watson home. Visitors to the home would climb a set of stairs and pass beside a gazebo situated on a landing before climbing a second set of stairs to an elaborate porch. Charles, a foundry manager, and wife Pauline moved from New York to Lenoir City in the town's early days.

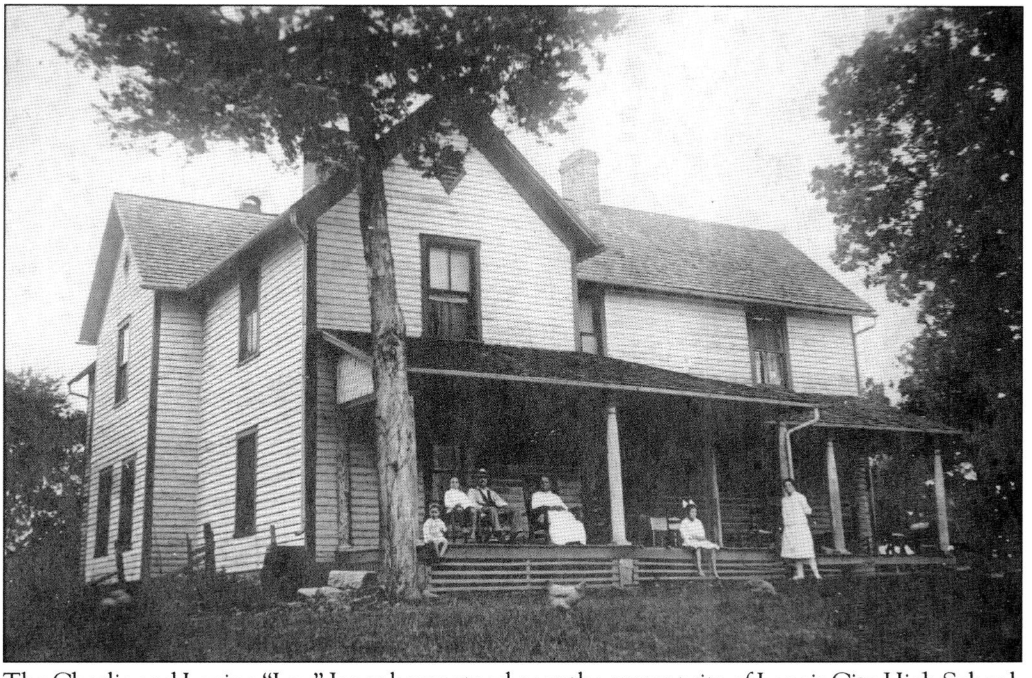

The Charlie and Lovina "Lou" Jones home stood near the present site of Lenoir City High School. Family members gathered on the generous front porch of the two-story farmhouse to enjoy the evening breezes in this photograph taken in the early 1900s.

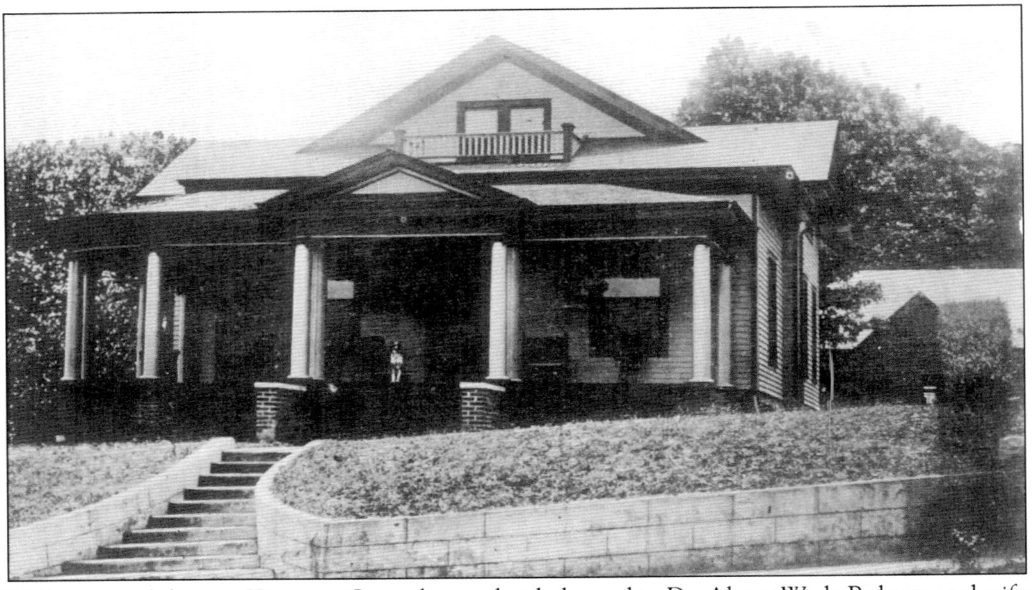

This postcard shows a Kingston Street home that belonged to Dr. Abner Wade Roberts and wife Ursa Mae Hall Roberts. Abner was a doctor of dental surgery and owned a private practice in Lenoir City. He was the son of Thomas and Mary Roberts of Williamson County, Tennessee.

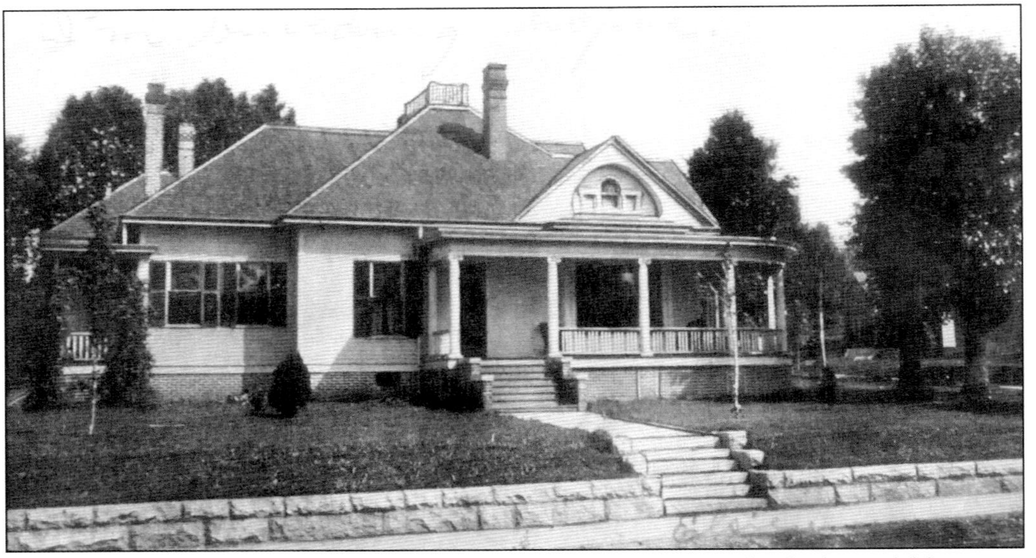

A romantic note is written on this postcard showing the side porch of a beautiful home on Kingston Street and Second Avenue in Lenoir City. It reads, "I'm building my hopes. Would you like this kind of a place?" The name "Elsie" is written in pencil on the steps, but it is unclear as to whether she is the sender or the recipient of the card.

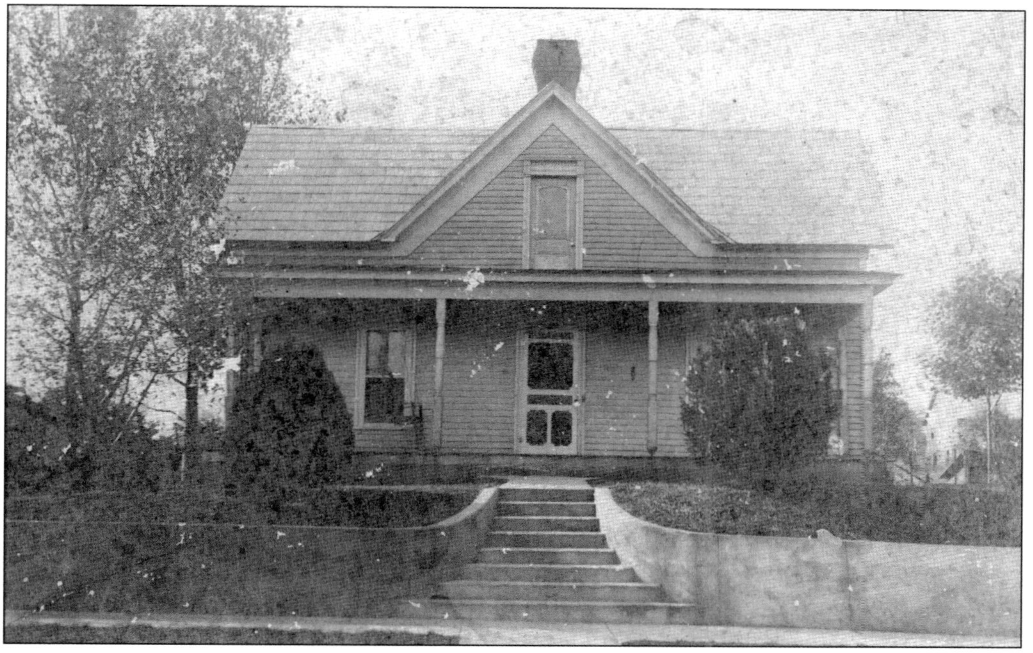

Written on the back of this photograph are the words, "Glandon Babb's House." Although no address is listed, the house is typical of many of the houses in Lenoir City with its concrete retaining wall and steps. There is a door over the porch, but with no railing, the person exiting there would have had to watch his or her step.

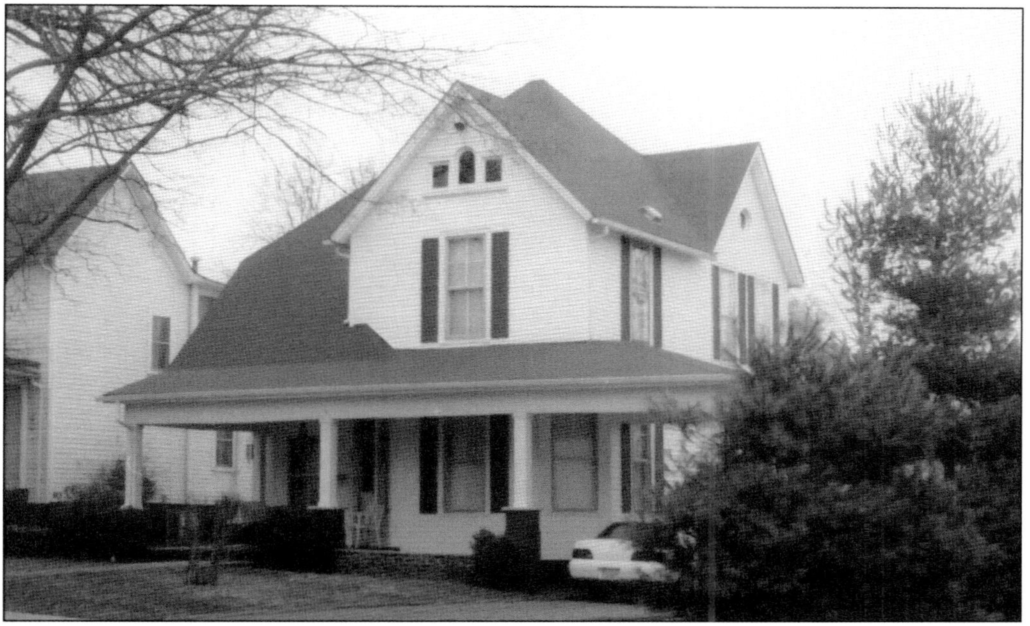

This home at 303 Kingston Street was built about 1884 by Col. Charles McClung McGhee, one of the founders of Lenoir City and one of the principle stockholders in the east Tennessee, Virginia, and Georgia Railroad. In 1918, McGhee sold the property to Dr. R. D. W. McDonald, a physician from North Carolina.

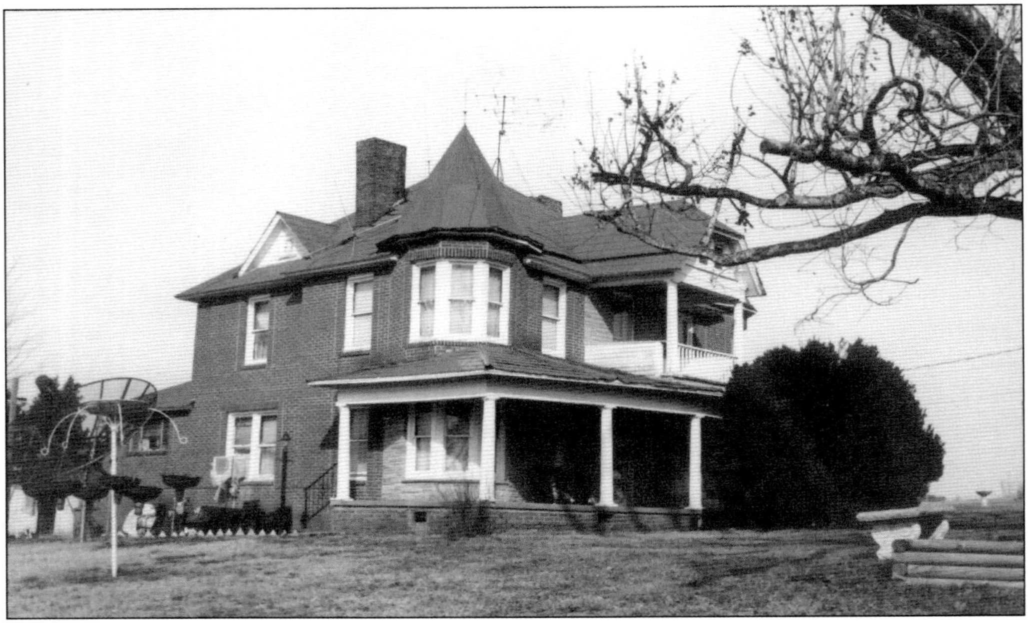

Located on Town Creek Road in Lenoir City, this Queen Anne–style home was constructed in the late 1880s. Although the builder is unknown, the home was originally part of a 100-acre farm. In the 1950s, the frame building was covered with brick, among other improvements.

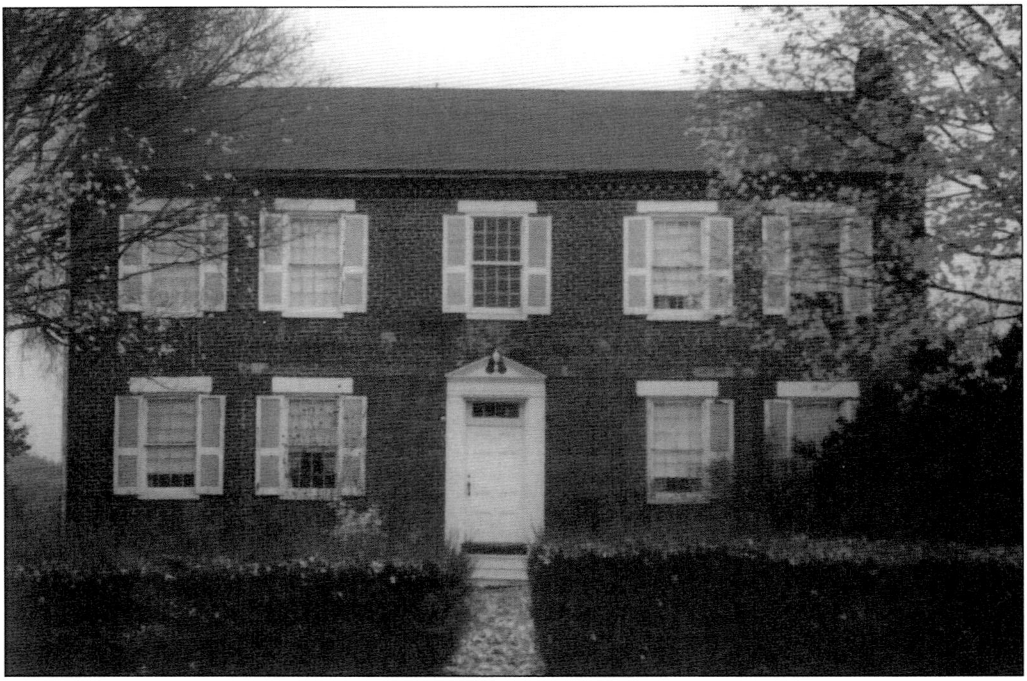

This Federal-style home was built by Joseph Browder more than 150 years ago. Handmade bricks and wooden pegs were used during its construction. During the Civil War, the house and farm were occupied by Union troops. Joseph and his cousin, John Browder, came to the Lenoir City area from North Carolina and settled on adjoining farms. They married sisters Ann and Minerva Matlock.

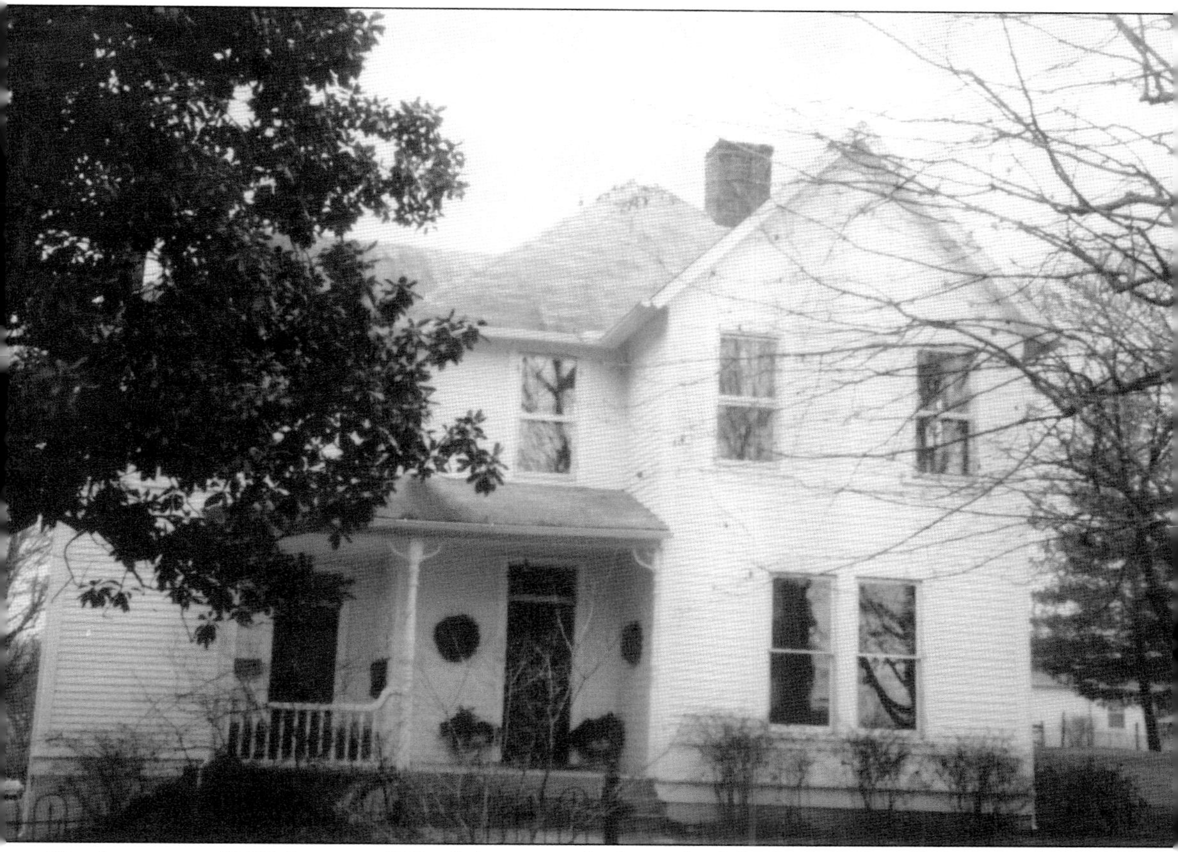

On the corner of Hill Street and Third Avenue is the home built by Dr. John Foute in 1891. The area in which the house was built was dubbed "quality hill," as many of Lenoir City's early affluent professionals, merchants, and wealthy industrialists chose to live there. The Queen Anne-style home is believed to have been designed by architect Samuel Sowards. The home sports many of its original attributes, such as double parlors, hand-painted stenciling, original floors, and detailed woodwork. The first floor has 10-foot-high ceilings, and there are 9-foot ceilings on the second floor. Dr. Foute's eldest daughter, Josephine, lived in the house until 1970.

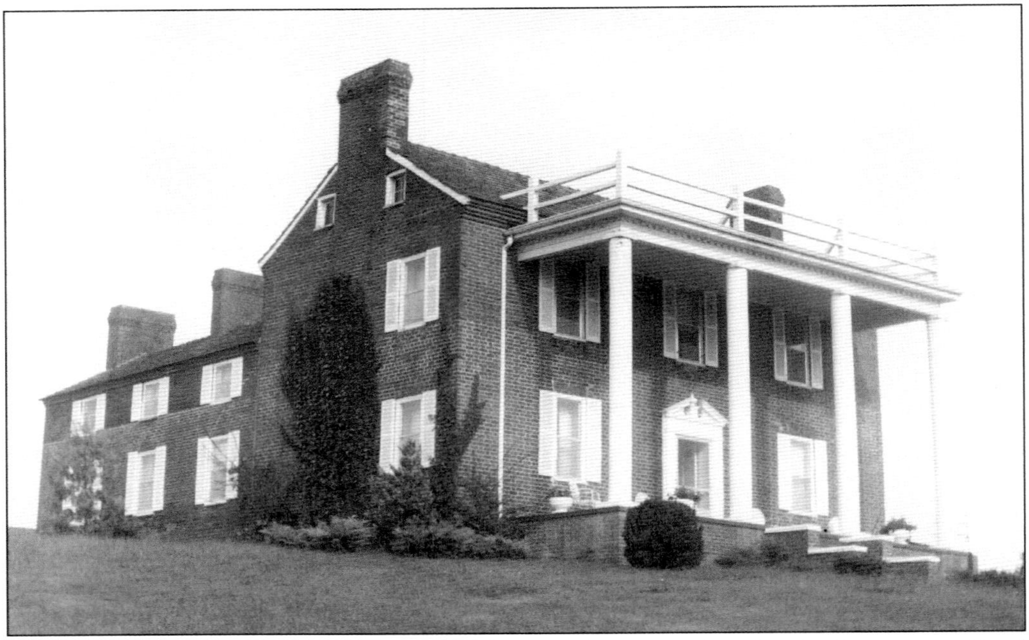

In 1797, Benjamin Franklin Prater and wife Nancy L. Prater purchased a 17-mile stretch of land along the Holston (now Tennessee) River. There they built themselves a home The house was built of bricks made by slave labor and had many special attributes, including brickwork done in a Flemish bond pattern and a corbelled cornice below the eaves. Although much of the house is original, like the granite doorknobs, the home has seen many renovations over the years, including the impressive two-story columned porch. According to local legend, the basement of Aquarelle, as the house has since been named, had rings in the basement where slaves were chained.

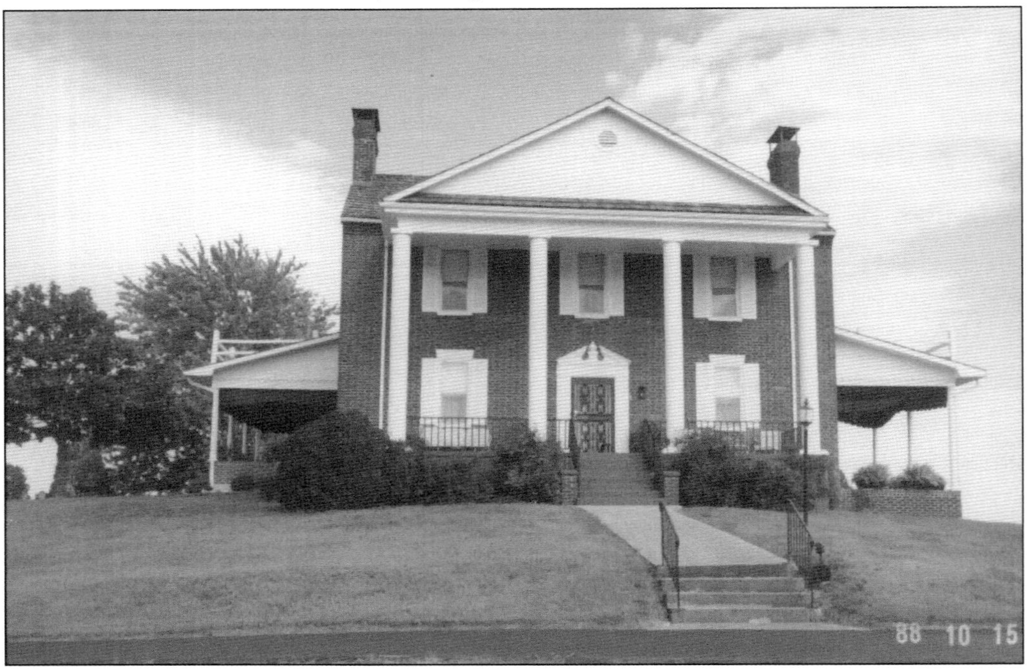

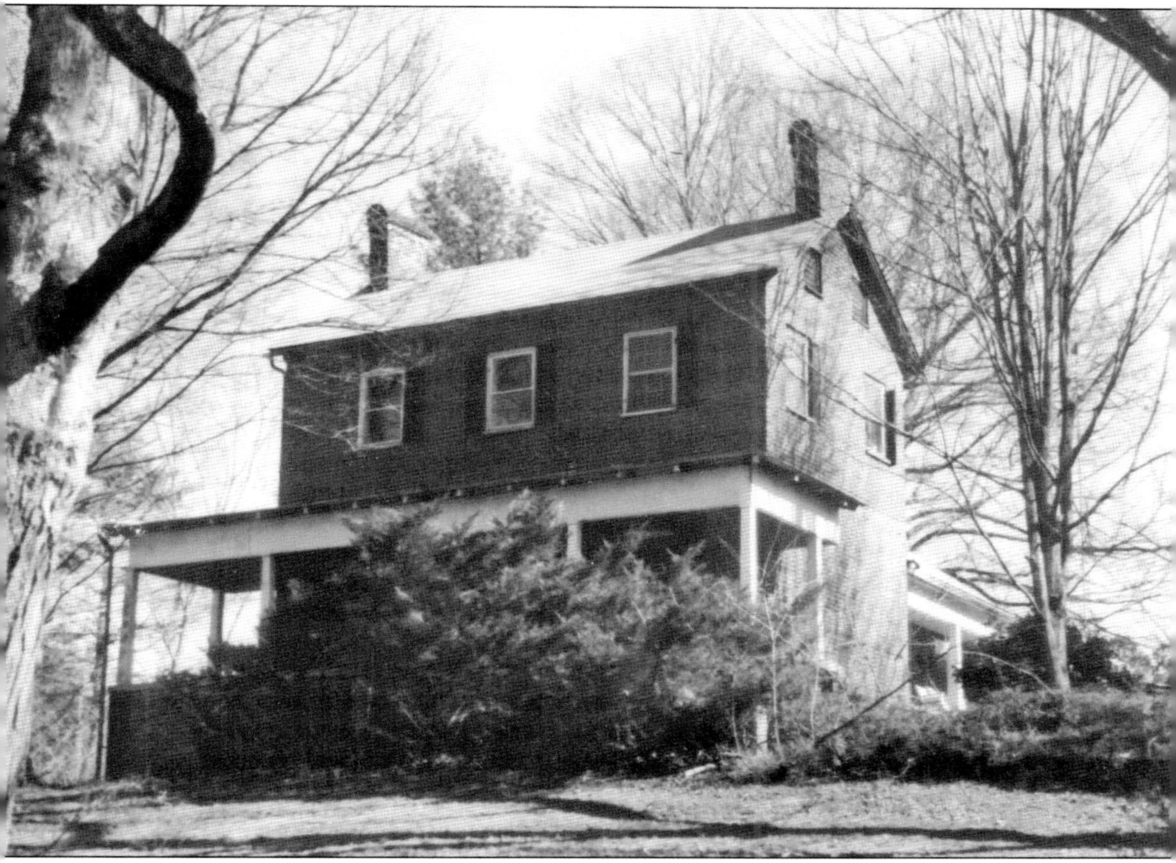

Built in 1830 by a contractor named Davis, this home was owned by Dr. Robert P. Eaton by 1870. Below the house, at the foot of the hill, sat a small building the doctor used as his office. Architectural elements, including two arched doors with handmade glass from the recently razed office, were used as doors for a built-in china press in the main house. Robert was the son of Andrew and Susan Eaton and was born in Roane County, a part of which later became Loudon County. He and his wife, Cornelia Boyd Eaton, had seven children, the eldest of whom, Andrew, also became a physician. The house has recently been demolished.

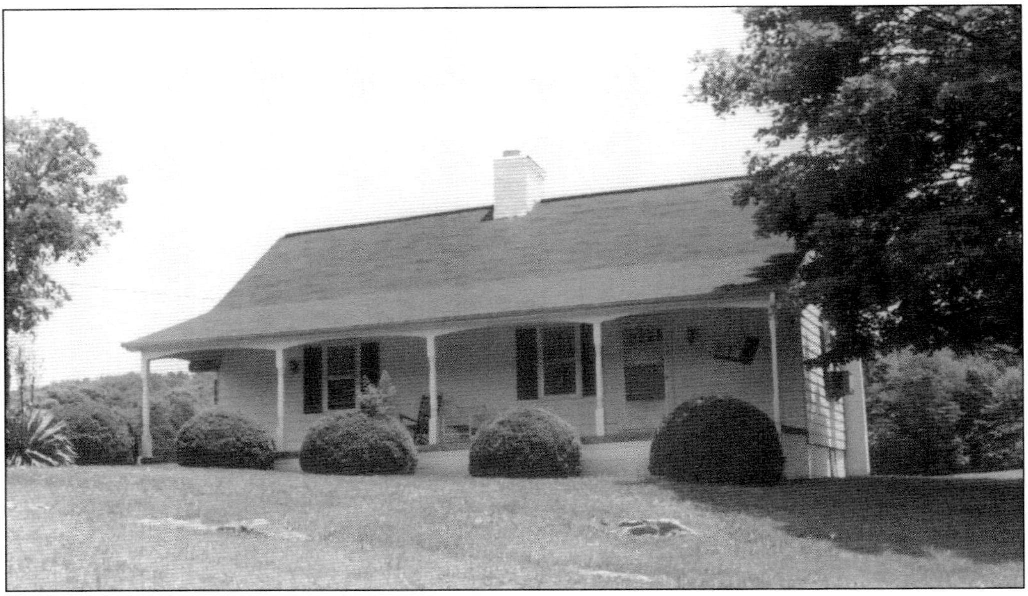

John Winton and wife Arabella Cunningham Winton came to Tennessee from Virginia, settling first in Dandridge before coming to the Martel community near Lenoir City in 1795. There they built a modest frame home, and John was ordained as a Methodist preacher. As the Winton family increased, so did their need for a larger home. They began work on a brick structure in 1812. The home, named Magnolia Manor in recent years, was completed in 1815 with bricks made by slaves who lived on the farm in log quarters. John was a large man, rumored to weigh nearly 500 pounds. He was also very devout in his religion and gave a portion of his land to establish the Muddy Creek Methodist Episcopal Church, now called Martel Methodist. Bishop Francis Asbury was often a guest in the little frame home.

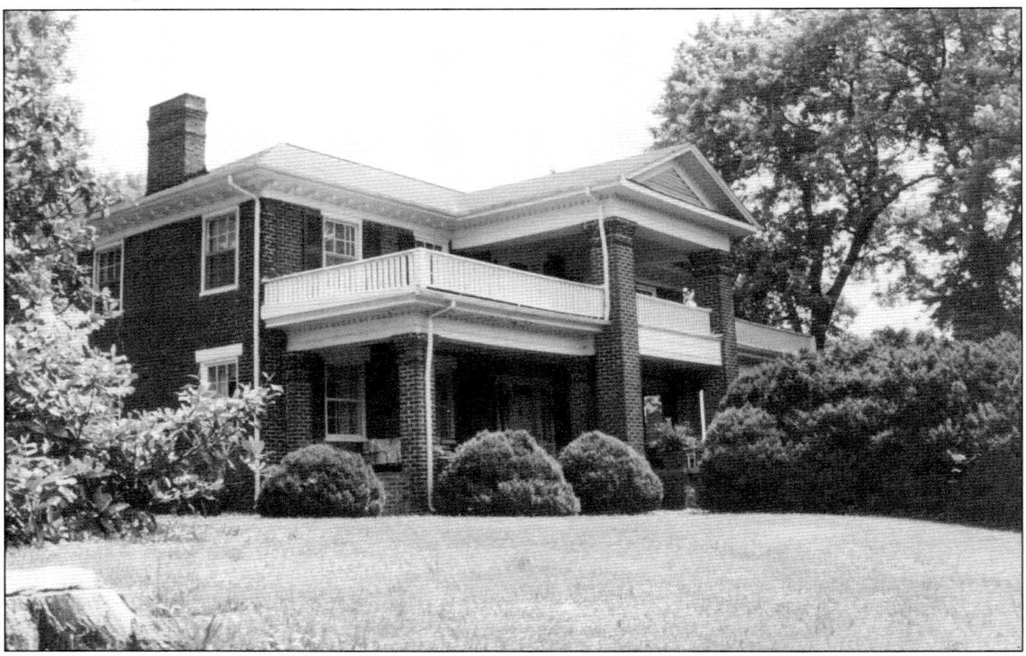

Ten

People

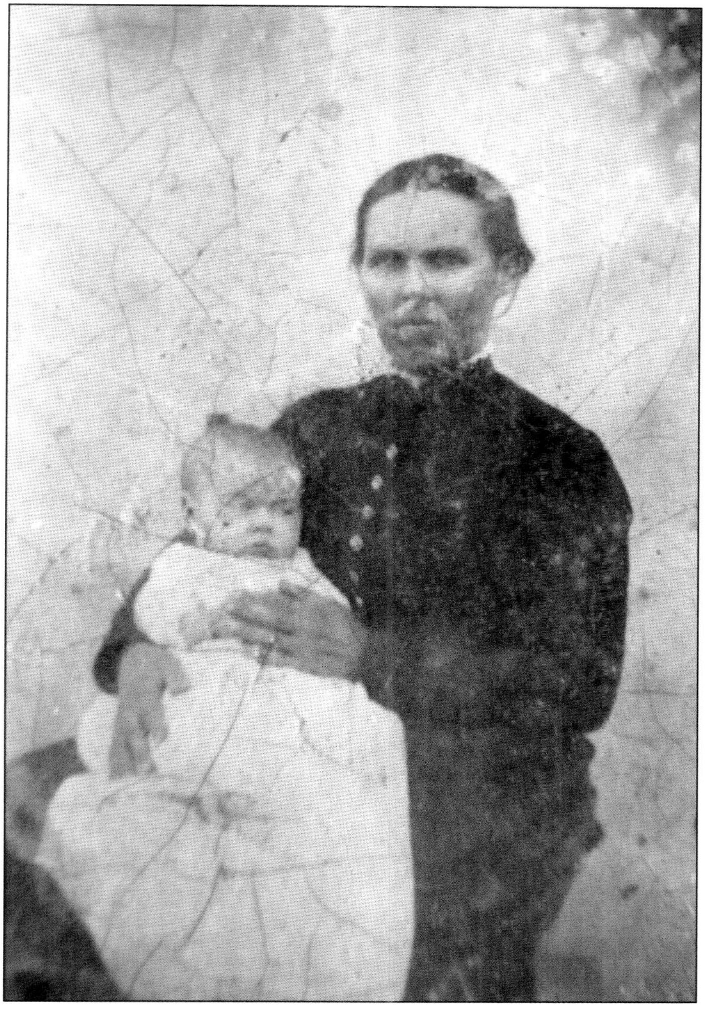

Alice Caledonia "Callie" Scarbrough Gibson holds her daughter, Julia Cleo Gibson, in this fragile photograph taken about 1889. Scarbrough married Daniel H. Gibson in 1867 when she was just 15. Gibson was a local farmer, justice of the peace officer, and circuit-riding preacher. The family lived on Third Avenue in Lenoir City.

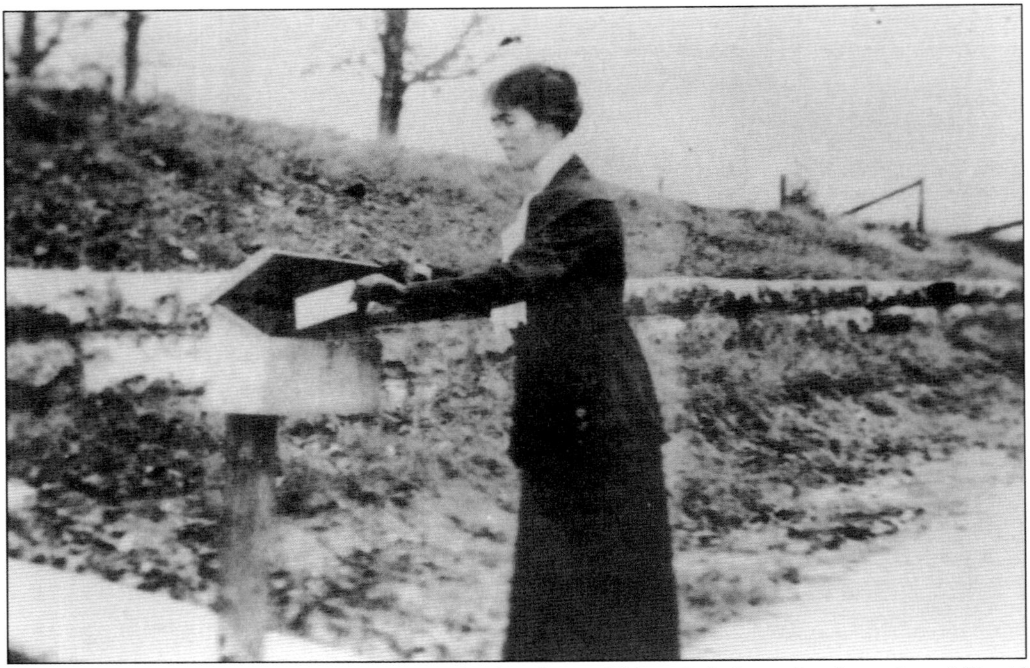

Julia Gibson was born about 1889 and was the daughter of Alice Caledonia Scarbrough and David H. Gibson. She later married Thomas E. Ghormley, and the couple ran a local Ford dealership in Lenoir City. This photograph, marked "mail service," was taken about 1920. Julia also worked at one time as a cashier at the bank according to the 1920 census.

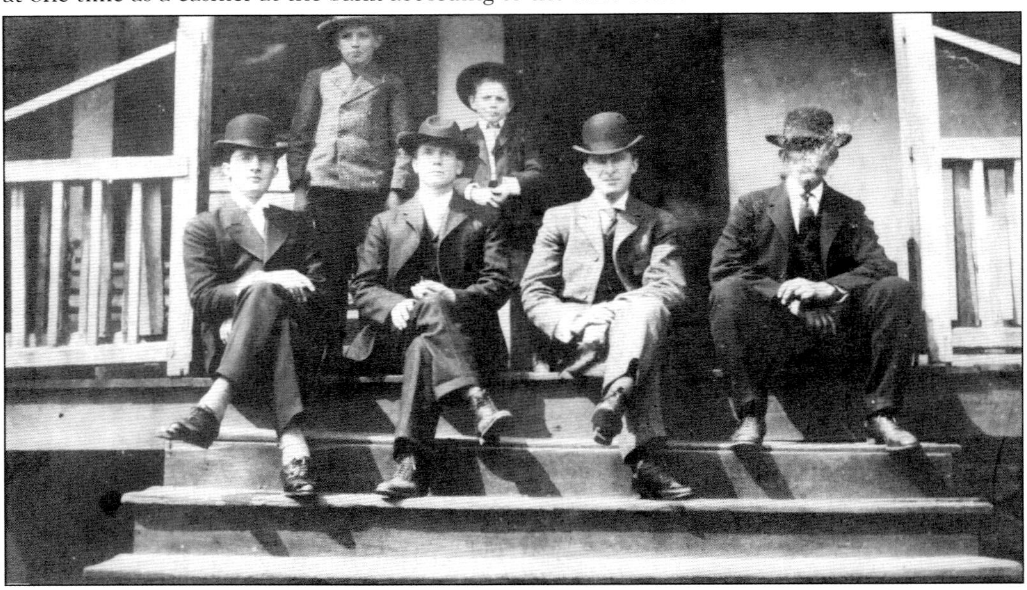

Written on the back of this photograph, taken in the early 1900s, is "E. [Edward] Fine, W. E. [Warham Easley], Zack, Clarence, Roy and Mark Alexander." All are members of the Fine family of Lenoir City. The gentlemen sat on the porch steps of a home built by Waightsill Avery Lenoir on Martel Road. In 1908, James Fine razed the Lenoir home and built his own. That house burned in 1915 and has since been replaced by yet another home.

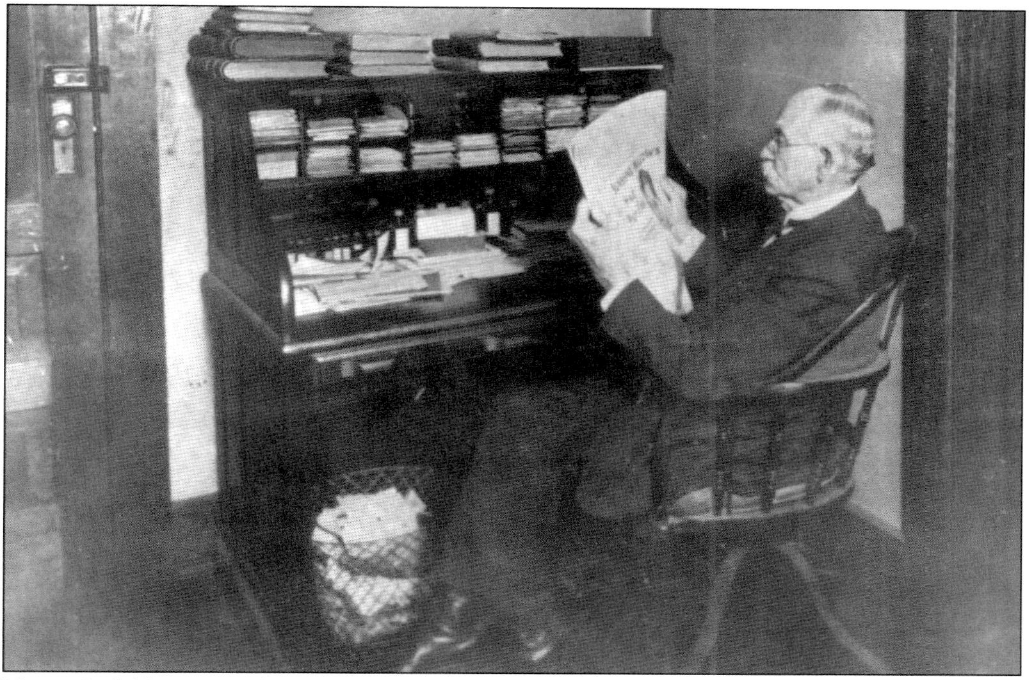

Horace Lydal Bacon was born March 27, 1869 in Loudon County to Susan and Allen Stokes Bacon. Horace was a real estate agent, county trustee, and also served as the Lenoir City treasurer. He married Tennessee Griffitts in 1912. The couple had a daughter, Elizabeth. Horace's desk appears to be well-stocked with papers, books, and other office supplies.

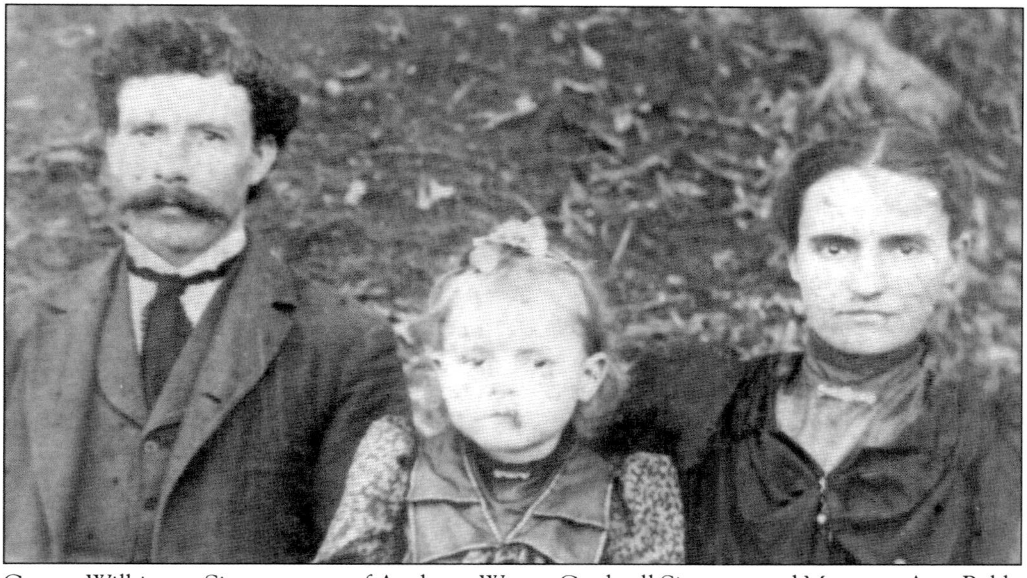

George Wilkinson Simpson, son of Anthony Wayne Cardwell Simpson and Margaret Ann Babb, married Nannie P. Gibson, daughter of Mason and Mary Gibson, in 1894. Their daughter, Volena, was born the following year. Volena died in 1900, and Nannie followed soon after in 1901. George was a farmer and jeweler. On the 1930 census, he and his second wife, Jennie (Phelps), are listed as living simply on "Old Dirt Road."

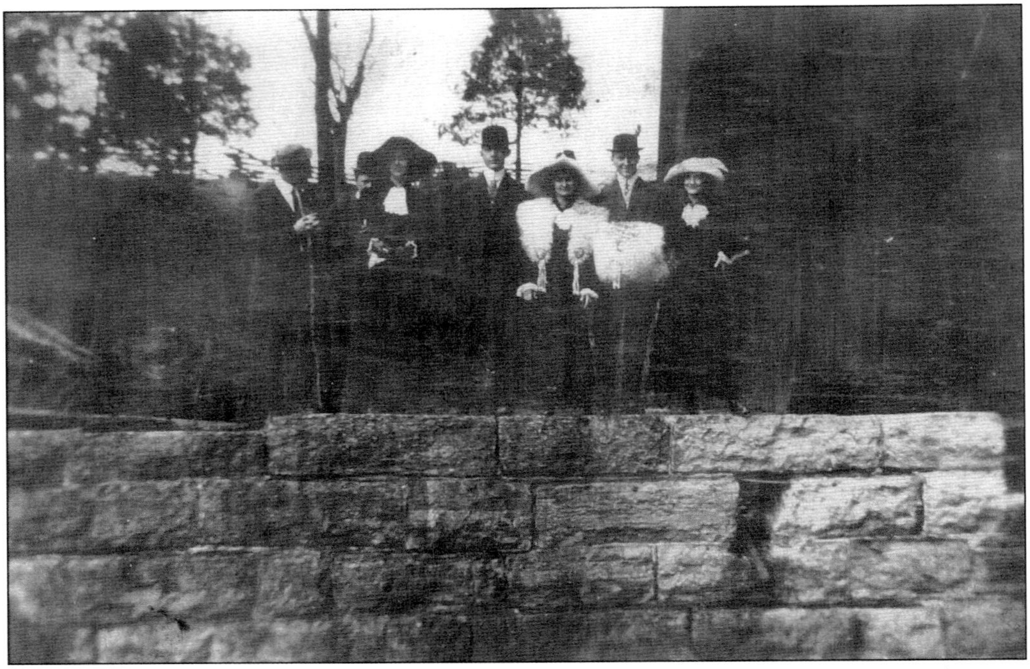

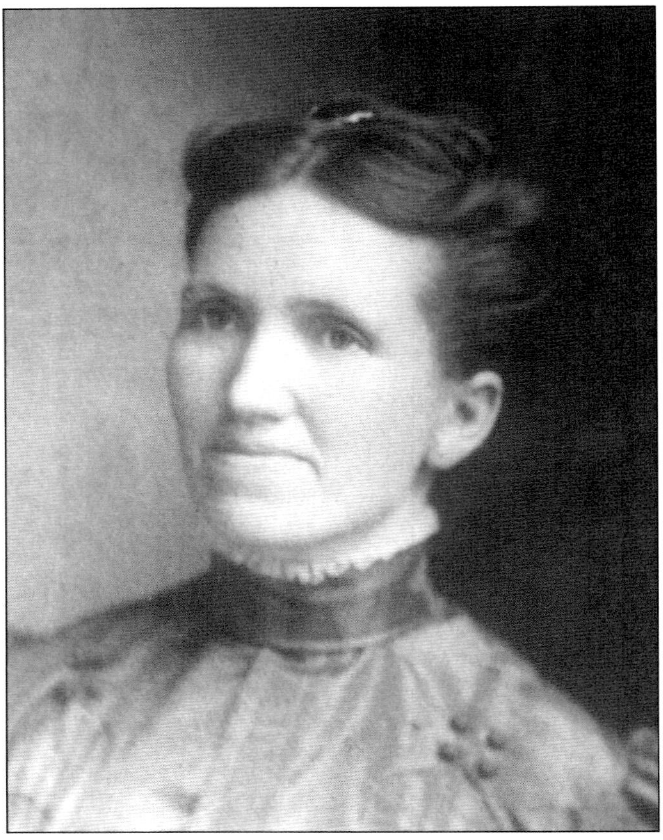

This handsome group of unidentified Lenoir Citians posed at the top of a rock wall that stood near either the flour or cotton mill. The photograph appears to be taken in the early 1900s, and both the men and women sport fine looking hats and clothing ready for a festive cold-weather event.

This photograph of Cornelia M. Cardwell was taken about 1900. Cornelia married John Wesley Cardwell, a hardware store owner and Methodist minister. The family made their home on Third Avenue in Lenoir City. John and Cornelia had nine children, seven sons and two daughters.

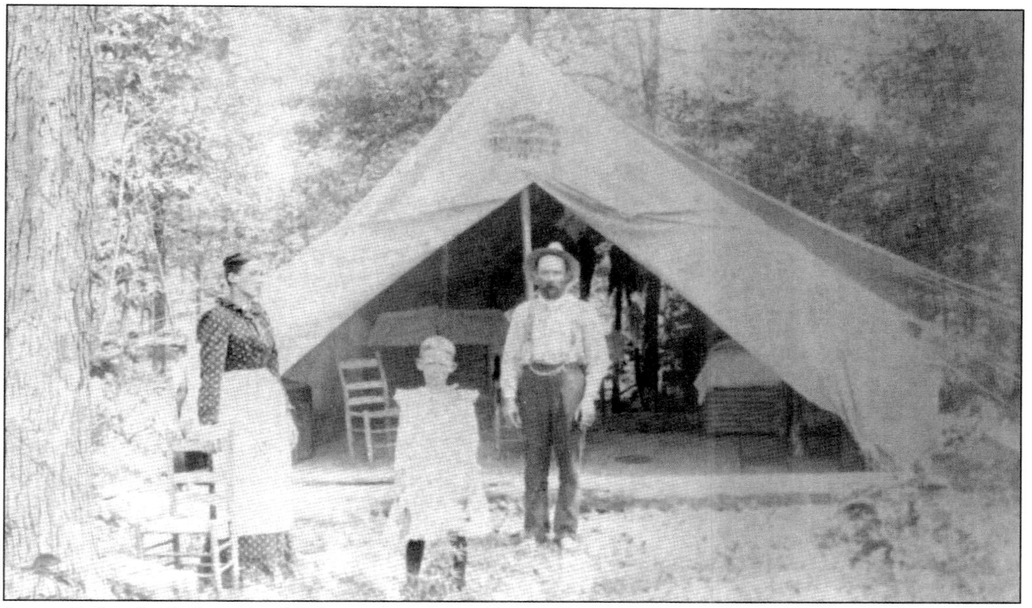

James Eubanks helped build the railroad, and he, wife Clara, and daughter Ruth moved around with his job through Georgia and Tennessee. The family often made their home in a tent outfitted with a wooden bureau and chairs and a full size bed with linens. Ruth was born on April 4, 1893, in Georgia. At age 22, Ruth married Charles Riggle, a lumberman, and she became a grammar school teacher. Before her 35th birthday, Ruth was a widow with three children. She was living with her widowed father, James; sister Nancy; and children Janie, Charles, and Ben Thomas on B Street in Lenoir City, according to the 1930 census.

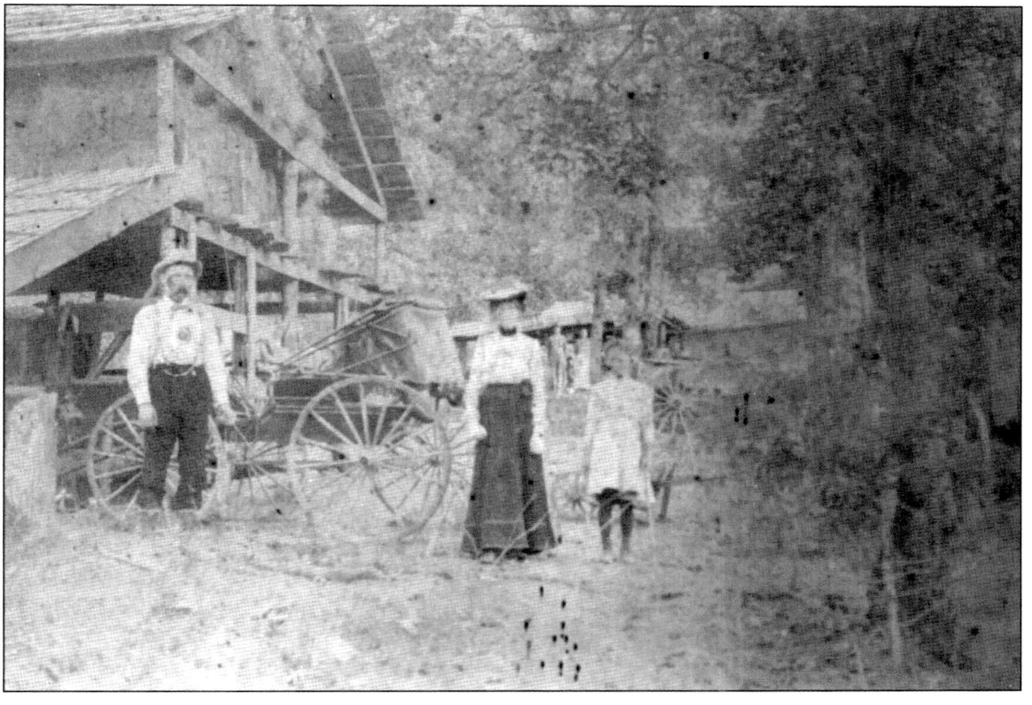

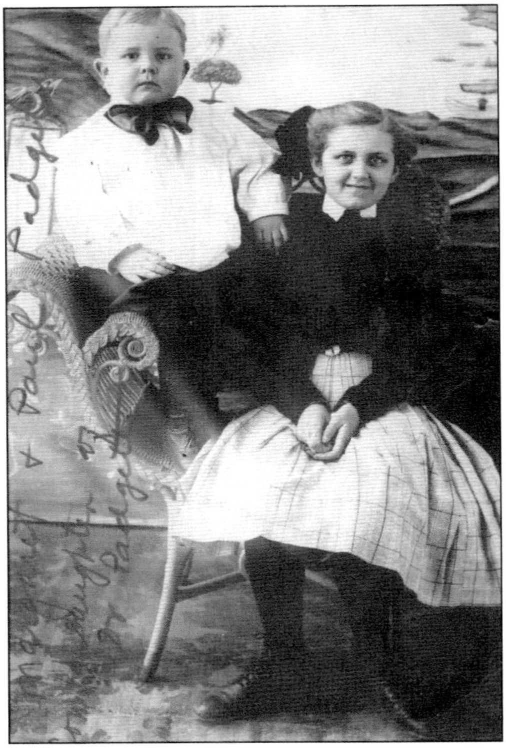

The writing on the back of this photograph postcard, made in 1906, reads, "This was taken the day Paul was four years old and he weighed 50 pounds. Margaret weighed 86 and she will be 10 in June. Hope this finds you all well. Your friend, Nellie M. Padget." The children are identified as Margaret and Paul Padget, children of Dr. William D. Padget and Nellie, the signer of the card.

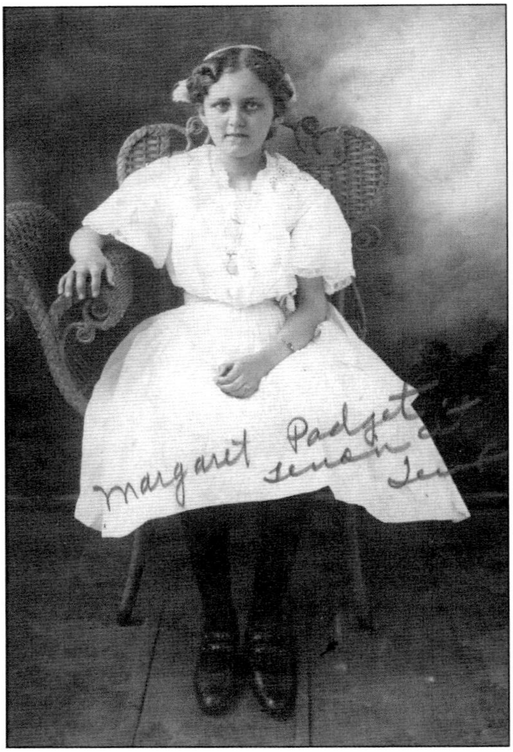

A second postcard of Margaret Padget sitting by herself reads, "Hello Freddie, how are you? I am crazy for you to come down. Be sure to bring your little doll. I want you to stay part of the time with me. Your friend, Margaret." Margaret may have been surprised at her own photographs as she wrote at the top of the card, "Does this look like me?"

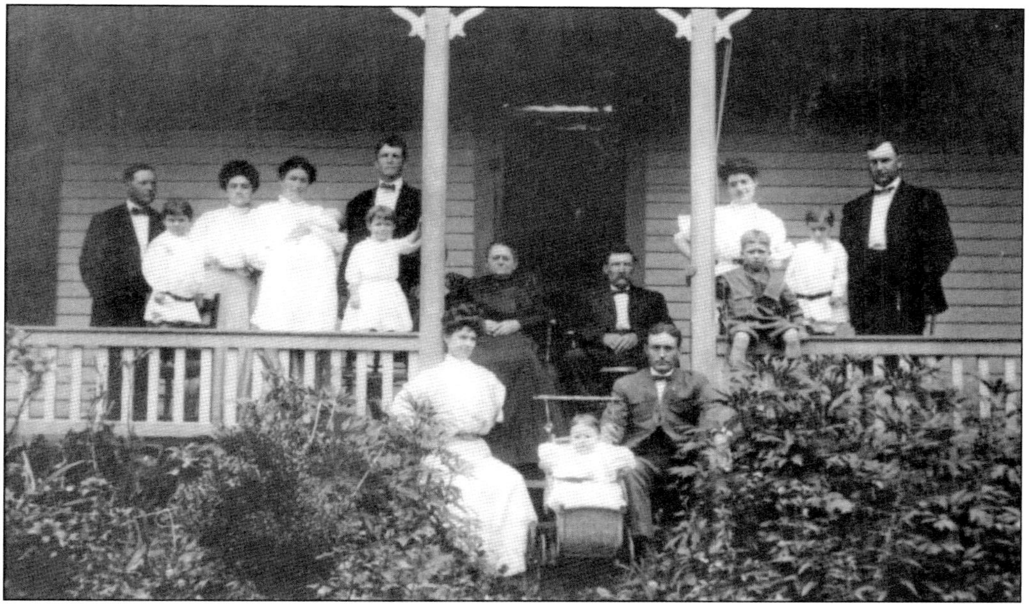

This photograph, taken about 1906, shows the Charlie and Lovina "Lou" Jones family. From left to right are the following: (first row) Bertie Jones, ? Jones, and John Jones; (second row) William Jones, Charles Jones, Gussie Jones, Laura Smith, Louise Smith, Bessie Mae Smith, Fred Smith, Lou Jones, Charlie Jones, Anna Harrison, Gordon Harrison, James Harrison, and Benjamin C. Harrison.

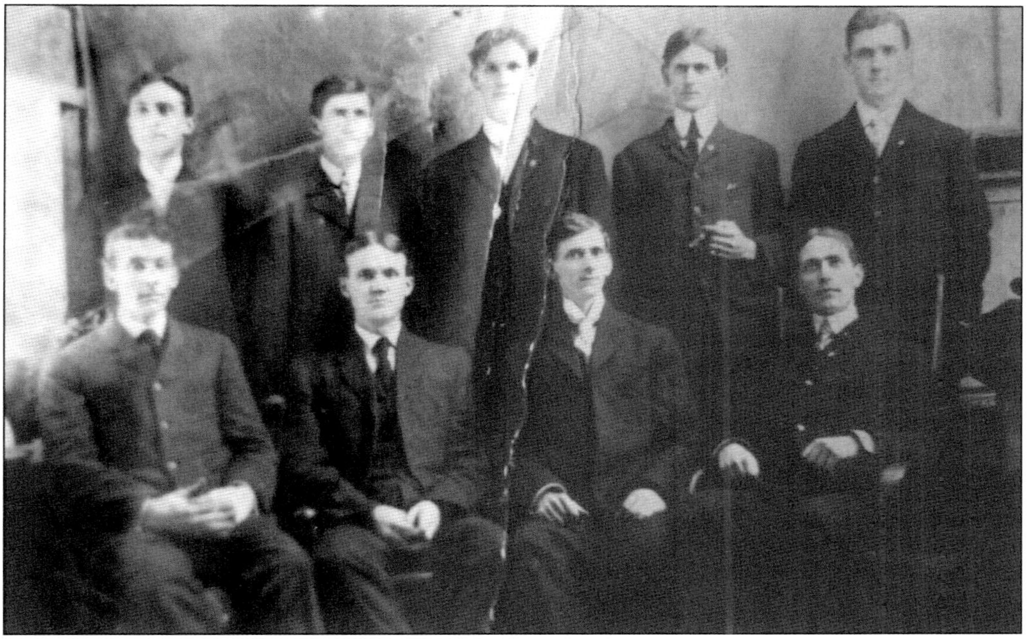

This photograph, taken about 1910, shows a group of local businessmen at an unknown Lenoir City event. From right to left are the following: (first row) ? Waller, Dr. Abner Wade Roberts, J. Boyd Porter, and unidentified; (second row) Warham Easley Fine, Ed Calloway, Dr. Gid Hall, Jim Jones, and unidentified.

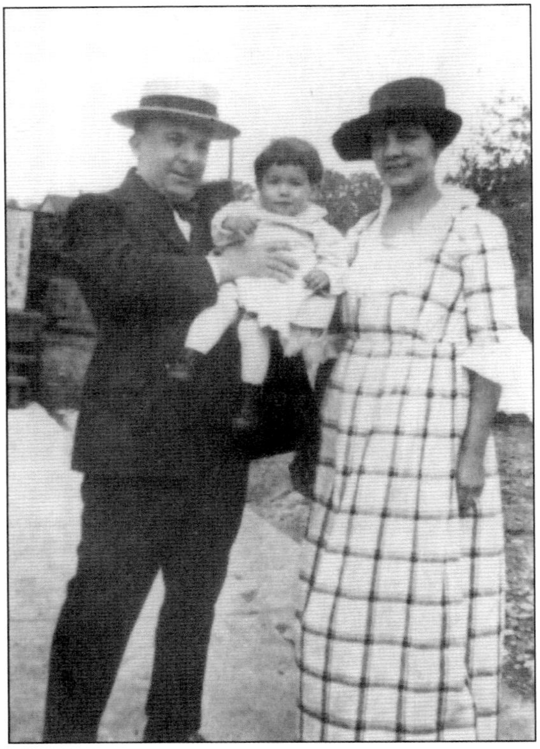

In this photograph, taken around 1915, Thomas E. Mills and wife Marie pose with daughter Margaret. The Mills family was originally from Virginia and made their home on B Street in Lenoir City. Thomas was a railway inspector with the East Tennessee, Virginia, and Georgia Railroad.

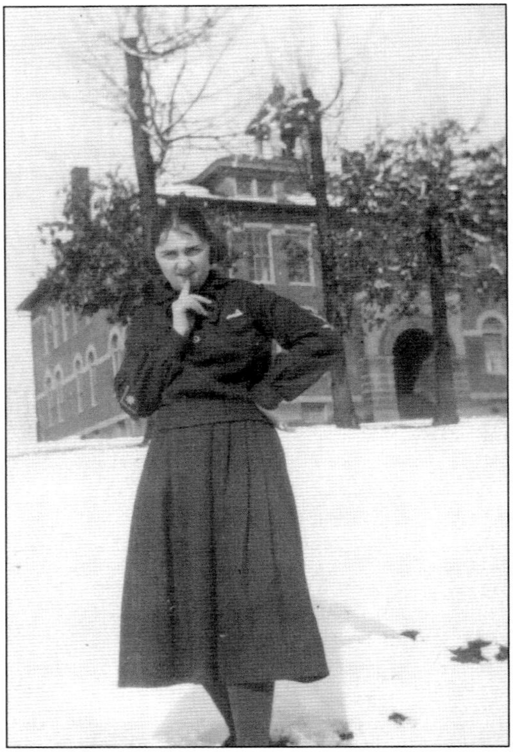

This unidentified Lenoir City High School student appeared to be deep in thought. Maybe she was pondering the snow in which she is standing, the school building behind her, or even her upcoming graduation. Since this picture appears to be taken in the early 1910s, she may have been a member of one of the first graduation classes.

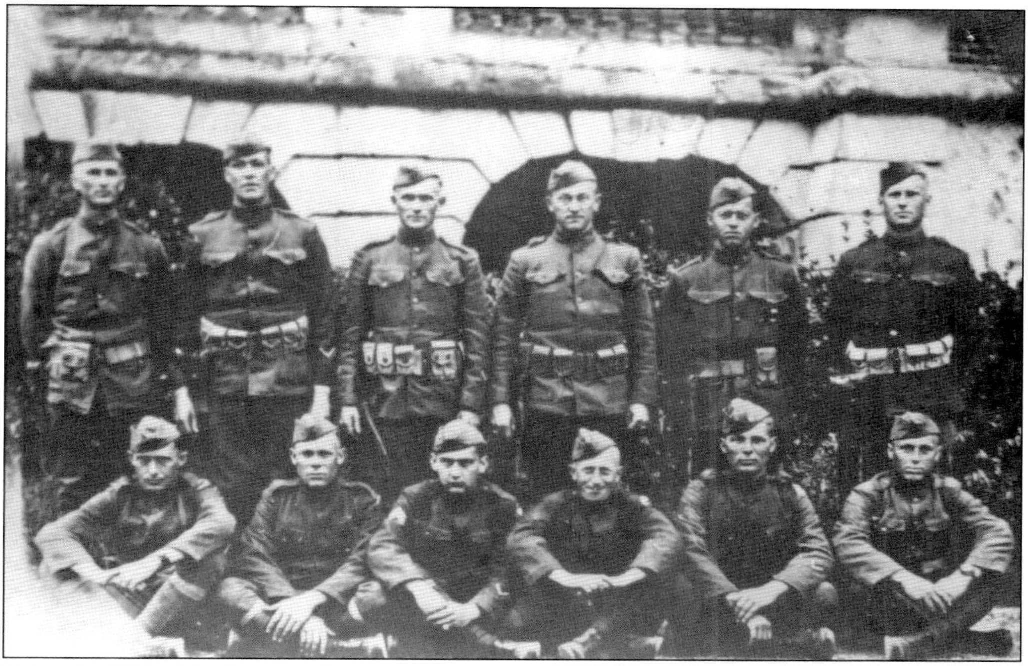

Taken in 1916, this photograph shows a group of World War I soldiers stationed in France. The only one identified is William Walter "Bud" Fisher (far left in the back row). Fisher later operated a clothing store in Lenoir City.

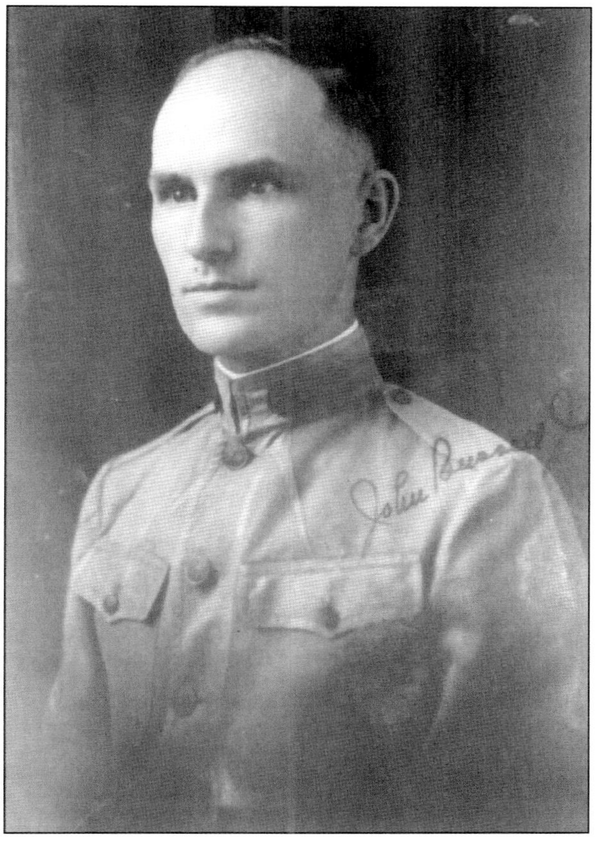

Shown here in 1917, this World War I soldier, John Bussell Jr., was born on May 29, 1890, to John William and Zoe Bussell. He was a banker at the First National Bank in Lenoir City, and according to his World War I draft card, he was considered tall with a medium build, brown eyes, and brown hair.

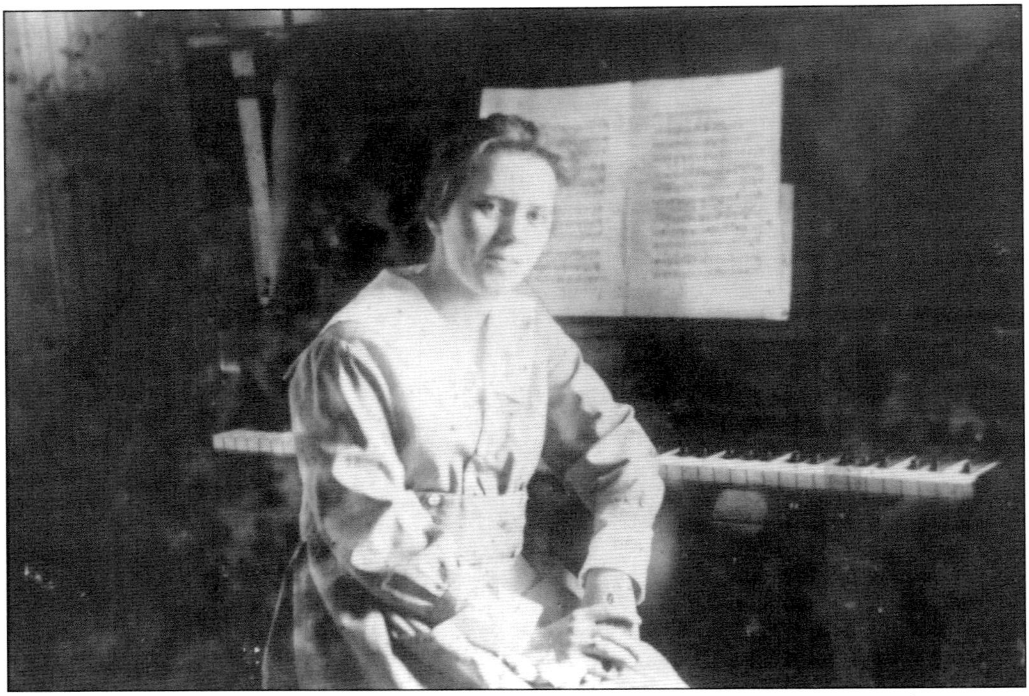

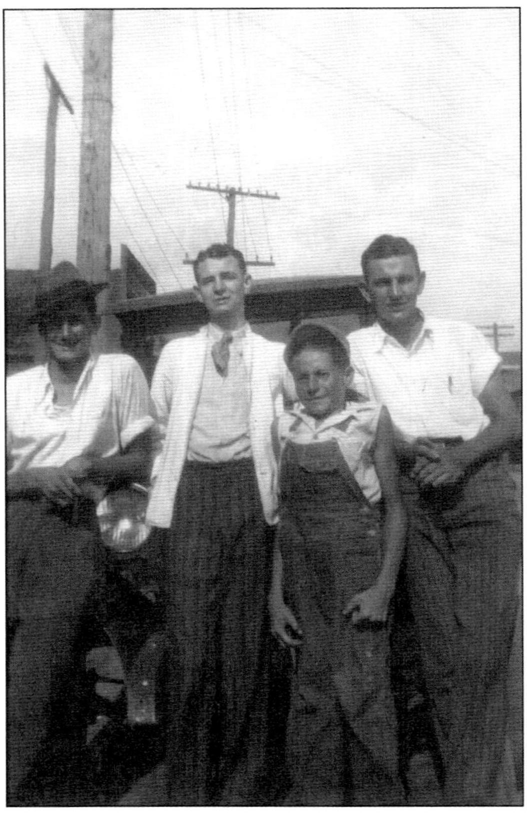

Jorea Spraker married Blaine Littleton on June 8, 1918. Soon after, Jorea and Blaine moved to Anniston, Alabama, where Blaine was employed at a steel plant. By 1930, the couple returned to Lenoir City where they raised their children Bianca Sue, Eugene Spencer, and Billy Joe. This undated photograph shows Jorea in front of her piano.

Paul Gossage, Edd Goodwin, Elwin Keener, and Henry Foster, pictured from left to right, were looking rakish in this 1929 photograph. The boys are undoubtedly posed in front of someone's car, as the headlight peeking from between Paul and Edd indicates. Maybe they all jumped in for a joyride as soon as the photograph was snapped. Henry later served as the Lenoir City recorder and treasurer.

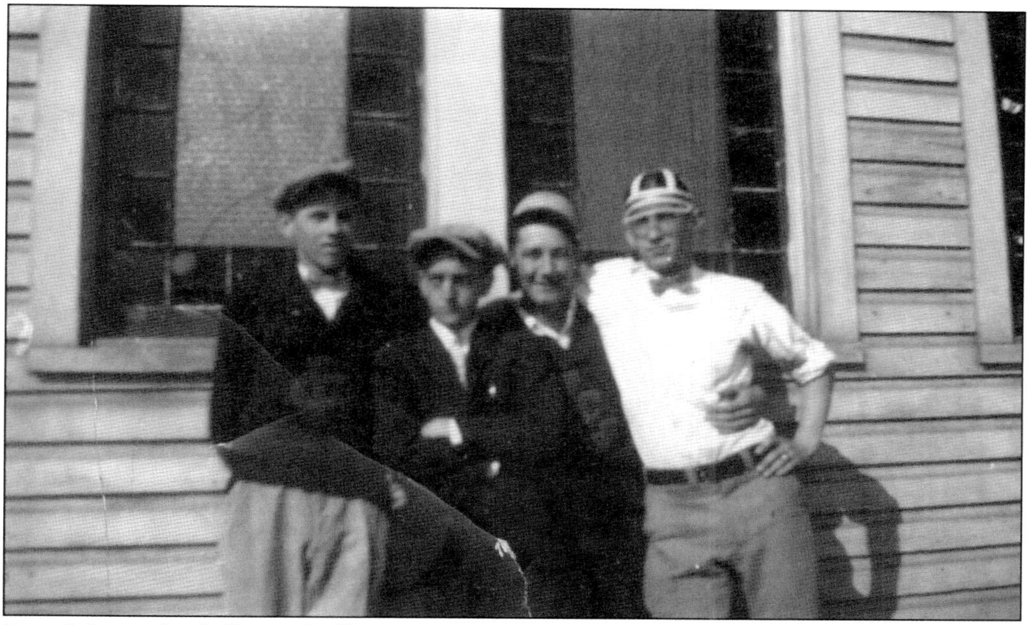

From left to right, Jefferson "Jeff" McAllister, Lester Brabson, Paul Gossage, and Harry Burns mug for this photograph taken in front of the Cumberland Presbyterian Church about 1925. According to the 1930 census, Paul worked as a serviceman at a local garage and Harry was employed as a drugstore salesman. Lester later worked as the manager of the Lenoir City Utility Board.

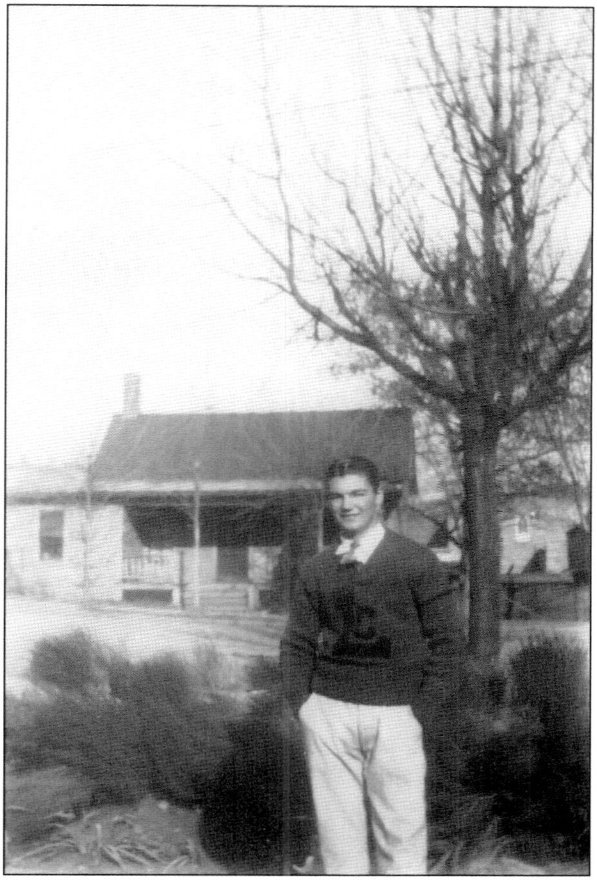

In this photograph taken about 1928, Roy "Snookie" DeRieux looked very collegiate in his Lenoir City sweater. Roy was born about 1912 to Frank P. and Mollie DeRieux. Frank died before Roy turned 8 years old. In addition to playing sports, Roy worked at the Porter and Campbell Grocery Store. The family lived on Broadway Street in Lenoir City.

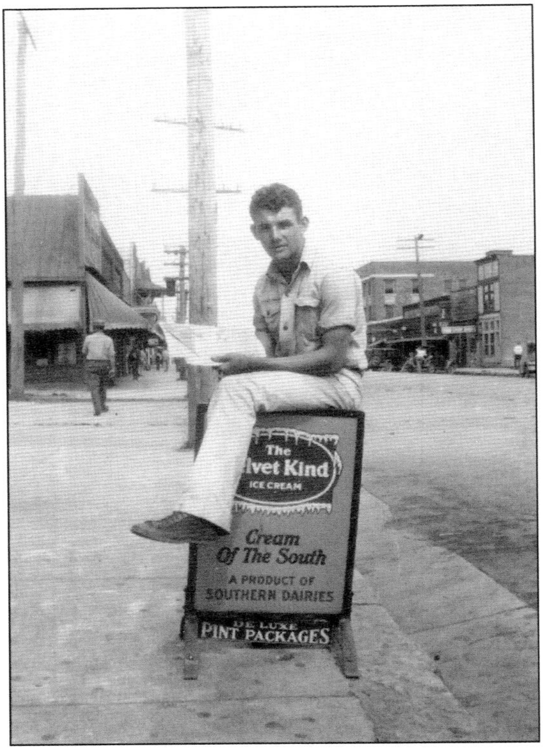

Taken on Broadway Street in Lenoir City during the late 1920s, this handsome young man had his leg slung over the top of a metal advertising sign placed at the edge of the sidewalk in front of the Goodwin Drug Store, where the sign read, "The Velvet Kind Ice Cream. Cream of the South. Product of Southern Dairies. De-Luxe Pint Packages."

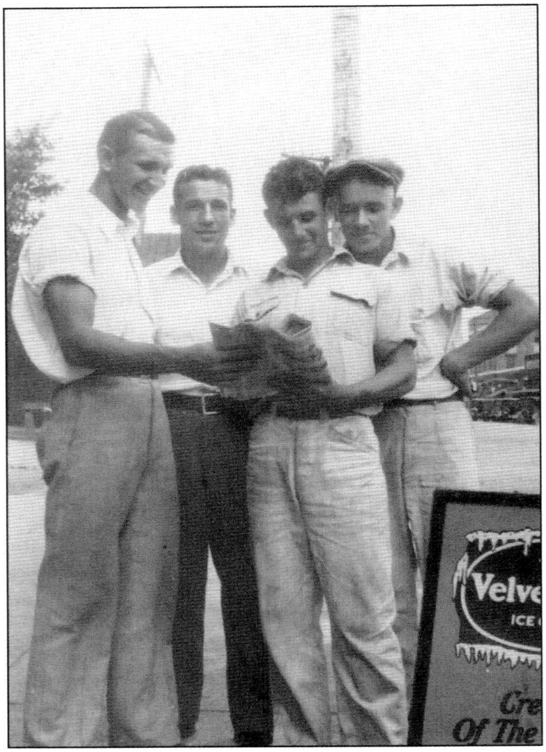

Written on the back of this photograph taken in the 1920s are the names, "Tom [Foster], Lew, Dan, and B. J." The young man third from the left is obviously the same person pictured in the photograph above. The group is standing near the same ice cream sign on Broadway Street in front of the Goodwin Drug Store, which burned in the 1920s. They appear to be reading a newspaper; maybe one of them is featured in the news of the day.

Henry Dyer Foster, born about 1909, was the son of Henry C. and Mattie (Dyer) Foster. Henry died before Thomas reached the age of 10. As a young man, Thomas worked in the shipping department at a local automotive store to help support his siblings and widowed mother. He became a grocer and eventually served as administrator of the Loudon County Hospital. This photograph was taken about 1928.

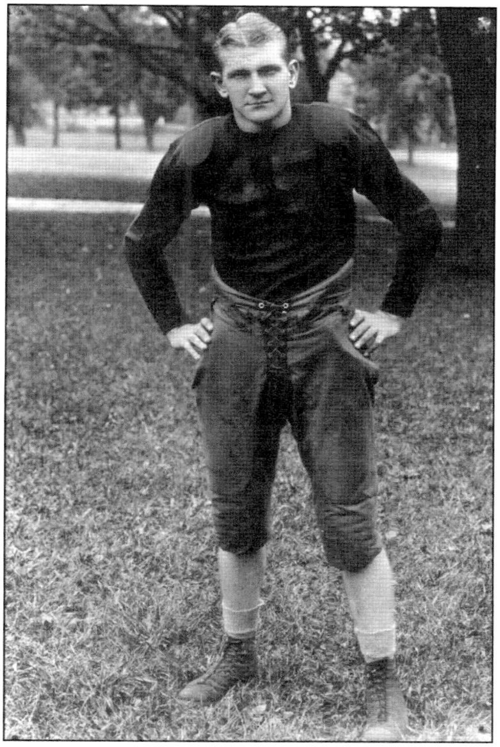

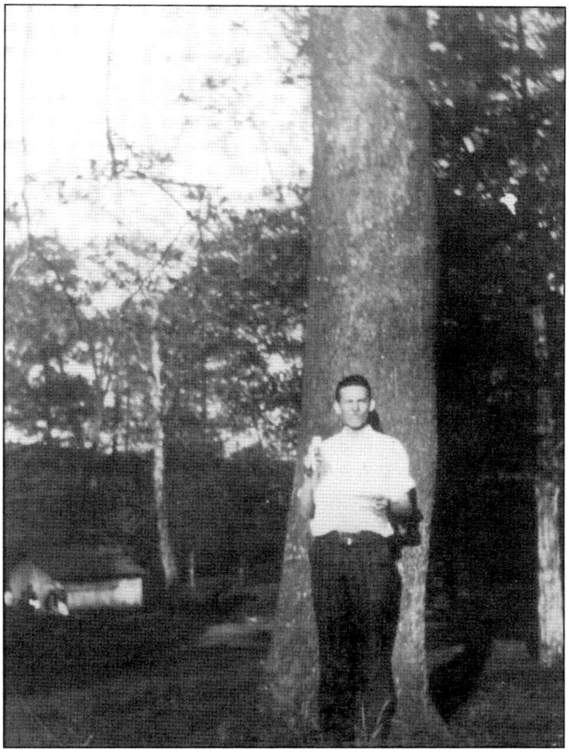

Clarence Blackburn, shown in this photograph taken about 1929, was born around 1911 to Elbert and Addie Lee Blackburn. The family lived on Second Avenue, and Elbert was the proprietor of a meat market. According to World War II enlistment records, Clarence was stationed at Fort Oglethorpe in Georgia in 1943.

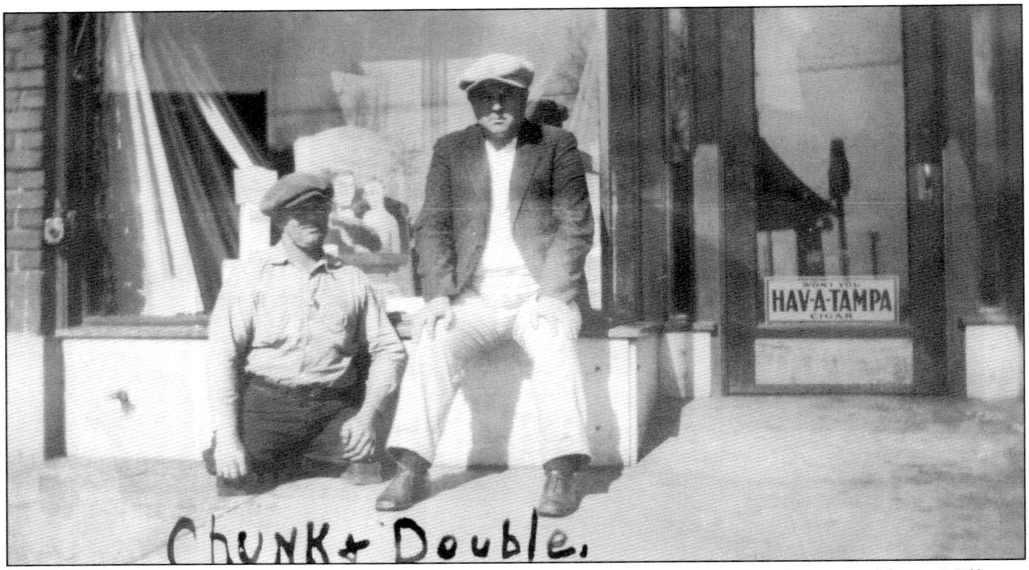

In this photograph taken in the early 1930s, Bobby "Crowder" Smith and John "Doublegut" Ellison hung out in front of the Goodwin Drug Store. Written on the front of the photograph are the words "Chunk and Double," no doubt in reference to the men's nicknames; although it appears Bobby had at least two nicknames. A sign in the door reads, "Won't you Hav-A-Tampa Cigar."

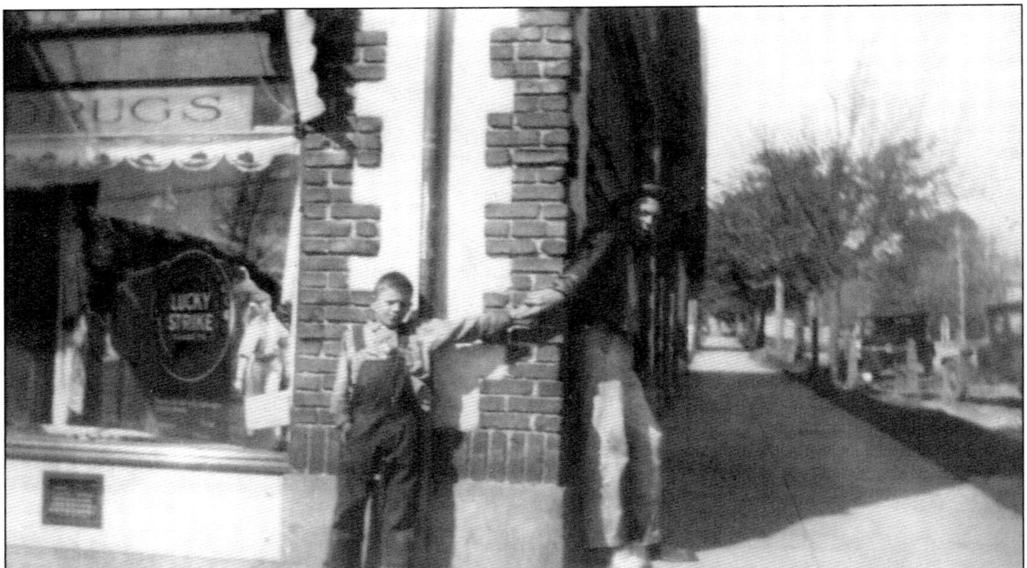

Robert "Snufflehead" Flannigan (left) and George W. Burdette stood at the corner of the Goodwin Drug Store in Lenoir City in this 1931 photograph. In the display window to Robert's left was a large sign for Lucky Strike cigarettes and a cardboard cutout of a baseball player. George appears to be wearing a tall stovepipe hat and black suit coat over jeans for an unknown occasion.

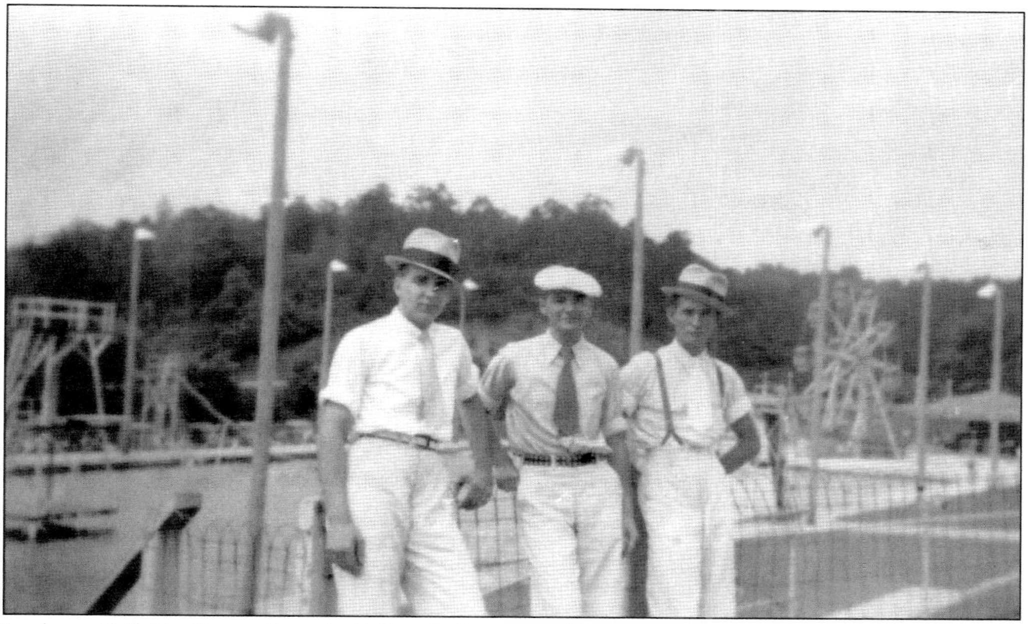

In the mid-1930s, Porter Campbell, Roy DeRieux, and John Worthy took a trip to an amusement park or fair, possibly the Chilhowee Park on Magnolia Avenue in Knoxville. In the background at the far right of the photograph, a Ferris wheel offered a bird's eye view of the surroundings. Dressed in hats and ties, the young men looked ready to take on the world.

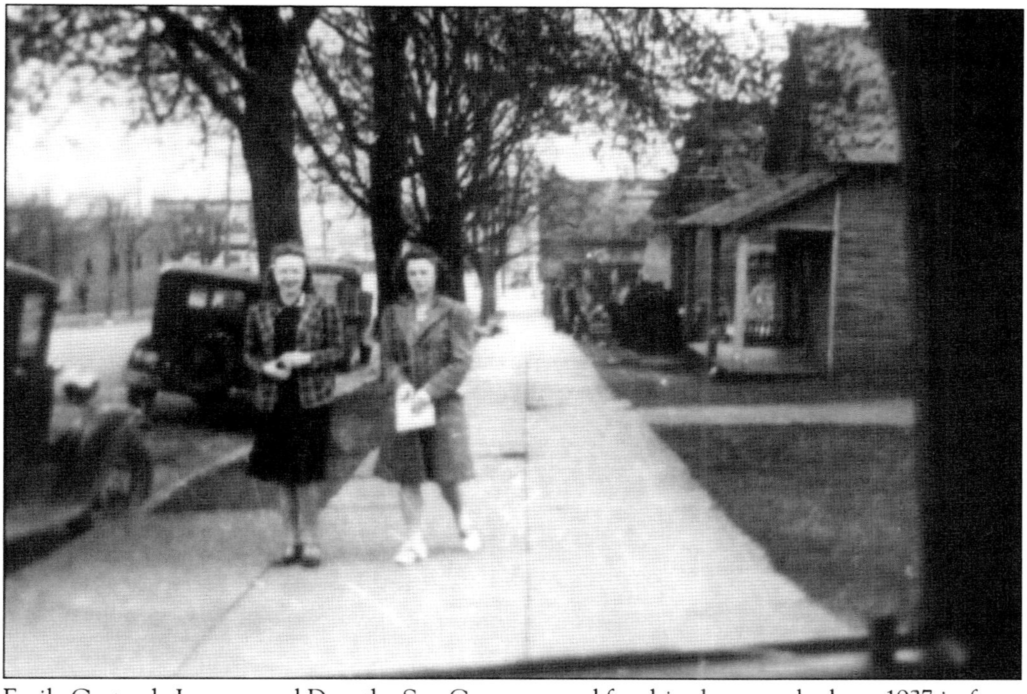

Emily Gertrude Lowery and Dorothy Sue Conner posed for this photograph about 1937 in front of a home at 110 B Street in Lenoir City. Emily later married Francis Burdette Gross on December 22, 1946, and Dorothy married James Arnold Monger on April 18, 1959.

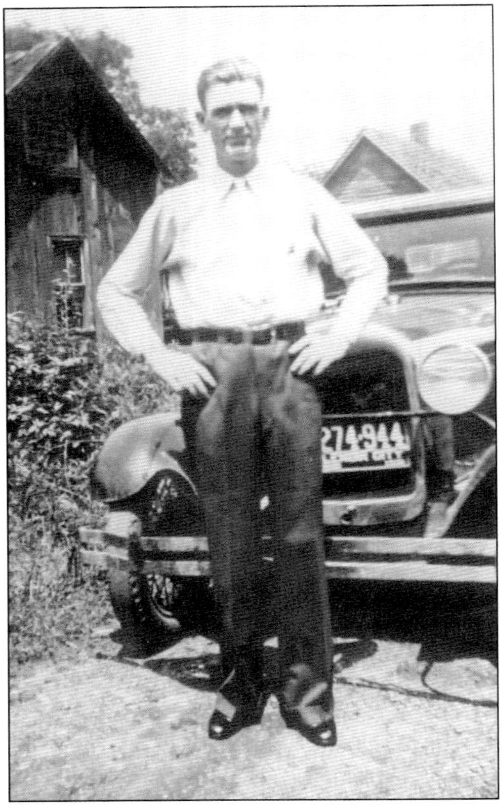

Gooden Welcome "G. W." Roberts stood proudly in front of his first new automobile, possibly a Ford Model A, in this 1929 photograph. He may have been dressed up to go courting with his sweetheart, Eva Mae Munsey; he and Eva married on June 3, 1939.

This 1940s photograph shows Ralph T. Simpson (right) with World War II general Douglas MacArthur (second from left). Simpson was, at one time, stationed in the Philippines. The other men are unidentified. In 1942, General MacArthur was made the supreme commander of Allied forces in the southwest Pacific.

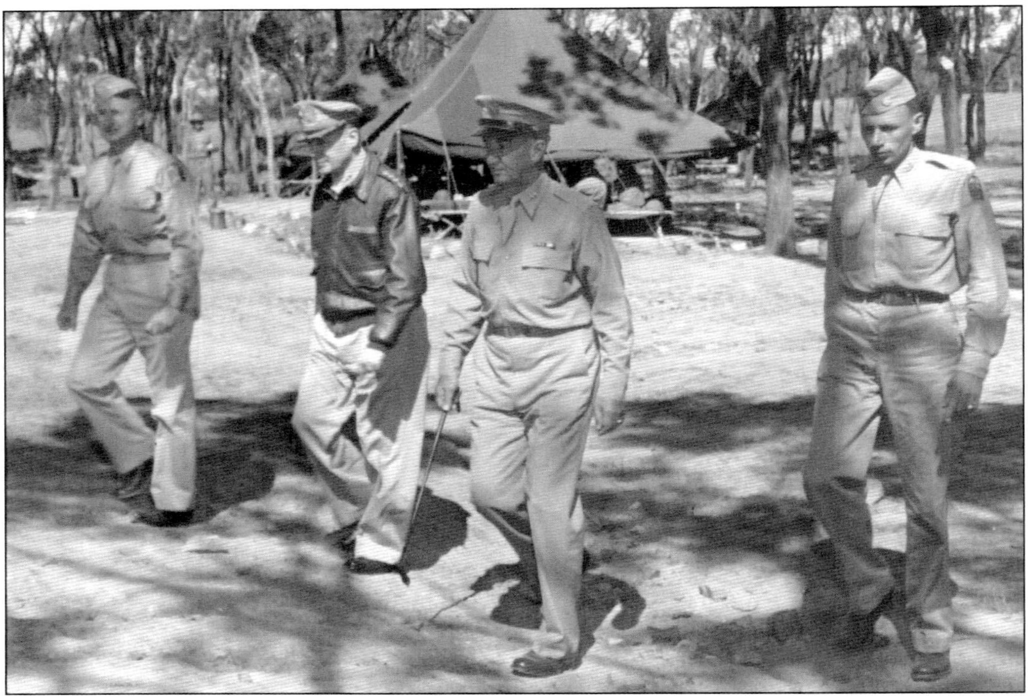

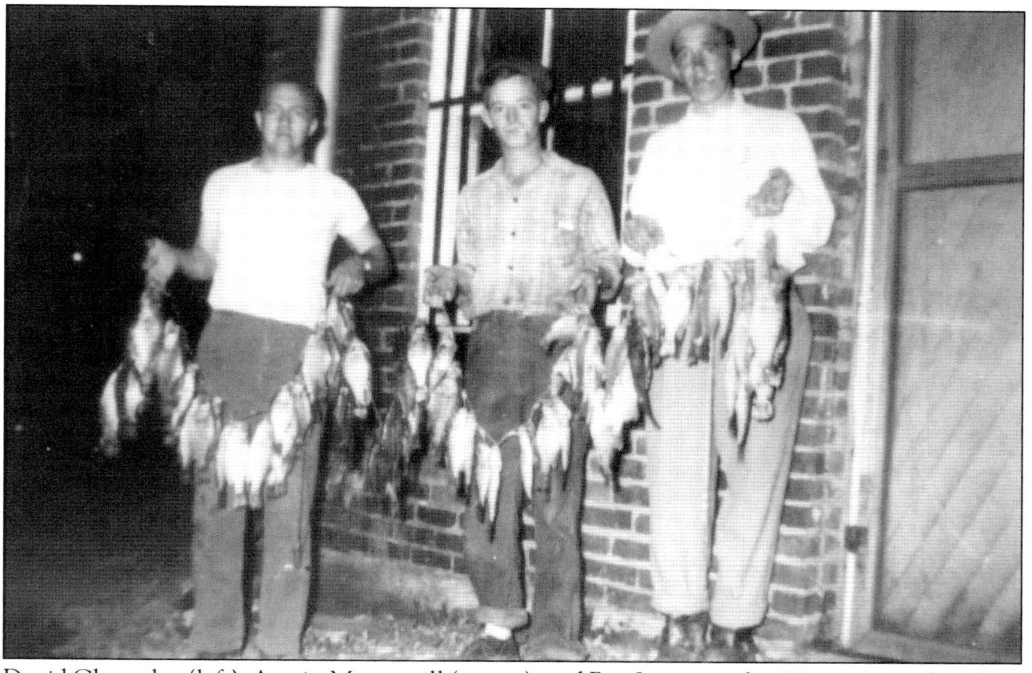

David Ghormley (left), Austin Massengill (center), and Ray Long caught 120 crappie in less than one hour in Watts Bar Lake. The year was 1949, and the fishermen certainly had a story or two to tell about their evening of fishing. Watts Bar Lake is a reservoir on the Tennessee River created by Watts Bar Dam as part of the Tennessee Valley Authority system.

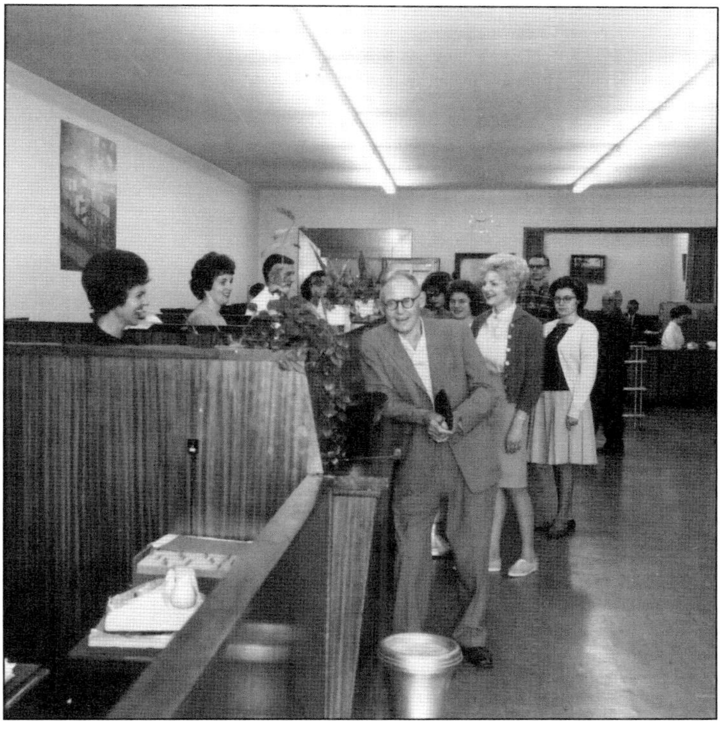

This photograph, taken in the 1960s, shows Albert A. "Shorty" Monger (center) and a group of Lenoir City High School students at the Bank of Loudon County on Broadway Street. The group was posed for an advertisement in the high school yearbook. The only other persons identified in this photograph are Anne Williams (second from left) and Patricia Fritz (standing at far right). Albert was the owner of a local furniture store.

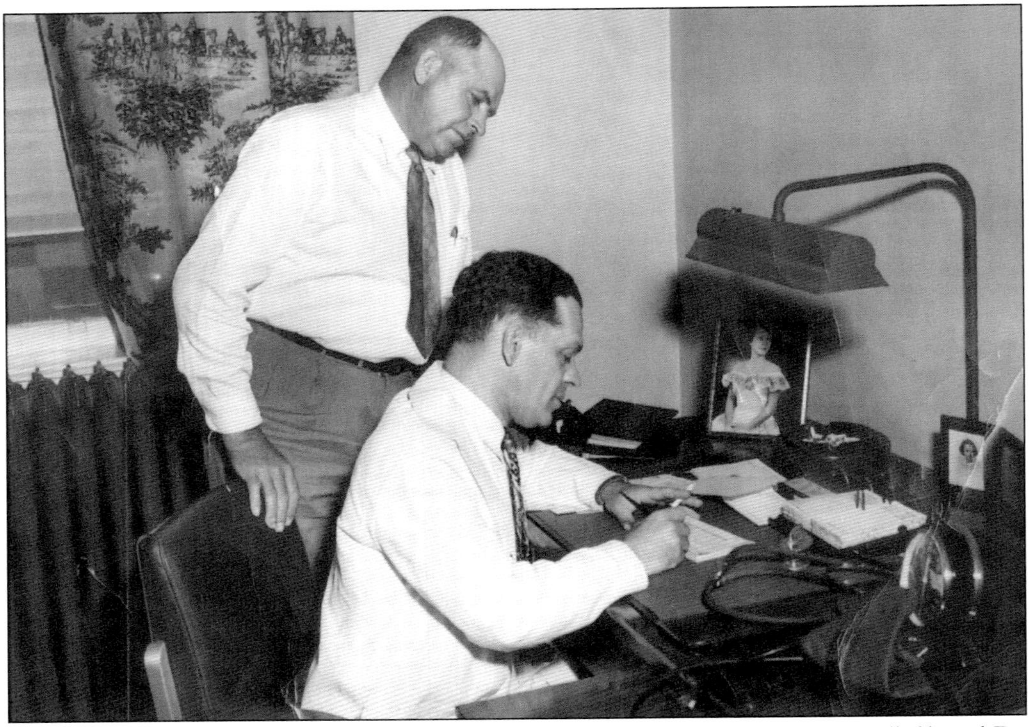

Taken sometime in the 1950s, this photograph shows William "Bill" J. Hamilton (left) and Dr. James Avery Leeper, who was a longtime Lenoir City physician. In addition to family photographs, a stethoscope and blood pressure cuff sat on Dr. Leeper's desk. Hamilton was a local contractor and also served a couple of terms as mayor of Lenoir City.

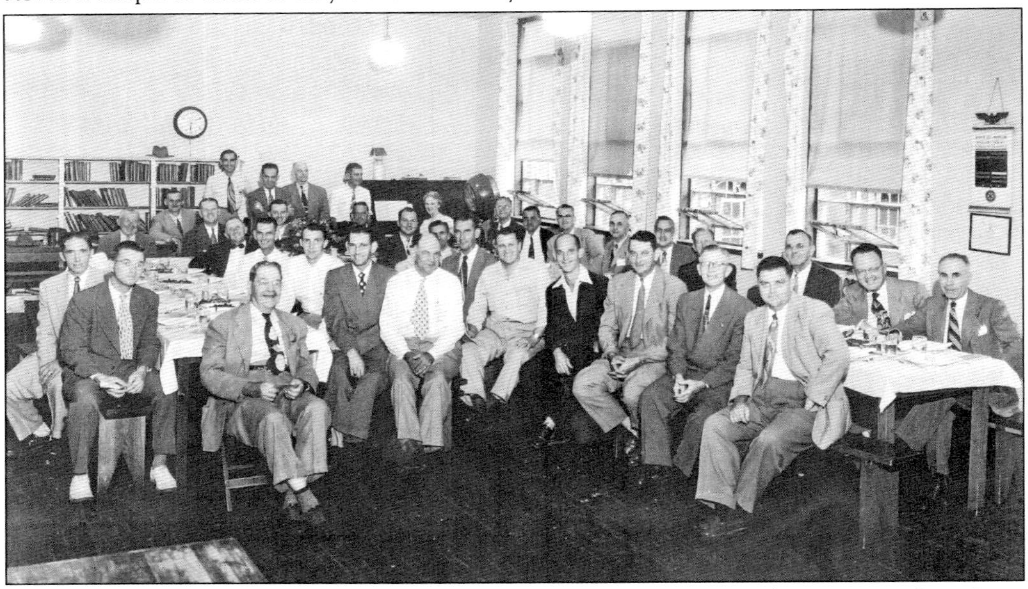

These unidentified men attended a Rotary Club dinner in Lenoir City. The event may have been held on a hot summer day, as the windows were open and a fan was set up near the piano player at the back of the room.

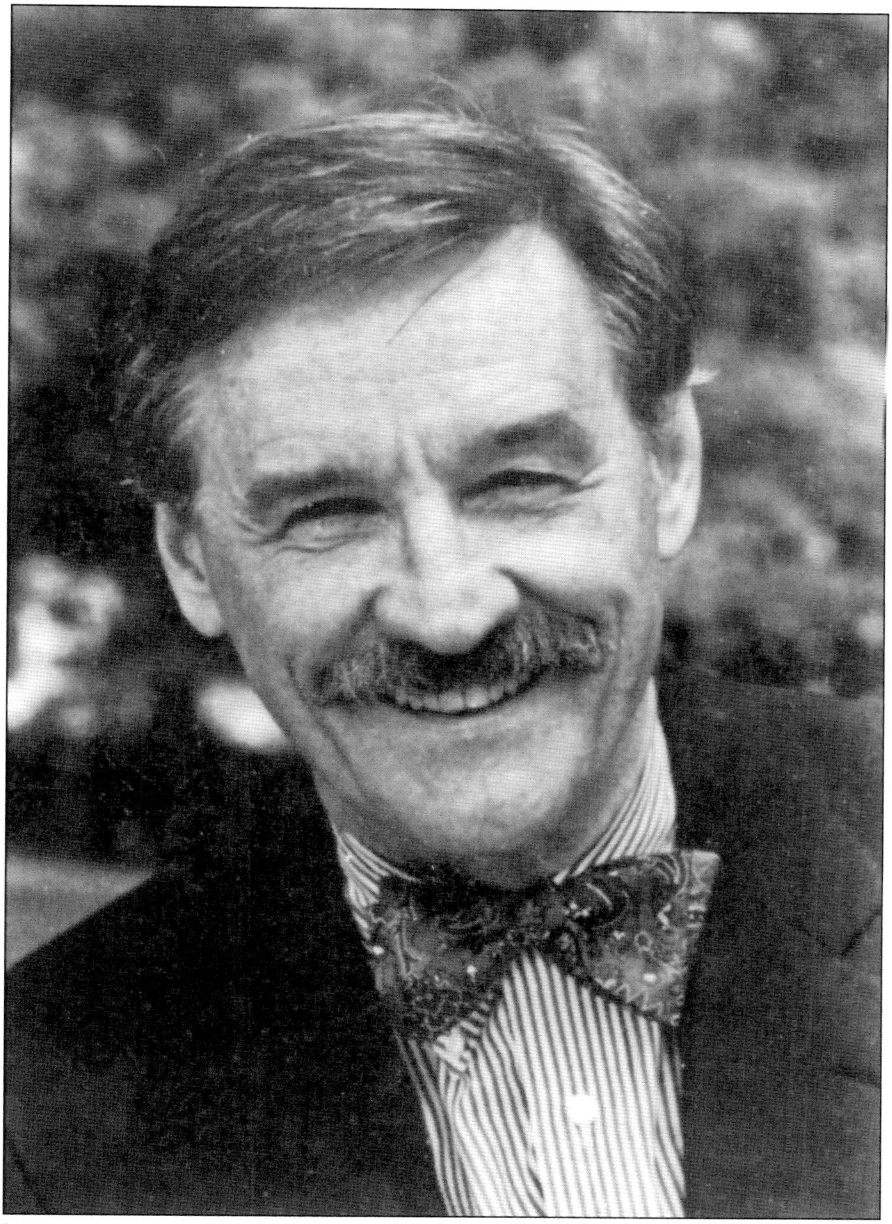

One of Lenoir City's most famous citizens would have to be Richard Curry Marius. Born in 1933 in the Martel community, Marius attended Lenoir City Schools and graduated from Lenoir City High School, where he was named "Most Likely to Succeed." He graduated summa cum laude in journalism from the University of Tennessee in 1954 and earned his B.D. from Southern Baptist Theological Seminary in 1958. However, Richard did not find the ministry to his liking, so he returned to school for his M.A. (1959) and Ph.D. (1962) from Yale. He taught history at Gettysburg College and the University of Tennessee before becoming director of expository writing at Harvard University, where he taught English until his death in 1999. Over the years, Richard wrote and edited novels and historical biographies, including one titled *An Affair of Honor* that was finished just a few months before he died from pancreatic cancer.

Consistent with our mission to preserve history on a local level, this book was printed in South Carolina on American-made paper and manufactured entirely in the United States. Products carrying the accredited Forest Stewardship Council (FSC) label are printed on 100 percent FSC-certified paper.

MADE IN THE USA